Navigating Sustainability in Asia

Navigating Sustainability in Asia

A Practical Guide for Leaders and Investors

Nana Li

Navigating Sustainability in Asia:
A Practical Guide for Leaders and Investiors

First published in 2026 by
Business Expert Press, LLC
222 East 46th Street, New York, NY 10017
www.businessexpertpress.com

ISBN-13: 978-1-63742-952-5 (paperback)
ISBN-13: 978-1-63742-953-2 (e-book)

Business Expert Press Environmental and Social Sustainability for Business Advantage Collection

First edition: 2026

10 9 8 7 6 5 4 3 2 1

EU SAFETY REPRESENTATIVE
Mare Nostrum Group B.V.
Doelen 72
4831 GR Breda
The Netherlands
gpsr@mare-nostrum.co.uk

Description

Asia's role in the global sustainability transition is too big to ignore—and too complex to oversimplify.

Navigating Sustainability in Asia is a practical playbook for business leaders, investors and policymakers who want to understand how sustainability is reshaping Asia's economies. Combining on-the-ground insight with practical tools, it shows how sustainability in Asia is not ideology but strategy—a driver of innovation, competitiveness and long-term value.

Whether you are a board member in Tokyo navigating governance reform, an executive in Singapore building climate-aligned supply chains or an investor assessing risks in India or Southeast Asia, the book translates lessons into decisions. Market analysis, case examples and end-of-chapter briefings help teams move from principle to practice.

By reframing sustainability as a source of advantage, the book offers a simple message: success belongs to those who combine persistence, cultural fluency and strategic adaptation. *Navigating Sustainability in Asia* is essential reading for corporates, executives, investors and the regulators shaping the environment in which they operate.

Contents

Acknowledgments

This book is the culmination of a journey shaped by the support, wisdom and kindness of many extraordinary people. To each of you, my deepest thanks.

First and foremost, this book would not have happened if not for my mentor, colleague, and dear friend, Helen Wong. Her sudden passing in 2022 was a profound loss. It also clarified my purpose and compelled me to embrace this project. Helen's legacy lives on these pages, and I hope they honor the brilliance and warmth she has brought to the world. My gratitude extends to Jamie Allen (Helen's husband), whose guidance as both a reviewer and a mentor has been invaluable—not only for this book but for every lesson he has taught me (so far). Also, I would like to extend my special thanks to all the 15 interviewees for their contributions to each market chapter, as well as to Jane Moir, Melissa Brown and Sharmila Gopinath for their kind assistance in reviewing and re-reviewing my draft without hesitation.

To Impax Asset Management, thank you for your unwavering support in making this book possible. I am equally grateful to my colleagues, Lisa Beauvilain, Chris Dodwell, Oscar Yang and Paul French, whose encouragement and flexibility made this idea a reality.

To my family—your love, patience and steadfast belief in me have been my anchor. Whether through quiet understanding or enthusiastic cheerleading, you gave me the courage to keep writing. You held the ladder while I built this—thank you.

A special acknowledgment to Business Expert Press, especially Scott Isenberg, Edward Stone, Robert Sroufe, Charlene Kronstedt, Cassie Kronstedt, and Dhinesh P for your support throughout this project. It is a real test of courage and conviction to publish this book at a time when sustainability has become contentious in the United States. Thank you for fostering thoughtful dialogue amid political headwinds and for standing by this project.

Finally, to you, my reader: the fact that you're holding this book means the world to me. I know Helen is grinning somewhere, saying, "See? I told you you could do it."

CEO Cheat Sheet

Why it Matters

- Asia is the growth engine and risk hotspot for climate, governance, and society.
- Regional choices define supply chains, capital flows, and legitimacy worldwide.

What Leaders Need to Know

- **Sustainability is strategy:** It underpins resilience, competitiveness, and capital.
- **No single playbook:** China, Japan, Korea, India, Southeast Asia, and Australia/New Zeland each follow different cultural, political, and regulatory paths.
- **Risks are mounting:** Climate, governance and social pressures.
- **Opportunities abound:** Renewables, digital solutions, sustainable food, circular models, and critical minerals put Asia at the heart of future industries.

How to Succeed

- **Respect differences:** Understand local norms and governance structures; avoid applying global approaches without adaptation.
- **Think long-term:** Tolerated practices today may become liabilities tomorrow.
- **Invest in relationships**: Trust with regulators, partners, and communities often matters as much as financial performance.
- **Stay adaptive:** Expectations shift quickly; agility and cultural fluency are essential.
- **Prioritize governance:** Dispersed ownership and global capital demand stronger governance foundations.

The Bottom Line

- Asia is not just a compliance challenge—it is a source of competitive advantage for those who approach it with persistence, humility, and strategic intent.
- Leaders who embed sustainability into their Asia strategy will capture growth, manage risk, and build enduring value.

Foreword

by Jamie Allen

It wasn't too long ago when buzzwords and phrases like ESG, net-zero targets, and sustainability were proudly displayed by corporations around the world in annual reports and environmental reports as a reflection of their commitment to improving the state of the world and addressing climate change. Financial institutions, on both the buy and sell sides, felt equally compelled to build ESG and sustainability expertise. For many years, it seemed that the tide was flowing in only one direction, and little could break this new consensus on the broader role of the corporation in global society.

We are now in a different world, ideologically speaking at least. ESG as a slogan is in retreat in major markets, the victim of populist politics and a degree of hubris on the part of its proponents. Large global financial institutions claim that they remain committed to their decarbonization targets, despite several withdrawing from net-zero industry alliances. The future looks decidedly bleaker as the tide retreats and the view becomes less pristine.

"Navigating Sustainability in Asia" presents a welcome tonic to such pessimism. Through a broad analysis of Asia's sustainability history, current regulatory developments in 13 key markets and numerous corporate case studies, the book makes the case that issues of climate adaptation and environmental protection, corporate governance reform, and an understanding of social norms remain as real and important for doing business in the region today as in the past. Indeed, it is likely that they will become more critical as continued economic development, combined with relatively large populations and weak governance institutions in certain jurisdictions, increases pressure on natural resources. While "Navigating Sustainability" does not make light of these challenges, it is firmly in the optimism camp and argues that the region has the ingenuity and intelligence to meet them head-on.

This book is a handy manual for both insiders and outsiders in Asia. Those at ease in the region will find it a rich source of context and insight on how different countries are responding to climate change and wider environmental and governance challenges. Those new to the region will find plenty of practical advice on the basics of doing business in a region that, although known by a single name—"Asia"—is extraordinarily diverse in terms of language, culture, religion, political economy, and history. Yet this is precisely what makes the region so fascinating.

Enjoy the read.

Jamie Allen
Founding/Former Secretary General,
Asian Corporate Governance Association

How to Use This Book

Navigating Sustainability in Asia is a practical playbook for corporates, executives, and investors operating or investing in Asia. It helps you make sense of the region's diverse sustainability landscape, adapt global principles to local practice, and build strategies for long-term value. Regulators may also find insight into how other stakeholders interpret policies.

Who This Book Is for

- Asian corporates embedding sustainability.
- U.S. and international executives navigating Asian markets.
- Global investors allocating capital and engaging in Asia.
- Regulators seeking cross-market perspectives.

How the Book Is Structured

- **Chapters 1–4**: Foundations—investor dialogue, education, and common missteps.
- **Chapters 5–10**: Market deep-dives with local context, regulation, case studies, and interviews with local experts.
- **Chapter 11**: The future: Asia's role in global sustainability and investments.

Chapters open with **audience labels**, enabling you to quickly identify their relevance.

Tools to Guide You

Every chapter contains:

- **Key Takeaways**—condensed lessons for reference.
- **Boardroom Briefings**—practical guidance for executive decisions.
- **Callout Boxes**—such as checklists and case studies.

How to Read This Book

You don't need to read sequentially. Executives can skip to Boardroom Briefings, investors to market chapters, and regulators to cross-market comparisons. This is a playbook to dip into as needed, not a linear story.

CHAPTER 1

Understanding Stakeholders and Groups

[CORPORATES] [INVESTORS] [REGULATORS]
[INTERNATIONAL EXECUTIVES] [U.S. EXECUTIVES]

This chapter is intended for corporates, investors, regulators, and executives (both United States and international) seeking to understand Asia's stakeholder landscape.

Asian Companies

Overview

The Asia-Pacific region is a study in contrasts. In this vast and varied landscape, hypermodern megacities coexist with ancient ecosystems, where rapid industrialization collides with the urgent need for sustainability. With over 2.2 billion urban residents and more than half of the world's urban population (UN, 2022), this region is not only growing but also defining the future of global economics, innovation, and environmental stewardship. Cities like Tokyo, Hong Kong, Shanghai, and Singapore are more than just economic powerhouses—they are testbeds for how societies can thrive amid density, scarcity, and technological disruption. Yet, to speak of "Asia" as a single entity is to overlook its staggering diversity. The corporate landscape alone reveals deep divergences: South Korea's tightly integrated *chaebols* (family-controlled conglomerates) operate on a scale and structure worlds apart from India's nimble, digitally native start-ups, while Vietnam's export-driven manufacturing boom follows a different playbook entirely. Generalizations fail here—Asia's strength lies in its multiplicity. This book is designed as a practical playbook for corporates, investors, and executives navigating Asia's sustainability realities—offering applied insights, decision-making tools, and region-specific guidance rather than abstract theory.

This complexity extends to its natural wealth. The region is home to 17 of the world's 36 biodiversity hotspots, a biological endowment that fuels industries from agriculture to pharmaceuticals. But this treasure is under siege. The same urbanization and industrialization that drive prosperity are also eroding forests, polluting waterways, and pushing species to the brink of extinction. The March 2025 earthquake in Myanmar, which killed thousands and sent economic shockwaves across Thailand, Laos, and beyond, was a grim reminder of how fragile this balance remains (WMO, 2024). Asia's growth story is inseparable from its environmental challenges—and increasingly, its solutions.

Economically, the region is the world's factory floor, its tech lab, and its most dynamic consumer market all at once. China, Japan, and South Korea dominate global supply chains, producing everything from microchips to electric vehicles. The Regional Comprehensive Economic Partnership (RCEP), established in 2020, has further cemented Asia's role in global trade by creating the world's largest trade bloc—a $26 trillion market encompassing 15 economies through tariff reductions, streamlined supply chains, and shared rules of origin.

But this system faces new pressures. The Trump administration's trade policies, emphasizing tariffs and reshoring, threaten to disrupt long-standing export flows. Ironically, external pressure could only amplify RCEP's role as members forge closer ties amid rising protectionism worldwide. Asia's history reveals a pattern: from colonial-era dismissals to modern-day trade wars, the region continues to adapt, outmaneuver, and emerge stronger.

Companies like Taiwan Semiconductor Manufacturing Company (TSMC) (leveraging U.S.–China tensions to create global investment opportunities) (TSMC, 2023) and Build Your Dreams (BYD) (pivoting from a battery maker to an electric vehicle [EV] leader during the climate crisis) illustrate how Asian firms convert existential threats into strategic advantages. Climate change poses a brutal reality here: Asia suffers more weather-related disasters than any other continent, from Bangladesh's drowning coastlines to the typhoons that regularly batter the Philippines (IPCC, 2022). But resilience is being engineered into the fabric of societies. China's world-leading renewable capacity (over 1,000 gigawatts [GW] as of 2023) and dominance in solar and wind supply chains demonstrate how Asian economies are converting decarbonization pledges into industrial reality (IEA, 2024). South Korea's Carbon Neutrality Act (2022)—the first in East Asia—binds chaebols, such as Hyundai, to mandatory emissions cuts while creating a $7 billion carbon market, demonstrating that regulatory teeth can drive corporate action (FSC, 2022). Even smaller players, such as Taiwan, have become global leaders in disaster-resistant architecture. This isn't just an adaptation—it's a quiet rewriting of the rules. These pressures converge into a set of common drivers that shape how corporate sustainability unfolds in Asia, as shown in Figure 1.1.

Figure 1.1 Sustainability drivers in Asia

The latest World Meteorological Organization (WMO) (WMO, 2024) State of the Climate in Asia 2024 report leaves no room for ambiguity: Asia is unequivocally warming at almost twice the global average, and 2024 was either the warmest or second-warmest year on record in the region, depending on the dataset. This accelerated warming continues to fuel more frequent and severe weather events—from heatwaves and glacial melt to coastal flooding. Across Asia, floods and storms remain the dominant threat, inflicting catastrophic losses on both human lives and regional economies. In 2024, floods in China alone displaced over 4.8 million people during one of the worst droughts in recorded history (WMO, 2024). Meanwhile, Myanmar reached a record high temperature of 48.2 degrees Celsius, and glaciers in the Himalayas lost mass at unprecedented rates, increasing water security risks in several countries.

Yet, the narrative of Asia as a passive victim of climate change or global economics is not just outdated—it's actively misleading. When Super Typhoon Rai devastated the Philippines in December 2021, the Association of Southeast Asian Nations (ASEAN) Humanitarian Assistance Center mobilized relief within 24 hours—far quicker than typical UN mechanisms—by deploying prepositioned supplies through a networked early-warning system. This response showcased institutional coordination and operational agility. Similarly, in India's capital region, smog episodes coincided with the rapid scaling of renewable energy capacity throughout 2023 and 2024—illustrating how crisis moments are driving structural shifts.

The reality reveals a more complex dynamic: a region that has developed unique resilience to volatility, increasingly converting crises into strategic pivots when institutions, capital, and innovation align. In practical terms, for business leaders in Asia, climate events are no longer distant planning scenarios—they are immediate threats and catalysts for action. Companies must integrate early-warning metrics, climate scenario modeling, and operational resilience into their core risk frameworks. A superficial nod to environmental sustainability is no longer sufficient; performance now hinges on real-time preparedness and strategic adaptation.

For sure, the challenges ahead are immense. Rising seas will redraw maps, trade wars will disrupt supply chains, and the tension between development and sustainability will only be sharpened. But Asia's corporate landscape contains pockets of extraordinary adaptability. While many traditional firms remain conservative, the vanguard (from Korean chaebols embracing circular economy to Southeast Asian start-ups leapfrogging legacy systems) indicates how institutional memory of past crises combines with a hunger for future opportunities. The West's persistent underestimation of this duality—entrenched caution and disruptive innovation—has always been shortsighted. Today, it's an outright liability.

The main stakeholder groups influencing ESG outcomes in Asia, together with illustrative regional dynamics, are summarised in Table 1.1.

Table 1.1 Key stakeholder groups in Asia's ESG landscape

Stakeholder Group	Role/Influence in ESG	Example Dynamic in Asia
Corporates	Implement ESG in operations; disclose sustainability data	Family-owned chaebols in Korea; Chinese SOEs (State-Owned Enterprises) aligning with "dual carbon" goals
Investors	Provide capital; set expectations via stewardship and voting	Japan's Government Pension Investment Fund (GPIF) blocklisting violators; Temasek linking financing to ESG performance
Regulators	Create mandatory disclosure and compliance frameworks	Hong Kong's climate reporting mandate; India's Business Responsibility and Sustainability Reporting (BRSR) requirements
International Executives	Adapt strategies to local sustainability norms; manage supply chain risk	LVMH–JD.com partnership; Beyond Meat's China entry
U.S. Executives	Bring capital, tech, and governance pressure; face geopolitical risk	Tesla Gigafactory Shanghai; Starbucks India JV

Challenges and Problems

Many Asian firms face significant challenges in adopting environmental, social, and governance (ESG) and sustainability practices due to a lack of basic knowledge and understanding. This knowledge gap is a major barrier, as companies struggle to integrate these principles into their operations effectively and to communicate what they are doing effectively for stakeholders who value the information. For instance, in my engagements with companies in the region, superficial target-setting for ESG performance often takes center stage in our discussions. This indicates a substantial need for education and capacity-building within the corporate sector to enhance ESG literacy and implementation.

The regulatory environment further complicates this picture, resembling a patchwork of conflicting priorities rather than a unified framework. In Japan, listed companies are subject to stringent Task Force on

Climate-Related Financial Disclosures (TCFD)-aligned reporting requirements, whereas Indonesia's guidelines remain largely voluntary (TCFD, 2021). The Stock Exchange of Hong Kong (SEHK) requires granular ESG disclosures, yet such transparency remains aspirational across the border in Vietnam. For multinationals operating regionally, these disparities force impossible choices—either overcomply in advanced markets or risk reputational damage in emerging ones. The result is a fractured approach to sustainability that benefits neither businesses nor the communities they impact.

Traditional top-down and often rigid corporate cultures in many Asian companies pose another significant challenge to adopting ESG values and compliance. While the Asian market has remarkably adaptive players, traditional structures present unique challenges for the adoption of ESG. Family-owned conglomerates and state-linked enterprises often exhibit deeply conservative decision making. However, promising shifts are emerging. Korean chaebols now tie executive bonuses to ESG metrics. At the same time, Thai conglomerates like the CP Group are now investing in blockchain-tracked shrimp and lab-grown protein, driven by pressure from younger-generation leadership. The key differentiator isn't corporate structure, but whether leadership recognizes sustainability as the new axis of competition.

In 2023, a Cambodian brick kiln worker stacked clay under a scorching sun, her hands cracked from labor, her freedom bound by a debt-bondage contract. Meanwhile, an asset manager in Singapore reviewed her factory's ESG report, which boasted a flawless "zero violations" record. The disconnect was glaring, but it was nothing new. Asia's labor-intensive industries have long struggled with human rights risks. Yet, the smartest companies now treat these challenges as strategic opportunities rather than compliance burdens. The 2013 Rana Plaza collapse was the wake-up call: when the Bangladeshi garment factory crumbled, killing over a thousand workers, global brands faced $30 billion in losses almost overnight. Having already trained local nongovernmental organizations (NGOs) to conduct surprise audits, Levi Strauss, the iconic American denim brand, had cut ties with Rana Plaza months earlier. Their proactive approach didn't just save lives—it saved them from financial ruin. By 2016, their expanded audit program reduced labor violations by 40 percent, proving that ethical supply chains aren't just morally sound—they're financially savvy.

Today, the stakes are even higher. Chin Poon Industrial (CPI), a major automotive electronics manufacturer based in Taiwan, was found to have migrant workers (primarily from Vietnam) paying recruitment fees of up to $6,150–$7,000 in 2022, which led to debt bondage risks. Their competitor, Intel Penang, avoided similar scandals by using blockchain to track payroll transparency, cutting violations by 85 percent in under two years (2019–2021). The lesson is clear: the old model of superficial audits is obsolete. When I visited a Chinese factory last year, the manager showed me how a simple QR-code grievance system reduced wage disputes by 60 percent while lowering turnover costs. "Happy workers stay," he said, "and staying workers make better products."

For executives and investors, the data speaks for itself. Since 2015, allegations of forced labor have cost Asian seafood exporters $1.6 billion in lost EU contracts (ILO, 2024). Factories with certified labor conditions see 25 percent higher productivity, according to a 2023 International Labor Organization (ILO) study (ILO, 2023). Companies that adopt wage transparency tools regain market access up to 18 months faster. New regulatory moves, such as Australia's planned strengthening of its Modern Slavery Act, suggest that supply chain transparency will become an increasingly explicit baseline expectation across the Asia-Pacific.

The question isn't whether to act—it's how quickly. Will your next supplier assessment be a routine checklist or a strategic advantage? For executives looking to turn supply chain oversight into a strategic advantage, the following checklist provides a practical framework.

Executive Checklist: Supply Chain ESG Risk Management in Asia

Use this list to test whether your company is managing supply chain risks effectively:

- **Supplier Mapping**—Do we have full visibility of *tier 1 and tier 2 suppliers*?
- **Labor Standards**—Are recruitment fees, working hours, and grievance systems monitored with independent checks?

(Continued)

(Continued)

- **Environmental Risks**—Are suppliers disclosing emissions, water use, and waste data, and are these audited?
- **Resilience Planning**—Do we stress-test critical suppliers against climate disruptions (e.g., floods, heatwaves)?
- **Cultural Fit**—Do our ESG expectations respect local norms while still aligning with international standards (e.g., International Sustainability Standards Board [ISSB], ILO)?
- **Crisis Protocols**—Do we have a plan if a supplier is linked to forced labor or environmental scandals?

A well-structured supply chain ESG framework can turn risk management into a competitive advantage—improving resilience, investor confidence, and regulatory readiness.

The tension between global sustainability standards and local realities demands nuance. Blind adoption of Western frameworks often stumbles on Asia's divergent priorities, where rapid industrialization collides with sustainability goals, or where state-directed capitalism reshapes stakeholder expectations. China's ESG reporting guidelines exemplify this balancing act: they incorporate global disclosure norms while embedding "Common Prosperity" objectives, creating a hybrid model that satisfies both international investors and domestic policymakers. This suggests that Asian ESG won't be imported, but iterated—adapted to developmental stages, governance structures, and cultural values.

The ISSB's global baseline represents a remarkable shift, not as a replacement for localized ESG approaches, but as a foundational layer enabling cross-border comparability (ISSB, 2023). While Asian companies will continue to tailor sustainability practices to regional priorities (as seen in China's blended reporting), the ISSB standards create a "floor" for disclosure rigor, particularly for small and medium enterprises (SMEs) that have previously lacked structured reporting (ISSB, 2023). Japan's rapid adoption of the ISSB and Singapore's climate risk disclosure mandates demonstrate how advanced Asian markets utilize these standards to enhance investor trust, while also accommodating domestic ESG nuances (ISSB, 2023). This dual trajectory—global alignment on transparency, local flexibility in implementation—may define Asia's next phase of ESG.

However, the implementation of ISSB standards faces delays in many markets due to political pushback in the United States (ISSB, 2023). The Securities and Exchange Commission (SEC)'s climate disclosure rule has faced significant opposition from conservative politicians and emissions-intensive corporate sectors, resulting in legal challenges and delays. This resistance has created a fragmented landscape, where the adoption of ISSB standards is uneven and slower than anticipated (ISSB, 2023). The political climate in the United States has also influenced other jurisdictions, causing hesitation and delays in fully embracing these standards. Despite these challenges, the growing support from investors and international bodies suggests that the ISSB's framework will eventually gain broader acceptance, albeit more slowly than initially hoped (ISSB, 2023).

Strategies and Solutions

Addressing the challenges faced by Asian companies in adopting sustainability practices requires more than just awareness—it demands embedding ESG into business operations. One key strategy is building practical ESG capability through targeted education and hands-on training programs. Rather than limiting efforts to theoretical literacy, companies should work with academic institutions, NGOs, and industry experts to design programs that focus on applying ESG principles in real-world contexts—such as integrating climate risk into supply chain management or aligning executive incentives with sustainability goals. A good example is the Singapore Exchange (SGX), which has gone beyond providing guidance by launching structured programs to help listed companies not only understand sustainability reporting requirements but also incorporate these frameworks into their business strategies and decision-making processes.

Regulatory harmonization in the Asia-Pacific region is essential for creating a consistent and supportive environment for sustainability practices. One key challenge is finding the right balance between regulatory interference and market function. Overregulation can stifle innovation and growth, while underregulation can lead to market failures and negative externalities. Some Asian markets, such as China, have long oscillated between regulatory overreach and underenforcement, creating a cyclical pattern of stagnation and instability.

The 2015–2016 "circuit breaker" mechanism in China illustrates how well-intentioned regulation can backfire if poorly designed. Introduced in January 2016, the mechanism was meant to calm extreme market volatility by halting trading when the CSI 300 Index fell by 5 percent, and suspending it for the rest of the day if losses reached 7 percent. In practice, the market hit the first threshold so quickly that trading was halted within minutes. On some days, it closed entirely within five minutes of opening. Instead of restoring confidence, it amplified panic selling, as investors rushed to exit positions before the thresholds were triggered. Within just four days, regulators scrapped the mechanism (China Securities Regulatory Commission, 2016), providing a cautionary lesson about the unintended consequences of overly rigid market interventions.

The 2016–2018 peer-to-peer (P2P) lending collapse, involving $150 billion in defaults from undersupervised platforms, evidences the risks of lax oversight. This "tighten-and-suffocate, loosen-and-chaos" (一管就死、一放就乱) dynamic persists today. Effective regulatory frameworks should aim to protect the public interest and support environmental and social equity, without imposing unreasonable demands on businesses.

A balanced regulatory approach requires adaptive precision, implementing Good Regulatory Practice (GRP) frameworks that calibrate oversight to market maturity. Take ASEAN's 2023 Harmonization Principles: rather than imposing rigid rules, they mandate transparent cost–benefit analyses (e.g., Indonesia's six-month public reviews for new fintech laws) and SME carve-outs (like Vietnam's two-year compliance grace periods for small exporters). This avoids China's extremes: unlike Beijing's retroactive tech crackdowns or laissez-faire P2P oversight, GRP aligns regulations with actual risk, such as Singapore's tiered licensing for digital banks, where capital requirements scale with operational complexity. The result? Rules that enable—rather than choke—growth.

Effective regulatory enforcement remains a persistent challenge across Asia, where institutional capacity and political disparities often create uneven compliance landscapes. While rule-setting has advanced, as we have seen in Malaysia's mandatory ESG reporting for public companies or India's Business Responsibility and Sustainability Reporting (BRSR) framework, enforcement often lags behind market expectations.

The fundamental drivers of adherence are increasingly coming from nonstate actors, such as institutional investors like Japan's Government Pension Investment Fund (GPIF), which now blacklists companies that consistently violate governance norms. At the same time, Singapore's Temasek Holdings ties financing terms to measurable ESG progress. Even China's much-publicized environmental inspections reveal a pragmatic approach—targeting visible violators to set examples while tolerating gradual compliance elsewhere. For regulators, the lesson is clear: pairing formal mandates with market-driven incentives (e.g., green bond subsidies, procurement preferences for compliant firms) can compensate for patchy enforcement capacity.

On the other hand, the disconnect between Asia's vibrant sustainability movements and corporate adoption is not a matter of cultural inertia, but one of incentives and structural design. While climate consciousness thrives among consumers and employees—evidenced by China's government-led zero-waste campaigns or Japan's surge in ESG-focused shareholder proposals—executive hesitance persists where sustainability is framed as a cost center rather than a value driver. The solution lies in recalibrating the mechanisms that shape corporate decision making.

Consider Indonesia's green taxonomy, a policy masterstroke that transforms ESG compliance into a financial advantage. Tying preferential loan rates and streamlined permitting to sustainability performance has spurred formerly reluctant miners and palm oil giants to adopt traceability systems, not out of idealism, but because clean operations now mean cheaper capital. Similarly, Japan's automotive supply chain reforms reveal how downstream pressure can trigger cascading change. When Toyota mandated Scope 3 disclosures, hundreds of Thai suppliers raced to install solar panels, recognizing that decarbonization had become a prerequisite for market access (Toyota, 2023).

The implications are clear for global investors and regional executives. The path forward requires neither Western-style activism nor passive cultural accommodation, but rather the strategic alignment of sustainability with Asia's distinct operational currencies: market access, cost efficiency, and intergenerational continuity.

Addressing human rights issues in labor-intensive markets requires more than just supply chain audits—it demands culturally attuned governance. Consider the cautionary tale of the Nissan-Renault Alliance (1999–2022): While not a labor rights case per se, CEO Carlos Ghosn's aggressive Western restructuring (e.g., abrupt plant closures in Japan, performance-based pay replacing seniority systems) triggered systemic backlash. His approach violated entrenched norms, such as *keiretsu* (corporate groups) loyalty and consensus-driven management. Ghosn's tenure ended dramatically when he was arrested in Japan in 2018 on charges of financial misconduct. He later escaped to Lebanon in 2019 while awaiting trial, where he remains a fugitive.

Adapting Western ESG standards to the Asian context involves recognizing the region's unique economic, social and cultural conditions. While adopting advanced Western standards wholesale may be tempting, a more effective approach is to develop localized ESG frameworks that address specific regional challenges. China upholds this balance. While its "dual carbon" goals (peak emissions by 2030, neutrality by 2060) mirror global ambitions, their implementation targets state-owned enterprises (SOEs) facing unique challenges. These include coal-dependent provincial governments resisting plant closures, and SOEs juggling decarbonization mandates with political directives to maintain employment. The result is a hybrid framework where global-aligned reporting coexists with localized solutions, such as "Just Transition" pilot zones that offer state-backed retraining for displaced workers. Such compromises are rarely seen in market-driven Western systems.

Investors in Asian Companies

Overview

Given the region's outsized role in global growth, savvy investors have long recognized Asia's strategic importance, accounting for over 60 percent of worldwide gross domestic product (GDP) expansion from 2013 to 2023 (IMF WEO, October 2023). Home to half of humanity (UN World

Population Prospects, 2022), Asia-Pacific economies combine scale with structural advantages: unrivalled manufacturing ecosystems (China produced 70 percent of global smartphones in 2022—International Data Corporation (IDC), [Statista, 2024]), leapfrogging digital adoption (India's Unified Payments Interface [UPI] processed 12.1B monthly transactions in Q3 2023—Reserve Bank of India [RBI] [Indian Ministry of Commerce 2021]), and rising research and development (R&D) investment (45 percent of global spending in 2023, per UNESCO Science Report, 2023).

While demographic headwinds challenge Japan (median age 49.1 in 2023—Statista, 2023) and South Korea (world's lowest fertility rate at 0.78 in 2022—KOSTAT, 2022), markets like India (median age 28.2 in 2023—UN) and Southeast Asia (projected 4.5 percent GDP growth in 2025—ADB Outlook 2023) offset this with youthful populations and productivity gains (Asia's financial services productivity grew 4.2 percent annually from 2015–2022—ILO). From China's green tech dominance ($4.3T climate tech revenue opportunity by 2030—BCG 2022) to India's tech unicorn boom (110+ unicorns as of March 2024—Hurun Report, 2024), the region rewards investors who tailor strategies to local realities.

The investor community in Asia is diverse, comprising institutional investors, high-net-worth individuals (HNWIs) and retail investors. Institutional investors, including pension funds, sovereign wealth funds, and insurance companies, are significant players, often seeking long-term, stable returns. HNWIs in Asia are renowned for their proactive investment strategies, striking a balance between caution and optimism regarding the region's growth prospects. Retail investors, driven by rising financial literacy and access to digital investment platforms, are also becoming more prominent, contributing to the overall vibrancy of the market.

Asian investors exhibit varied preferences, often influenced by regional economic conditions and market dynamics. Real estate remains a favored asset class, particularly in markets like Japan, India, and Singapore, where core and core-plus investment strategies are prevalent. The technology and health care sectors are also desirable, driven by the region's innovation capabilities and growing demand for digital and health care services. The sudden rise of DeepSeek, with its cost-effective and high-performing models, has made investors more likely to invest in artificial intelligence

(AI) in Asia, demonstrating the region's potential to lead in innovative and accessible AI technologies. Also, there is a notable interest in sustainable investments, with ESG considerations becoming increasingly important in investment decisions.

On the other hand, the maturity level of investors in Asia varies significantly across different markets. Developed markets like Japan, South Korea, Hong Kong, and Singapore have well-established investment ecosystems with sophisticated regulatory frameworks and high levels of investor sophistication. In contrast, emerging markets such as Vietnam, Indonesia, and the Philippines are still developing their financial infrastructures, offering not only high growth potential but also higher risks. This diversity in market maturity provides a wide range of opportunities for investors with different risk appetites and investment horizons.

Investment styles in Asia are equally diverse, ranging from conservative, income-focused strategies to aggressive, growth-oriented approaches. Institutional investors often favor conservative strategies, seeking stable, long-term returns through investments in blue-chip stocks, government bonds, and real estate. Conversely, venture capital and private equity firms are more inclined toward aggressive strategies, such as investing in high-growth start-ups and innovative sectors, including fintech, biotech, and infrastructure projects. The rise of angel investment networks in Southeast Asia further highlights the region's self-motivated investment landscape, supporting early-stage ventures and fostering entrepreneurial growth.

Challenges and Problems

Investing in Asian companies, however, presents a unique set of challenges and problems that could deter potential investors. One of the primary issues is low transparency and accessibility. Many less-developed Asian markets lack the robust disclosure practices seen in Western markets, making it difficult for investors to obtain reliable and comprehensive information about companies' financial health and operational practices. This lack of transparency can lead to increased risks and uncertainties, as investors may not have a clear understanding of the companies they are investing in or the resources to conduct on-site visits.

Weak shareholder protections in Asia have taken a dangerous turn with the rise of dual-class shares—a well-intentioned reform now testing the limits of investor trust. When Hong Kong Exchanges and Clearing Limited (HKEX) revived these structures in 2018 to compete for tech initial public offerings (IPOs), it opened a Pandora's box: 81 percent of Chinese tech firms listing in New York with dual-class shares at the time would have violated Hong Kong's own 10:1 voting ratio cap, revealing a regulatory arbitrage game (HKEX, 2024). Take Xiaomi's IPO that same year: founders retained 54.7 percent voting control with just 29.4 percent equity, a disparity that has become commonplace. Investors are right to worry. The dangers aren't theoretical. Alibaba's nonstandard partnership structures show how super-voting rights can sideline shareholders. At the same time, Singapore's lighter-touch 2018 rules lack the teeth to punish abuses. Yet the real issue lies deeper, as most Asian investors lack experience assessing these risks, leaving them exposed in markets like Hong Kong, where derivative lawsuits rarely succeed. As exchanges race to attract listings, Asia's shareholder protection framework risks becoming collateral damage.

The immature legal environment in many Asian countries further compounds these challenges. Inadequate enforcement of corporate governance standards and investor protection laws can leave investors vulnerable to fraud and mismanagement. The 2023 CG Watch rankings reveal stark contrasts: while Australia scored highest for the "Investor" category (69 out of 100), markets like China (22) and Indonesia (20) struggle with entrenched ownership structures that dilute minority voices. Notably, Hong Kong's middling score reflects the reality: strong formal rights on paper, but limited practical influence when confronting controlling families or state-linked entities. Such disparities force investors to navigate a patchwork of protections, with active stewardship often constrained by local business norms and practices. These structural realities underscore why sound legal frameworks must be paired with cultural willingness to enforce them—a lesson reinforced by recent clashes over related-party transactions in India and Thailand.

Additionally, Asia's fragmented regulatory landscape presents distinct hurdles for cross-border investment. Foreign investors face multilayered challenges, from language barriers in Japan's consensus-driven culture to opaque licensing regimes in Vietnam's provincial bureaucracies. In South Korea, "gye" (relationship-based) networks often dictate access to dealmaking, while India's state-level regulatory variations complicate pan-market strategies. Even advanced markets like Singapore, despite English-language advantages, require nuanced navigation of unwritten rules around government-linked enterprises. These structural complexities explain why firms like Uber struggled with Indonesia's cash-based economy and why Walmart exited Japan after failing to adapt to its *keiretsu* distribution systems.

The Evergrande collapse (2021–2024) serves as a cautionary case study in the consequences of weak governance and speculative excess in Asia's corporate sector. China's shadow banking system and implicit state backing enabled the developer's aggressive debt-fueled expansion, reaching $300 billion in liabilities by 2021. However, Beijing's abrupt 2020 "Three Red Lines" policy (capping developer debt ratios) exposed Evergrande's unsustainable model. Critical failures included: (1) misaligned incentives (executives prioritized land hoarding over liquidity); (2) opaque financial disclosures (hiding liabilities through off-balance-sheet vehicles); and (3) disregard for homebuyer protections (presales of unbuilt units funded 35 percent of its debt). The January 2024 Hong Kong liquidation order revealed systemic flaws: despite 18 months of state-led "restructuring theater," political constraints prevented meaningful debt haircuts or asset sales.

The unraveling of Evergrande offers hard-won lessons for those navigating Asia's corporate landscape. At the heart of the crisis sat a glaring governance failure: founder Hui Ka Yan ruled the property giant like a personal fiefdom for years, controlling 70 percent of shareholder votes while stacking the board with loyalists. This lack of independent oversight allowed reckless expansion to continue even as liabilities ballooned past the repayable level, until Hui's abrupt 2023 detention laid bare the perils of concentrated power.

Equally jarring was Beijing's regulatory whiplash. Preselling unbuilt apartments—a practice accounting for 35 percent of Evergrande's debt—was standard industry procedure for decades. Yet the 2020 policy change abruptly recast these obligations as existential threats, demonstrating how quickly state priorities can render entire business models obsolete.

Perhaps most sobering was the aftermath. When liquidation finally came in 2024, foreign bondholders recovered pennies on the dollar—a gruff reminder of Asia's patchwork insolvency systems. As creditors watched helplessly, politically connected stakeholders jumped the queue, exposing the urgent need for coordinated creditor protections in Asia.

Strategies and Solutions

Addressing the challenges that investors face in Asian companies requires a comprehensive approach that enhances transparency, strengthens shareholder protection, and improves regulatory frameworks. Central to this effort is active investor stewardship, where institutional investors leverage their ownership stakes to engage companies on governance, strategy, and sustainability. In Asia, effective stewardship often involves one-on-one discussions with companies to address ESG shortfalls, collaborating with peer investors to amplify influence, and directing capital toward leaders in corporate accountability.

The introduction of stewardship codes in Asia marked a pivotal shift toward stronger corporate governance. However, their effectiveness varies by the level of regulatory rigor. Japan pioneered this movement in 2014 with its voluntary Stewardship Code, urging institutional investors to engage with companies for long-term value creation—a model later adopted by most major economies of the region. However, these frameworks can easily be found toothless; compliance remains voluntary, and concentrated ownership structures (e.g., family conglomerates in Hong Kong or state-linked entities in Singapore) can dilute investor influence. In contrast, India's approach stands out: its Securities and Exchange Board of India (SEBI) mandates adherence to stewardship principles for asset managers, requiring detailed disclosures of engagement activities and voting records. This binding model, coupled with SEBI's enforcement of independent director quotas and shareholder rights, offers a more actionable template for aligning investor-company interests in Asia's complex governance landscape.

Investors can engage directly with companies and regulators to advocate for better governance practices and sustainability initiatives. This includes participating in annual general meetings (AGMs), voting on key issues, and engaging in dialogue with company management to influence corporate behavior (if access is available). Active stewardship helps hold companies accountable and fosters a culture of transparency and long-term value creation. For instance, the Asian Corporate Governance Association (ACGA) has been instrumental in promoting active stewardship among institutional investors in the region.

The rise of shareholder activism in Asia has gained momentum in recent years, with high-profile campaigns targeting underperforming companies. Activist investors, such as Elliott Management and Oasis Management, have made significant inroads in Japan and South Korea, markets traditionally resistant to external pressure. Notable examples include Elliott's 2017–2020 campaign against Samsung Electronics, which successfully pushed for governance reforms, including a $10 billion share buyback and board restructuring; and Oasis Management's 2023 engagement with Japanese retailer Unizo, resulting in a 40 percent premium buyout offer from a private equity firm.

These cases demonstrate that activism can unlock value: targeted Asian companies saw an average share price outperformance of 12 percent postcampaign (Lazard, 2023 data). However, success often hinges on navigating local norms, as seen when Elliott's aggressive tactics failed with Hyundai Motor. At the same time, collaborative approaches at Toshiba led to a successful spin-off of its memory chip business.

Strengthening shareholder protection is another pressing strategy. Regulatory bodies must enforce stricter governance standards to safeguard shareholders' rights. As mentioned earlier, introducing dual-class share structures in markets like Hong Kong and Singapore has raised concerns about governance and control. To mitigate these risks, regulators could implement mandatory sunset clauses that limit the duration of dual-class shares, as well as enhanced disclosure requirements to ensure transparency in voting rights and control structures. For example, the HKEX introduced stricter entry requirements for companies with dual-class shares to protect the interests of minority shareholders.

Effective regulation enforcement is essential to ensure compliance and deter malpractices. Regulatory agencies must be equipped with the necessary resources and authority to monitor and enforce compliance.

This includes conducting regular audits, imposing penalties for noncompliance, and fostering cross-border cooperation to address regulatory arbitrage. The SEBI has been proactive in enhancing corporate governance standards and enforcing compliance through stringent regulations and penalties. Such measures can serve as a model for other markets in the region.

International Businesspeople (Non-U.S.) Doing Business in Asia

Overview

International businesspeople in Asia come from diverse backgrounds and industries, reflecting the region's dynamic economic landscape. These individuals include executives from multinational corporations, entrepreneurs, investors, and consultants, all seeking to capitalize on Asia's rapid growth and vast market potential. The community comprises professionals from Europe, Australia, Canada, and other regions, each bringing unique perspectives and expertise to the Asian business environment.

International businesspeople in Asia often prefer sectors with high growth potential, such as technology, finance, health care, and consumer goods. Many are drawn to the region's burgeoning middle class and increasing purchasing power, which presents significant opportunities for market expansion and innovation. Additionally, the rise of digital transformation and e-commerce in Asia has attracted tech-savvy entrepreneurs seeking to leverage the region's advanced technological infrastructure and large user base.

Business styles among international professionals in Asia are influenced by both their home cultures and the local environment. However, common traits include a strong emphasis on relationship-building and networking, which are crucial for success in many Asian markets. In countries like China and Japan, the concepts of "*guanxi*" (networks/relationships) and "*nemawashi*" (consensus-building) play a vital role in dealings. Understanding and respecting local culture can significantly enhance business interactions and foster long-term, mutually beneficial partnerships.

Navigating Asia's business landscape demands the flexibility of rubber—stretching to fit local customs without snapping under pressure. Experienced executives toggle between communication codes: the crisp efficiency of a Singaporean boardroom, the "nemawashi" patience of Japanese consensus-building, and the relationship-first rhythm of a Chinese negotiation. While Westerners might charge ahead like a bouncing basketball, Asia often prefers the steady roll of a bicycle tire—smoother, quieter, and far less likely to startle the room (and let's face it: in some meetings, you'll feel like you're spinning your wheels anyway). The key isn't mimicking traditions but mastering the pivot—knowing when to grip firmly and when to roll with resistance.

Famous case studies highlight the complexities and successes of international business operations in Asia. The partnership between the French luxury goods company LVMH (Moët Hennessy Louis Vuitton) and the Chinese e-commerce giant JD.com illustrates how global firms can thrive in the Asian market. In 2017, LVMH collaborated with JD.com to enhance its online presence in China, leveraging JD.com's extensive logistics network and deep understanding of local consumer behavior. This partnership enabled LVMH to reach a broader audience and offer a seamless shopping experience, seamlessly combining luxury with convenience. The collaboration has been highly successful, demonstrating the potential of international firms to adapt to the Asian market by forming strategic alliances with local partners.

Challenges and Problems

International businesspeople face numerous challenges when operating in Asia, stemming from diverse factors such as language and cultural barriers, unstable political systems, corruption, and geopolitical risks. These challenges can significantly impact business operations, requiring strategic approaches to navigate effectively.

Language and cultural barriers extend beyond mere communication issues. They encompass a deep understanding of local traditions, business etiquette, and societal norms. For instance, in South Korea, hierarchical relationships are highly valued and understanding the nuances of these relationships is needed for effective interactions. The concept of "*nunchi*", which refers to the ability to gauge others' moods and intentions, plays a significant role in the culture. Misinterpreting these subtle cues can lead to misunderstandings and strained relationships.

Moreover, in countries like India, the diversity of languages and cultures within the country itself adds another layer of complexity. Each region has its own language, customs, and business practices. For example, business practices in Mumbai might differ significantly from those in Chennai or Kolkata. This diversity requires international businesspeople to be adaptable and sensitive to regional differences even within the same country.

Political instability in Asia takes many forms: a sudden regulatory shift in Vietnam, a protest shutting down factories in Myanmar, or an overnight policy reversal following a Malaysian election. Take Indonesia, where the 2019 election turmoil saw riots paralyze Jakarta's business district for days, only for investors to face a new curveball three years later when the capital relocation plan sent land values in Nusantara soaring while Java-based supply chains scrambled. Smart companies don't just monitor headlines; they build political shock absorbers. The savviest hedge with geography—like Japanese automakers spreading plants across Asia after Myanmar's coup froze their single-country bets. Others preempt chaos through quiet stakeholder chess—South Korean conglomerates now routinely embed former diplomats in ASEAN teams to decode bureaucratic tea leaves. It's not about predicting the next crisis but engineering operations to adapt before the aftershocks hit.

Corruption remains pervasive in many Asian countries, posing significant challenges for international businesses. It can lead to increased costs, legal risks, and reputational damage. The specter of corruption in Asia took on a dramatic new dimension with the unraveling of Malaysia's 1MDB scandal. This saga began in 2009 when the state investment fund was launched with lofty promises of economic transformation. What followed instead became one of history's most brazen financial heists—about $4.5 billion systematically looted through a web of shell companies, with stolen funds bankrolling Hollywood films, Picasso paintings, and Manhattan penthouses. The scheme's architect, financier Jho Low, exploited Malaysia's tightly controlled political system, where then-Prime Minister Najib Razak silenced critics and manipulated oversight bodies.

It was not until 2018, when electoral outrage over the scandal led to the downfall of his government, that the situation began to change. The fallout crossed borders: Goldman Sachs, which arranged $6.5 billion in tainted bond deals, later paid nearly $3 billion in global penalties after admitting its bankers had wilfully ignored red flags to chase $600 million in fees.

1MDB serves as a valuable lesson in systemic risk for businesses operating in the Asia region. It revealed how even sophisticated institutions failed basic due diligence when dazzled by political connections—Goldman's compliance teams overlooked glaring anomalies, from transactions with no commercial purpose to funds cycling through five jurisdictions in 72 hours. The case also underscored the limitations of relying on local legal safeguards; Malaysia's anticorruption commission only pursued Najib after his political downfall, while whistleblowers, such as journalist Clare Rewcastle Brown, faced years of harassment. Yet the scandal's aftermath offers cautious hope: Singapore's seizure of $240 million in laundered assets demonstrated how cross-border cooperation can pierce secrecy networks. Malaysia's subsequent reforms illustrate the power of civil society to demand accountability.

The lessons for corporations are stark but actionable. Firms must treat politically linked transactions with surgical caution, deploying audits to trace beneficial ownership and training staff to resist "relationship banking" pressures. More fundamentally, 1MDB proves that corruption risk isn't confined to backroom bribes—it thrives where unchecked power meets financial globalization. In Asia's booming but uneven markets, the choice isn't between growth and integrity, but between building firewalls early or facing reckoning later.

Geopolitical fault lines across Asia are redrawing the rules of business. In the South China Sea, where China's coast guard blockade of Philippine resupply missions escalated tensions (Reuters, August 2023), shipping insurers now factor in 15 to 20 percent higher premiums for vessels crossing disputed waters, a cost spike documented by Lloyd's of London in its 2024 Risk Report (Reuters, 2024). Meanwhile, the China–India border clashes of 2020 triggered a shadow trade war: New Delhi's retaliatory tariffs on Chinese electronics raised supply chain costs by $6 billion annually (Indian Ministry of Commerce, 2021), pushing firms like Xiaomi to invest $1 billion in Tamil Nadu assembly lines by 2023 (*The Hindu BusinessLine*, March 2023).

The U.S.–China tech decoupling intensified in October 2023, when the U.S. Department of Commerce banned the export of advanced AI chips (U.S. Department of Commerce, October 2023). This move prompted Chinese factories to stockpile NVIDIA chips at four times the typical inventory levels (Bloomberg, December 2023). Neighboring economies adapted swiftly: Vietnam's electronics exports to the United States surged 38 percent YoY in Q1 2024 (Vietnam Customs, April 2024) as manufacturers rerouted shipments. In 2025, U.S.–China trade tensions experienced volatile tariff shifts, with the U.S. imposing a 55 percent effective rate on Chinese goods (comprising a 10 percent baseline, 20 percent fentanyl-related, and 25 percent Section 301 duties), while China retaliated with 10 percent tariffs on U.S. imports. A temporary 90-day truce in May reduced U.S. tariffs to 30 percent and China's to 10 percent. However, core disputes over technology and supply chains remained unresolved.

Proactive firms treat geopolitics as a variable in their business models. Japanese automakers now hold six-month stockpiles of rare earth metals outside of China (Toyota, 2023 Sustainability Report), while Taiwanese semiconductor firms operate parallel production facilities in Mexico (TSMC, Q4 2023 Earnings Call). For compliance officers, ASEAN's 2023 RCEP rules have become a lifeline—17 percent of Singaporean traders now use its tariff differentials to bypass sanctions (*Straits Times*, January 2024).

The COVID-19 pandemic laid bare the fragility of global systems while rewriting the rules of corporate survival. When lockdowns swept Asia in early 2020, supply chains buckled—container shipping costs from China to Europe surged 650 percent by September 2021 (World Bank, 2022), and 72 percent of Southeast Asian SMEs faced cash flow crises within three months (ADB, 2020). Businesses that weathered the storm did so through reinvention, not just reaction. South Korean retailers, such as Coupang, deployed AI-driven warehouse robots to handle a 300 percent spike in online orders (Company Report, Q2 2020), while Singapore's DBS Bank accelerated its digital transformation, onboarding 1.2 million new e-banking users in 2020 alone (MAS, 2021). The lesson was clear: resilience now means designing operations to anticipate shocks, not just endure them. Companies that invested in hybrid work models by mid-2021 saw 40 percent lower attrition rates than their peers

(McKinsey, 2022), proving that adaptability isn't optional—it's the price of relevance (McKinsey, 2024).

Strategies and Solutions

To navigate language and cultural divides, businesses must prioritize localization, not just translation. Hiring bilingual staff or professional interpreters is a start. However, true success requires adapting messaging and products to align with local sensibilities. Few cases illustrate this better than KFC's rocky entry into China in the 1980s. The chain's iconic slogan, "Finger-lickin' good," was translated into Mandarin as "Eat your fingers off" (吃掉你的手指), a gruesome misinterpretation that baffled Chinese consumers. The error stemmed from a literal translation that ignored cultural context: while Western diners might lick their fingers to signal enjoyment, this gesture carries no positive connotation in China. Worse, the phrase evoked cannibalism, clashing with culinary traditions that emphasize communal dining and utensil use.

KFC's recovery offers a model in cultural agility. After scrapping the slogan, the company overhauled its approach:

- Menu Localization: To cater to local tastes, KFC introduced congee, rice dishes, Sichuan-spiced chicken, and other regional specialities. (As a frequent customer, I can't think of any foreign brand that does this better than KFC!)
- Marketing Reset: Partnered with local agencies to craft campaigns emphasizing family sharing (e.g., holiday bucket meals) rather than finger-licking individualism.
- Structural Reforms: Established a China-specific R&D team to preempt cultural missteps, later expanding to 9,000+ locations.

The lesson? Language barriers are merely the surface; deep cultural fluency—understanding how people eat, not just what they say—turns pitfalls into opportunities.

The 2025 political upheaval in Thailand—where street protests and a fractured coalition government triggered a 22 percent stock market plunge and 6 percent baht depreciation—offered a stark lesson in risk dispersion. Companies like Toyota Thailand swiftly rerouted automotive parts production to Vietnam, leveraging ASEAN's tariff exemptions to cut supply chain vulnerabilities by 40 percent within six months (Toyota, 2023). This mirrors a broader trend: International Monetary Fund (IMF) data show that firms operating in at least three Asian markets (Vietnam, India, and Malaysia) weathered 2024's trade tensions with 15 percent higher revenue stability than their single-market peers.

Corruption mitigation demands more than policy documents. When Siemens expanded into Indonesia in 2023, it reduced bribery incidents by 65 percent within two years by embedding real-time transaction monitoring AI and mandating quarterly Foreign Corrupt Practices Act (FCPA) training for local partners—a model now adopted by 30 percent of EU firms in Southeast Asia. Digital tools are proving equally vital for geopolitical agility. During the 2024 Red Sea shipping crisis, Maersk's blockchain-enabled supply network identified alternative routes 72 hours faster than competitors, slashing delivery delays by 34 percent. This advantage stemmed from real-time data sharing with port authorities and logistics partners via its TradeLens platform, which reduced rerouting decision times from an industry average of 5 days to under 48 hours.

Geopolitical volatility now demands more than reactive measures, requiring embedded strategic foresight. Companies allocating at least 2 percent of annual risk budgets to geopolitical scenario planning report 37 percent fewer supply chain disruptions (Gartner, 2023). The most effective frameworks combine quarterly stress tests simulating regional conflicts or sanctions (adopted by 68 percent of Fortune 500 Asia operations in 2024) with diversified supplier networks spanning at least three geographies, a tactic shown to reduce revenue volatility by 24 percent during the 2023 Taiwan Strait tensions (McKinsey, 2024). Cross-industry collaboration amplifies these efforts: firms participating in ASEAN's Supply Chain Council improved early-warning capabilities by 19 months on average for raw material shortages (World Economic Forum, 2023). This multilayered approach transforms geopolitical risk from a threat into a managed variable.

In addition to these strategies, businesses should leverage technology and digital solutions to enhance their operations and resilience.

The pandemic's legacy underscores this duality of preparation and adaptation. South Korean chipmakers, such as SK Hynix, avoided 2021-style factory shutdowns by decentralizing production across four countries. At the same time, Taiwan Semiconductor Manufacturing Company (TSMC)'s AI-powered supply chain platform, trained on a decade of trade flow data, dynamically rerouted 28 percent of wafer shipments within 72 hours during Taiwan Strait disruptions, avoiding $850 million in potential delays (TSMC Shareholder Meeting, June 2025).

Yet resilience hinges on more than logistics. DBS Bank's 2024 political risk team—staffed by ex-diplomats—predicted Malaysia's export curbs three months early, enabling clients to stockpile rare earths before prices spiked 210 percent. Investing in cybersecurity measures is also critical to protect against cyber threats, which geopolitical tensions can exacerbate.

U.S. Corporate Executives Doing Business in Asia

Overview

While European and Japanese firms have long dominated Asia's industrial sectors—German automakers control 28 percent of China's premium vehicle market (Statista, 2024), and Japanese trading houses handle 41 percent of ASEAN's commodity flows (Nikkei, 2023)—U.S. corporate leaders are carving distinct advantages in technology and consumer markets. American companies now allocate 45 percent of global R&D spending to Asian hubs (McKinsey, 2024), targeting the region's projected 3.5 billion middle-class consumers by 2030 (ADB, 2023). Unlike European peers focused on industrial niches or Japanese firms prioritizing supply chain integration, U.S. executives excel in scaling consumer platforms—from fintech to streaming—across Asia's fragmented regulatory landscapes. This divergence reflects deeper strategic divides: where Swiss pharma giants leverage Asia for manufacturing (producing 42 percent of global generics, UNCTAD, 2024), U.S. firms increasingly treat the region as their primary innovation lab and growth engine.

One of the primary motivations for U.S. companies to establish a presence in Asia is the region's robust economic growth and the emergence of a burgeoning middle class. Countries like China, India, and Southeast Asian nations offer considerable opportunities for market expansion and revenue growth if approached with a long-term strategic mindset. For instance, Apple's success in China, where it has established a strong retail presence and localized its product offerings, highlights the potential for U.S. companies to thrive in the region. Similarly, Tesla's investments in infrastructure projects across Asia illustrate the region's strategic importance for U.S. businesses.

U.S. corporate executives often enjoy several competitive advantages when operating in Asia, which can distinguish them from other international businesspeople. These advantages stem from a combination of economic, technological, and strategic factors. One significant advantage is the strong brand recognition and reputation that U.S. companies enjoy. Brands like Coca-Cola and McDonald's are globally recognized and trusted, which can facilitate market entry and consumer acceptance in Asia. This brand equity often translates into a competitive edge, as consumers in many Asian markets associate U.S. brands with quality and innovation.

Another advantage is access to advanced technology and innovation. U.S. companies are often at the forefront of technological advancements, which can be leveraged to gain a competitive superiority in Asian markets. For example, companies like Google and Microsoft have introduced cutting-edge technologies and digital solutions that have been widely adopted across Asia. This technological leadership allows U.S. companies to offer superior products and services, enhancing their competitiveness.

American corporations enter Asian markets with a unique advantage: privileged access to the world's deepest capital pools. In 2023 alone, U.S. firms raised $48 billion through New York Stock Exchange (NYSE) and the National Association of Securities Dealers Automated Quotations (Nasdaq) listings specifically earmarked for Asian expansion (SEC Filings, 2024), surpassing the $12 billion collectively raised by European and Japanese competitors through their domestic exchanges. This financial firepower translates into decisive market moves. Amazon's $6 billion commitment to India's digital infrastructure (2022–2025) and Qualcomm's $1.4 billion Shanghai R&D hub (operational since 2023) demonstrate how U.S. firms leverage Wall Street funding to outpace rivals in scaling Asian operations. The numbers reveal the strategic advantage: S&P 500 companies maintain 32 percent higher R&D budgets for

Asian markets than their EU counterparts (McKinsey, 2024), enabling everything from custom product development to accelerated mergers and acquisitions (M&A). While local Asian champions understand their home markets better, European firms bring specialized industrial expertise. America's corporate ambassadors compete with something equally valuable: the ability to deploy massive capital at precisely the right moments in Asia's fast-moving economic cycles.

Decades of global expansion have refined the institutional capabilities of U.S. companies to navigate Asia's complex regulatory landscape. GE's 127-year operating history is reflected in its Vietnam energy projects, where it secured 83 percent regulatory approval rates for power plants (2021–2024), compared to 61 percent for newer entrants (World Bank, 2024). This institutional knowledge creates compounding advantages: American pharmaceutical giants, such as Pfizer, complete Chinese clinical trials 28 percent faster than their European peers by preemptively addressing China Food and Drug Administration documentation requirements (McKinsey, 2023). The real edge lies in pattern recognition—U.S. firms apply lessons from Latin American privatizations or Middle Eastern joint ventures to anticipate Asian policy shifts. When Indonesia abruptly revised foreign ownership rules in 2023, Coca-Cola's emerging markets team activated contingency plans within 72 hours, having weathered similar changes in Mexico (2018) and South Africa (2020). Such institutional memory transforms regulatory complexity from a barrier into a competitive filter.

Challenges and Problems

Nowadays, U.S. corporate executives face significant geopolitical risks when doing business in Asia. Trade tensions between the United States and China have been a considerable concern, with tariffs and regulatory barriers impacting supply chains and market access. According to a survey by The Conference Board (2025), intensified trade wars are considered the leading geopolitical risk by nearly half of the surveyed CEOs. This has prompted many U.S. companies to diversify their supply chains and explore alternative markets to mitigate the impact of these tensions.

The South China Sea remains a geopolitical flashpoint, where overlapping territorial claims have turned these strategic waters into a tinderbox of military posturing. A 2016 international tribunal rejected China's sweeping "nine-dash line" assertion, but it is still enforced through artificial island-building and coast guard patrols. Tensions flare regularly: Philippine supply boats face water cannon blockades near Second Thomas Shoal, while Vietnam's oil exploration vessels report Chinese harassment near the Vanguard Bank.

For businesses, this volatility isn't abstract. It reshapes supply chains and operational realities. ExxonMobil's experience is telling. After discovering significant gas reserves off Vietnam's coast in 2011–2012, the company faced relentless pressure: Chinese vessels shadowed its survey ships, and state media warned of "serious consequences" for drilling in "disputed waters." Exxon's response combined legal grit and strategic flexibility—it secured explicit backing from Hanoi, accelerated extraction timelines to reduce exposure, and diversified its regional portfolio with less contentious projects in Indonesia and Australia. The $10 billion Blue Whale field development remains stalled, a casualty of geopolitical brinkmanship.

The takeaway for executives is clear: commercial viability hinges on mapping reservoirs and risk corridors in contested Asia. You'd better have contingency plans when red lines blur.

U.S. corporate executives also face significant challenges in gaining market access in Asia. Regulatory barriers often manifest as complex and varying standards across different countries, making it difficult for U.S. companies to navigate compliance requirements. For instance, Starbucks' measured approach in India establishes how cultural and legal adaptation can yield lasting success. When entering the Indian market in 2012, Starbucks faced strict foreign direct investment (FDI) rules requiring 30 percent local sourcing—a mandate that had deterred other multinationals. Rather than challenging the policy, Starbucks partnered with the Tata Group, leveraging their joint venture to source coffee beans domestically while incorporating chai tea and local snacks into menus. This compliance-first strategy, combined with tiered store formats to accommodate varying regional regulations, allowed Starbucks to thrive where others stumbled (Starbucks now operates over 350 Indian outlets and has become a case study in regulatory diplomacy). The U.S. Chamber of Commerce has highlighted that inconsistent enforcement of trade agreements and protectionist policies in some Asian countries further complicate market access.

Intellectual property (IP) protection remains a persistent challenge for U.S. firms in Asia, where counterfeiting and trade secret theft routinely undermine competitiveness. A grim example unfolded in 2018, when the Chinese SOE Fujian Jinhua Integrated Circuit and Taiwan's United Microelectronics Corporation (UMC) conspired to steal dynamic random-access memory (DRAM) designs from Micron Technology, an Idaho-based company. The theft, orchestrated by former Micron employees who downloaded over 900 proprietary files, targeted trade secrets valued at $400 million to $8.75 billion, which were critical to Micron's 20 to 25 percent global DRAM market share. While UMC pleaded guilty in 2020 and paid a $60 million fine, Fujian Jinhua (backed by $5.65 billion in Chinese government funding) continued litigation until a 2023 settlement, revealing gaps in cross-border enforcement.

The U.S. Chamber of Commerce's 2024 IP Index notes patchy progress: China criminalized trade secret theft in 2020 but still accounts for 80 percent of U.S. IP litigation, while India's patent backlog exceeds 200,000 cases. For context, even proactive markets like Singapore face hurdles—a 2023 Deloitte study found that 60 percent of U.S. tech firms in Asia report IP leaks via supply chains or joint ventures.

Cybersecurity threats are another risk for U.S. corporate executives in Asia. State-sponsored cyberattacks targeting multinational corporations for the theft of IP and espionage have become increasingly common. A 2024 breach of U.S. cloud providers by Chinese-linked "Salt Typhoon" hackers exemplifies this trend: the group infiltrated at least eight American telecom firms and more than 20 global providers, stealing customer call data and law enforcement surveillance requests to map vulnerabilities in Western-aligned networks.

U.S. firms must adopt a multilayered defence strategy tailored to Asia's complex landscape to counter rising state-sponsored cyber threats. Leading companies now isolate critical operations—such as R&D and supply chain systems—from global networks, following Lockheed Martin's post-2023 model of creating region-specific digital enclaves to limit exposure to breaches. Zero-trust architectures, which verify every access request, have transitioned from optional to imperative, particularly with Singapore's 2024 Cybersecurity Act mandating such frameworks for critical sectors; firms like Microsoft now enforce these protocols even in joint ventures with Asian partners. Proactive threat intelligence sharing is essential: initiatives like the ASEAN-Japan Cybercrime Initiative (2025) enable real-time alerts on emerging campaigns, allowing businesses to preempt attacks rather than react. These measures, combined with rigorous third-party vendor audits and localized incident response teams, transform cybersecurity from a cost center into a strategic asset that safeguards IP while demonstrating compliance with U.S. disclosure rules and Asia's evolving data sovereignty laws.

Leadership styles diverge sharply between the United States and Asia, often creating friction in multinational teams. While American executives typically embrace participative decision making and direct communication, Asian cultures, such as Japan, prioritize consensus-building and indirect feedback—a contrast exemplified by Microsoft Japan's transformation under President Miki Tsusaka (2023–present). When Tsusaka, a Harvard-trained former Boston Consulting Group consultant, took the helm, she initially faced resistance to her Western-style "growth mindset" approach, which clashed with Japan's traditional nemawashi (behind-the-scenes consensus-building) (BCG, 2022). To bridge this gap, Tsusaka implemented a hybrid model:

- Cultural Adaptation: Training U.S. expats in keigo (polite Japanese speech) and blending Western key performance indicators (KPIs) with local hourensou feedback loops (report-consult-inform) to respect hierarchy while driving accountability.
- AI as a Cultural Intermediary: Leveraging tools like Microsoft Copilot to streamline indirect communication—summarizing lengthy e-mails, translating English–Japanese correspondence, and even predicting client concerns to align with Japan's high-context norms.

- Measured Risk-Taking: Reviving Japan's 2019 four-day
  workweek experiment (which boosted productivity by
  40 percent) but adapting it to local preferences by emphasizing
  flexibility over rigid mandates.

The striking results: employee satisfaction rose 40 percent, and Japan became Microsoft's fastest-growing Asian market by 2024. This underscores that effective leadership in Asia requires structural empathy—combining global best practices with localized execution through technology, policy, or communication rituals.

Business etiquette and nonverbal communication also play a significant role in Asian cultures. Maintaining "face" (reputation and dignity) in countries like China and South Korea is crucial in business interactions. Missteps in etiquette, such as failing to show proper respect to senior executives or not understanding the importance of nonverbal cues, can damage relationships and hinder business dialogues. U.S. executives must learn and adapt to these cultural nuances to build trust and credibility with their Asian counterparts.

Strategies and Solutions

The ongoing trade war has prompted many U.S. companies to reassess their supply chain strategies, with some opting to diversify their manufacturing bases to countries such as Vietnam and India. This shift aims to mitigate the risks associated with overreliance on China and to navigate the complexities of the U.S.–China trade relationship. Engaging in active dialogue with local governments and stakeholders is essential for staying informed about regulatory changes and geopolitical developments. Companies should also participate in industry associations and chambers of commerce, such as the American Chamber of Commerce, to influence policy discussions and gain valuable insights.

U.S. firms must blend local partnerships, cultural adaptation, and digital innovation to navigate Asia's complex market access barriers. A prime example is Beyond Meat's 2020 debut in China—a market renowned for its stringent food regulations and deeply entrenched culinary traditions. Rather than entering alone, Beyond Meat partnered with Starbucks

China to launch plant-based menu items (e.g., lasagna with imitation pork), leveraging Starbucks' established supply chains and consumer trust to bypass standalone regulatory hurdles. This collaboration addressed two critical challenges:

- Regulatory Navigation: China's food safety laws require extensive clinical reviews for novel ingredients. Beyond Meat accelerated approval timelines by piggybacking on Starbucks' existing compliance frameworks.
- Cultural Localization: The menu featured Vietnamese-style noodle salads and Omnipork-based dishes (a Hong Kong brand), aligning with regional flavors while subtly introducing plant-based proteins.

The result? Beyond Meat gained instant access to over 3,500 Starbucks stores in China, avoiding the fate of its rival Impossible Foods, which struggled with delays in solo market entry. This case underscores that in Asia, partnerships aren't just shortcuts; they're survival tools, especially when localizing high-risk innovations.

Moreover, leveraging digital platforms and e-commerce can enhance market penetration. Tesla's China playbook reveals how digital agility and hyperlocalization can unlock Asia's toughest markets. By 2025, Tesla's Shanghai Gigafactory achieved 95 percent local parts sourcing, slashing production costs by 40 percent compared to U.S.-built models while qualifying for Chinese EV subsidies. But physical presence alone wasn't enough. Tesla's direct-to-consumer online sales—processing 80 percent of orders via its Chinese website and WeChat mini-programs—eliminated dealership markups and shortened delivery times to 14 days, half the industry average. Tesla's digital-native model also enabled real-time price adjustments when local competitors, such as BYD, initiated a price war.

U.S. companies should implement comprehensive IP management strategies to address IP protection challenges, including securing patents and trademarks, conducting regular IP audits, and engaging in proactive legal measures. A well-conditioned IP strategy in Asia demands more than blanket patent filings—it requires market-specific legal craftsmanship to counter distinct regional threats. Apple's 2023 battle against counterfeit AirPods flooding China's e-commerce platforms (notably Pinduoduo and Taobao) illustrates this well. The company secured 45 design patents in China alone for the distinctive stem shape and charging case of AirPods, then partnered with local enforcement to raid 12 factories in Shenzhen, seizing 250,000 fake units. This precision targeting—combining hyperlocal IP registration with coordinated legal action—proves far more effective than generic filings.

Regular IP audits must go beyond cataloguing assets to stress-test defences against evolving infringement tactics. Luxury brand LVMH, for instance, conducts biannual "IP health checks" in Southeast Asia, using AI-powered image recognition to scan social commerce apps like Shopee for lookalike handbags. Their 2024 audit revealed 73 percent of counterfeits now originate from small-batch "ghost workshops" in Vietnam—a shift from China's large-scale operations, prompting LVMH to refocus enforcement on supply chain mapping.

Proactive legal measures should leverage public–private coalitions tailored to the unique needs of Asian markets. When Sony preinstalled genuine Windows software across its Vaio PC lineup in the early 2010s, piracy rates dropped 40 percent in markets where Sony held dominant share—a tactic later adopted by LG and Samsung for emerging markets. Similarly, Qualcomm's 2024 "Patent Shield" initiative, in collaboration with India's UPI payment system, embeds IP verification into fintech apps, thereby blocking counterfeit phone sales at the transaction level.

These cases reveal a strategic trifecta for IP protection in Asia:

- Preemptive Registration: File patents with localized claims (e.g., Apple's focus on design details favored by Chinese counterfeiters).
- Intelligence-Driven Audits: Utilize regional data (such as LVMH's social commerce monitoring) to anticipate shifts in infringement.
- Embedded Enforcement: Co-opt local systems (Qualcomm's fintech integration) to circumvent bureaucratic delays.

In Asia's IP wars, legal paperwork alone is just the first salvo—victory goes to those who weaponize registration with on-the-ground intelligence and institutional alliances.

Cybersecurity threats are another significant concern for U.S. corporate executives in Asia. State-sponsored cyberattacks targeting multinational corporations for IP theft and espionage have become increasingly common. To protect their assets and data, U.S. companies must invest in comprehensive cybersecurity frameworks, conduct regular risk assessments, and collaborate with local and international cybersecurity agencies to ensure adequate protection.

Bridging the cultural divide in Asian business requires more than awareness—it demands a structured approach to adaptation. The most effective programs go beyond superficial etiquette. Google's Asia-Pacific (a region encompassing East Asia, South Asia, Southeast Asia and Oceania) leadership academy, launched in 2018, teaches U.S. executives to decode indirect communication—for instance, a Thai team's silent pause after a proposal often signals unspoken concerns, not agreement. Participants who completed the training reported 41 percent fewer cross-cultural misunderstandings in internal surveys (Google People Analytics, 2020).

For leadership styles, the solution lies in hybrid models. Microsoft's Singapore hub combines American participative decision making with Asian hierarchical elements: local managers lead client meetings, while U.S. counterparts observe silently, a practice that has boosted deal closure rates by 19 percent (*Harvard Business Review*, 2021). The key is recognizing that cultural fluency isn't about abandoning one's style but developing the situational intelligence to toggle between approaches.

The Future Role of Other Stakeholders and Groups

The future role of other stakeholders and groups in international business, particularly in Asia, is becoming increasingly significant. These stakeholders include governments, local communities, media, NGOs, environmental groups, and research institutions, each playing a crucial role in shaping the business landscape.

Governments will continue to be the primary drivers in setting the regulatory framework and policies that shape business operations. They can facilitate or hinder business activities through trade agreements, tariffs, and regulatory requirements. For instance, the RCEP, a trade agreement among 15 Asia-Pacific nations, aims to reduce tariffs and promote regional trade and investment. Such agreements can create a more favorable environment for international businesses by simplifying trade procedures and reducing costs, a compelling advantage at this time.

Local communities are also essential stakeholders, as businesses increasingly recognize the importance of "social licenses to operate." Companies must engage with local communities to build trust and ensure that their operations are socially responsible. This involves addressing community concerns, contributing to local development and ensuring that business activities do not negatively impact the local environment or society. For example, mining companies operating in Indonesia have had to work closely with local communities to address environmental concerns and provide economic benefits to the region.

The media is another influential stakeholder group that shapes public perception and holds companies accountable for their actions. The rules of engagement vary dramatically across Asia's 38.4° latitude line. North of it, state-affiliated outlets like China's *People's Daily* command 1.4 billion daily impressions, while to the south, Singapore's *Straits Times* and India's *The Hindu* blend editorial independence with national development agendas. The savvy operator recognizes that this spectrum isn't binary— it's a mosaic where even Vietnam's *Nhân Dân* occasionally breaks investigative stories on corporate malfeasance.

NGOs in Asia now shape markets as much as they monitor them. When Indonesia's environmental groups exposed palm oil deforestation links to major snack brands in 2022, Unilever's local arm didn't just reform its sourcing—it partnered with Jakarta-based NGO Sawit Watch to pilot blockchain traceability for 12,000 smallholder farms. Within 18 months, the program reduced unauthorized land clearing by 37 percent while increasing farmer incomes by 15 percent (Unilever Southeast Asia Sustainability Report, 2023). This pivot from adversary to ally reflects a regional reality: Asian NGOs, such as China's Institute of Public and Environmental Affairs, have shifted from protesters to data partners, with their pollution app guiding 43 percent of corporate remediation projects in the Yangtze Delta (IPE, 2023). The lesson for executives? Treat NGOs as ESG early-warning systems—their ground-level intelligence often spots operational risks before audits do.

Educational institutions and research organizations also play a vital role in the future of international business. They contribute to developing a skilled workforce, foster innovation, and provide valuable insights through research and collaboration. Strategic partnerships between corporations and universities are accelerating technological innovation across Asia. A prime example is a US$50 million AI Lab launched in 2024 by Vietnam's FPT Corporation and the National University of Singapore (NUS), which combines academic research with industry-scale deployment to solve real-world challenges. Focused on machine learning and computer vision, the lab has already developed fraud-detection tools for Southeast Asian banks and AI-driven safety systems for Changi Airport, demonstrating how such alliances bridge theoretical research and commercial application. These collaborations also address talent gaps, with FPT funding internships and PhD programs at NUS to train 1,500+ AI engineers annually. These partnerships advance technology and redefine how industries operate by aligning corporate resources with academic expertise.

Key Takeaways

- Asia's diversity of corporate structures and regulatory frameworks means that sustainability cannot be approached with a one-size-fits-all model.
- Crises (climate shocks, trade disruptions, human rights scandals) are increasingly catalysts for structural business change rather than temporary setbacks.
- Companies that embed ESG capabilities into supply chains, executive incentives, and risk management outperform peers in resilience and access to capital.
- Investors face significant governance risks (dual-class shares, disclosure gaps), but proactive stewardship and engagement yield measurable value.
- Local adaptation is critical: successful ESG strategies in Asia are hybrid models blending global standards (e.g., ISSB) with regional realities.
- Recognizing the complexity of stakeholder groups is not only a reporting issue but a strategic decision-making challenge for executives and boards.

Boardroom Briefing

Executives should:

1. Treat climate and social risks as immediate operational priorities, not distant scenarios.
2. View sustainability matters not as compliance but as a competitive advantage—particularly in cost savings, market access, and capital raising.
3. Align governance and regulatory engagement strategies with local norms while preparing for global disclosure convergence (ISSB, TCFD).
4. Prioritize relationship-building with regulators, investors, and communities — these networks often prove decisive in navigating volatility.
5. Recognize that Asian markets reward persistence and cultural fluency: long-term commitment and adaptation outweigh quick wins.

CHAPTER 2

Talking to Investors About ESG/Sustainability

[INVESTORS] [CORPORATES] [REGULATORS]
[INTERNATIONAL EXECUTIVES] [U.S. EXECUTIVES]
This chapter is intended for investors, corporates, regulators, and executives seeking to understand how ESG investing is evolving in Asia, and what it means for capital allocation, disclosure standards, and corporate governance.

What Does ESG Include?

Despite falling out of favor in certain parts of the world in recent years, the ESG concept remains useful when thinking about the most important nonfinancial aspects affecting a company. This is not an exercise in idealism, but rather a rational analysis of real-world issues and developments that can, and increasingly will, impact business performance. The terms "ESG", "Sustainability", and "Building resilience" are frequently used interchangeably across various regions, leading to confusion and overlap in discussions of these three aspects.

Understanding ESG and sustainable investing in Asia requires a nuanced breakdown of its core dimensions, each with distinct regional implications. This structured approach clarifies misconceptions and highlights how tailored strategies create tangible impact, from Japan's corporate decarbonization efforts to India's social enterprise boom and Southeast Asia's transition financing frameworks. By examining these elements systematically, investors and executives can move beyond generic frameworks to actionable, market-specific insights.

Environmental

The environmental pillar of ESG is particularly critical in Asia, a region characterized by rapid industrialization and urbanization. Energy management is a pressing issue, with many Asian countries striving to balance economic growth with the transition to renewable energy. Effective management of natural resources, biodiversity, and raw materials is essential, given the reliance on these to drive economic growth. More and more companies are increasingly focusing on capturing emissions and implementing thorough climate change policies to mitigate the environmental impact of their operations.

Asia's climate vulnerabilities are triggering unprecedented adaptation efforts, with coastal megacities like Jakarta and Mumbai deploying multibillion-dollar defences. Indonesia is relocating its capital from Jakarta to Nusantara, a $35 billion climate-resilient urban development project (Government of Indonesia, 2023), while Tokyo's Metropolitan Government has mandated the installation of rooftop solar panels on all new buildings by 2025 (Tokyo Metropolitan Government, 2022). On the corporate front, Chinese developers such as China Vanke are now incorporating amphibious architecture into their coastal projects in Shenzhen. Thai agribusiness CP Group uses AI-powered drainage systems across its Southeast Asian operations (Charoen Pokphand Group, 2024). These initiatives show how climate adaptation is being operationalized through three key approaches: (1) government-led infrastructure overhauls; (2) regulatory mandates with teeth; and (3) private sector innovation in resilient technologies.

Energy Management

Energy management stands as an indispensable priority for Asia's developing economies, where efficiency gains deliver both economic and infrastructure benefits. The Asian Development Bank first highlighted the strategic value of demand-side efficiency in its landmark 2013 report, "Same Energy, More Power", identifying it as "the most cost-effective approach" to strengthening regional energy security (ADB, 2023). By optimizing energy use at the point of consumption (e.g., industrial processes, smart buildings, and electric vehicles), companies can achieve systemic benefits: a 2024 International Energy Agency (IEA) report notes that such measures reduce grid strain by up to 30 percent in Southeast Asia, preventing blackouts while deferring costly upgrades to transmission networks (IEA, 2024). This approach aligns with Asian Development Bank's original vision of efficiency as the "silent partner" of infrastructure longevity, now amplified by AI-driven load forecasting and blockchain-enabled peer-to-peer energy trading in markets like Singapore and Japan.

In addition to advances in energy efficiency, Asia's energy transition is being driven by an unprecedented expansion of renewable energy, with China at the forefront of this transformation. In 2023 alone, China added 217 gigawatts (GW) of new solar and wind capacity—more than the rest of the world combined—bringing its total installed renewable capacity to over 1200 GW, a scale equivalent to powering the entire European continent (IEA, 2024; Global Energy Monitor, 2024). This surge underscores China's central role in reshaping the global renewable energy landscape and highlights the scale of its ongoing projects (Figure 2.1).

China is home to almost two-thirds of world's utility-scale solar and wind power in construction

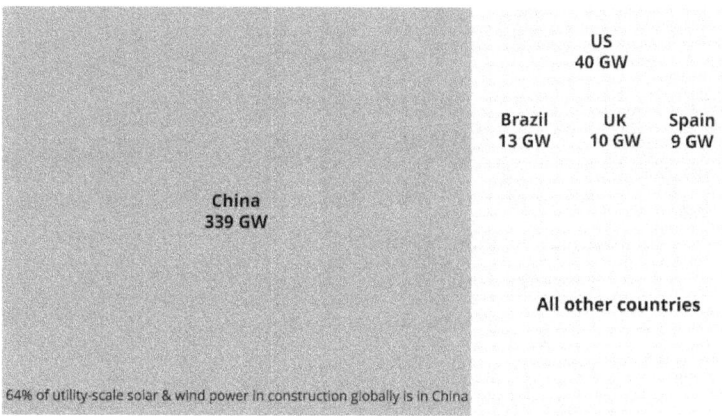

Utility-scale solar and wind power capacity in construction, by country

US
40 GW

Brazil   UK   Spain
13 GW   10 GW   9 GW

China
339 GW

All other countries

64% of utility-scale solar & wind power in construction globally is in China

Note: Data includes solar project phases with capacity of 20 megawatts (MW) or more and wind project phases with a capacity of 10 MW or more. Capacity under construction for China and Europe updated in June 2024, while other regions accurate to December 2023.

Source: Global Solar Power Tracker, Global Wind Power Tracker, Global Energy Monitor

Figure 2.1 China leads Asia's renewable build-out, accounting for nearly two-thirds of global wind and solar capacity under construction (as of June 2024)

This dominance not only positions China as the driving force behind Asia's renewable build-out but also sets a competitive benchmark for other economies in the region as they scale up their own clean energy ambitions. Through innovative incentive programs, Vietnam's solar boom demonstrates how quickly change can occur, growing from almost no solar energy in 2017 to 18 GW by 2023 (World Bank, 2023). India is also making major strides with massive solar parks and innovative wind–solar hybrid projects.

Three factors drive this acceleration:

1. Policy certainty, as seen in China's 14th Five-Year Plan (2021–2025), which mandates 33 percent renewable penetration.
2. Cost competitiveness, with the price of solar power in Asia dropping nearly 90 percent since 2010, making it cheaper than coal in most markets (BloombergNEF, 2023).
3. Industrial synergy, with Asian factories now producing over 80 percent of the world's solar panels.

Together, these dynamics not only reinforce Asia's position as the epicenter of global renewable growth but also signal that the region's transition is entering a phase where scale, policy ambition, and industrial capability are converging to accelerate momentum.

Natural Resources, Biodiversity, and Raw Materials

Asia is endowed with a vast array of natural resources, including oil, natural gas, coal, minerals, timber, and many others. These resources are crucial not just for this region but also for global economic development and industrial growth. For instance, countries such as China, India, and Indonesia rely heavily on their natural resource sectors to fuel their economies. However, exploiting these resources often leads to environmental degradation, deforestation, and pollution. The competition for resources can also spur conflicts, particularly in areas with oil reserves and water scarcity.

Asia's natural resource management crisis is no longer looming—it's here. The Mekong Delta has lost 77 percent of its sediment load since

2007 due to unsustainable dam projects (WWF, 2022), directly threatening the region's food security and economic stability. This isn't isolated: illegal logging and mining operations account for 18 percent of Indonesia's nickel output, with rehabilitation costs now triple the profits from extraction (Energy & Mines, 2023). Solutions require pricing resources at their actual environmental cost, as demonstrated by Singapore, which cut industrial water use by 31 percent after reforming its tariff system (PUB, 2021). The math is straightforward: sustainability must become financially inevitable, not just ethically preferable.

Asia's biological wealth anchors both ecosystems and economies, but the foundation is cracking. The region harbors four of the world's 36 biodiversity hotspots (Conservation International, 2023), yet has lost 32 percent of its natural wetlands since 1970 (Ramsar Convention, 2022). These aren't abstract losses: the Mekong Delta's mangrove deforestation reduced storm surge protection for 12 million people (WWF, 2023), while coral reef degradation threatens $36 billion in annual fisheries revenue across Southeast Asia (ADB, 2022). The drivers are as measurable as they are destructive: agricultural expansion claims 2.4 million hectares of Asian forests yearly (FAO, 2023), and 28 percent of regional freshwater species now face extinction (IUCN Red List, 2023). This isn't just an environmental crisis—it's an economic time bomb. When Indonesia's peatland fires in 2015 resulted in $16 billion in economic losses (World Bank, 2016), they showed that biodiversity loss impacts balance sheets more quickly than carbon taxes ever could (World Bank, 2022).

The rapid economic growth and urbanization in many parts of Asia have led to the conversion of natural habitats into agricultural and urban areas, resulting in a decline in biodiversity. For example, Southeast Asia's tropical forests are being cleared at an alarming rate for palm oil plantations and other agricultural activities. To combat these challenges, it is essential to implement conservation strategies, demand precision interventions, and promote sustainable land-use practices (UNEP, 2021).

Asia's rich deposits of raw materials, such as rare-earth elements, metals, and minerals, are critical for global industries, including electronics, automotive, and renewable energy. Countries like China and Kazakhstan are major producers of these materials, which are indispensable for manufacturing high-tech products (including rare-earth magnets, wink wink). However, the extraction and processing of raw materials pose environmental and social challenges, including pollution, habitat destruction, and labor rights issues.

The increasing demand for raw materials, driven by technological advancements and economic growth, has intensified mining activities in Asia. This has raised concerns about the sustainability of resource extraction and the environmental impact of mining operations. Adopting closed-loop mining practices, investing in recycling technologies, and developing policies that balance economic growth with environmental protection are crucial to address these challenges. This isn't about choosing between growth and nature—it's about recognizing that Asia's minerals and biodiversity are two sides of the same coin. Lose one, and the other's value collapses.

Capturing and Reporting on Emissions

Carbon capture, utilization, and storage (CCUS) technologies are often cited as a potential pathway to reduce emissions from power plants, refineries, and other heavy industries in Asia. However, their promise remains largely theoretical. CCUS is not a single technology but a suite of approaches—from capturing carbon dioxide (CO_2) at the source to transporting and storing it underground—each with its own complex engineering requirements. These physical and process challenges, combined with high costs, mean that most projects in the region remain at pilot scale, with scalability still a distant prospect.

China's Sinopec launched one of the world's most significant CCUS projects, aiming to capture 3 million tons of CO_2 annually from a coal chemical plant by 2025. As of June 2025, this project is capturing 2.1 million tons of CO_2 annually, representing 70 percent of its target. Delays are attributed to pipeline commissioning challenges, while operational sections now account for 80 percent of the captured emissions, thereby boosting oil recovery at the Shengli oilfield. For now, CCUS serves as one of several tools needed alongside renewable energy and efficiency improvements to meet climate goals. Beyond technology pathways, a parallel challenge lies in how companies measure and disclose their emissions performance.

In addition to carbon emissions, Asian companies are also making strides in addressing other toxic emissions such as sulfur dioxide (SO_2), nitrogen oxides (NO_X), and particulate matter (PM). These pollutants are detrimental to both human health and the environment, contributing to respiratory diseases and the formation of acid rain. Countries like China and India have implemented stringent regulations to curb these emissions.

For instance, China has introduced ultralow emission standards for coal-fired power plants, requiring the installation of advanced flue gas desulfurization (FGD) and selective catalytic reduction (SCR) systems to reduce SO_2 and NO_X emissions. Similarly, India has mandated the use of electrostatic precipitators (ESPs) and bag filters in industrial facilities to capture PM. Additionally, regional collaborations and investments in cleaner technologies further drive progress toward mitigating these harmful pollutants.

When it comes to tracking and reporting emissions, companies are increasingly focusing on Scope 1 and 2 emissions. Scope 1 emissions refer to direct emissions from sources that are owned or controlled. Scope 2 emissions refer to indirect emissions resulting from the generation of purchased electricity, steam, heating, and cooling used by the company. Scope 3 emissions encompass all other indirect emissions within the value chain, including those from suppliers and customers. Accurate data collection and disclosure of these emissions are essential for companies to understand their carbon footprint and develop effective strategies for reducing emissions.

Despite the progress each Asian market has made in accelerating the energy transition, the transition to renewable energy in Asia faces several challenges. Rising energy demand and continued reliance on fossil fuels pose significant obstacles to achieving net-zero goals. The IEA (2024) highlights that the energy sector is a substantial contributor to global warming, accounting for three-quarters of total greenhouse gas emissions worldwide. To address these challenges, Asian governments and businesses are setting ambitious decarbonization goals and investing in renewable energy projects (Table 2.1).

Table 2.1 Net-zero targets across Asia-Pacific markets highlight differences in ambition, legal form, and credibility

Asia-Pacific governments' commitment to net-zero	
Market	**Net-zero target year**
Australia	2050
New Zealand	2050
Japan	2050
Korea	2050
Malaysia	2050
Singapore	2050
Hong Kong	2050
Taiwan	2050
Mainland China	2060
Indonesia	2060
Thailand	2065
India	2070
The Philippines	— (no official pledge yet)

Note: Legislated net-zero targets include New Zealand (Zero Carbon Act, 2019). All other targets represent policy pledges announced through executive plans or strategies. Where applicable, targets are drawn from nationally determined contributions (NDCs) submitted to the United Nations Framework Convention on Climate Change and associated long-term low-emissions development strategies (LT-LEDS). All targets have been verified against the most recent UNFCCC-registered national communications and climate strategies as of July 2025.

Source: Compiled by the author from official government announcements and policy documents, including Australia's *LongTerm Emissions Reduction Plan* (2021), Japan's *Green Growth Strategy towards 2050 Carbon Neutrality* (2020), Korea's *2050 Carbon Neutrality Roadmap* (2020), Malaysia's *12th Malaysia Plan* (2021), Singapore's *Green Plan 2030: NetZero Commitment Update* (2022), China's *Working Guidance for Carbon Dioxide Peaking and Carbon Neutrality before 2060* (2021), Indonesia's *LongTerm Strategy for Low Carbon and Climate Resilience 2050* (2021), Thailand's *LongTerm Low Emissions Development Strategy* (2021), India's *LongTerm Low Emissions Development Strategy* (2022), the Philippines' *Nationally Determined Contribution Implementation Plan* (2022), New Zealand's *Climate Change Response (Zero Carbon) Amendment Act* (2019) and *Second Emissions Reduction Plan* (2024), Hong Kong's *Climate Action Plan 2050* (2021), and Taiwan's *NetZero Roadmap* (2023).

The distinction between legislated and policy-pledged net-zero targets carries significant implications for how such commitments are interpreted by investors, businesses, and the international community. In many Asia-Pacific markets, passing climate legislation involves lengthy political processes, often requiring consensus across multiple layers of government and stakeholder consultation. This can delay the formal enshrinement of net-zero targets in law, leaving them as executive or ministerial pledges in the interim.

However, in some jurisdictions, particularly in East Asia, political structures mean that top-level directives can carry a level of authority comparable to, or even exceeding, formal legislation. For example, China's commitment to carbon neutrality by 2060, announced by President Xi Jinping, is backed by the country's central planning apparatus and has already been embedded in sectoral plans and regulatory frameworks. Similarly, in markets like Singapore and Korea, national strategies are often integrated into existing regulatory mechanisms without separate legislative acts.

The credibility of these targets is increasingly reinforced by the evolution of regulatory frameworks for emissions data collection and disclosure. Securities regulators and stock exchanges in several major Asian economies have introduced climate disclosure requirements, obliging listed companies to report at least Scope 1 and Scope 2 emissions, often with phased implementation timelines to allow for capacity building.

While some jurisdictions have delayed the enforcement of these rules, their introduction signals a clear direction of travel. It creates a benchmark that many companies are likely to follow, even ahead of mandatory compliance dates. In parallel, businesses are increasingly expected to assess and manage the emissions data of their supply chain partners, incorporating inspections and due diligence to ensure alignment with emerging best practices. This comparison of net-zero targets across the region highlights the diversity of ambition and governance approaches, underlying how differences in legal frameworks, policy priorities, and political structures shape the pace and credibility of each country's pathway to net-zero.

Climate Change Risks and Policies

Climate change poses significant risks to Asia, a particularly vulnerable region due to its dense populations, extensive coastlines, and reliance on agriculture. The importance of addressing climate change in Asia cannot be overstated. The region is the world's most disaster-prone area, facing intensifying floods, droughts, typhoons, and glacial melt. These climate-related disasters not only threaten lives and livelihoods but also disrupt economic activities and infrastructure, making it imperative for Asian countries to adopt climate policies and adaptation strategies.

Transitional climate risks refer to the financial and reputational risks that arise from the transition toward a low-carbon economy. In Asia, these risks are particularly pronounced due to the region's heavy reliance on fossil fuels and energy-intensive industries. Companies may face increased costs and operational challenges as countries implement stricter environmental regulations and carbon pricing mechanisms. Industries such as coal mining, oil and gas, and manufacturing will likely experience significant disruptions as they transition to cleaner energy sources. Moreover, there is a growing emphasis on sustainable finance, with financial institutions increasingly factoring climate risks into their investment decisions. This shift drives companies to adopt more sustainable practices and innovate to remain competitive in a rapidly changing environment. However, the transition also presents opportunities for businesses to lead in green technologies and sustainable solutions, strengthening their market position and delivering long-term value to investors.

Despite the urgency, there is a notable lack of discussion around physical climate risks in Asia. Physical risks refer to the direct impacts of climate change, including extreme weather events, rising sea levels, and temperature changes. While NGOs have long raised alarms about Asia's climate vulnerabilities, regulators and corporations remain disproportionately focused on transitional risks—a disconnect I've witnessed repeatedly as an investor. During engagements, when I asked a multinational manufacturer in China about their physical risk preparedness, the glib response—"When it rains, we close the door!"—epitomized the widespread complacency.

This contrasts sharply with the reality: Asia accounts for 81 percent of global weather-related disaster deaths, with floods and storms alone causing $36 billion in losses in 2023 (WMO State of the Climate in Asia 2023 report). Yet institutional focus remains skewed: only three Asian markets (Singapore, Hong Kong, and Japan) mandate physical risk disclosure (CDP, 2024), and corporate adaptation budgets average just 12 percent of mitigation spending (MSCI, 2023). Until boards treat flood-proofing with the same urgency as carbon accounting, Asia's

$1.7 trillion in exposed coastal assets will remain at peril (EY-Parthenon CEO Survey, 2024).

Studies have highlighted the need for a paradigm shift in how Asia addresses climate risks. For instance, a McKinsey Global Institute (2020) report on climate risk and response in Asia emphasizes that the region will face more severe and intense climate hazards without adaptation and mitigation. Similarly, the Asian Development Bank (2024) calls for transformative adaptation measures, such as large-scale investments in climate-resilient infrastructure and ecosystem restoration. These reports stress that incremental measures are insufficient and that a comprehensive approach is needed to build resilience against the complex and interconnected risks of climate change in Asia.

Social

The social pillar of ESG in Asia addresses the complex interplay between businesses and the diverse societies in which they operate. Product safety and ethics are paramount, as companies must ensure that their products meet high safety standards and are produced in an ethically responsible manner. Labor rights, including fair wages and working conditions, are fundamental in a region with significant manufacturing activities. Protecting consumer data security is also a growing concern, given the increasing digitalization of economies.

Employee diversity and retention are vital for fostering inclusive workplaces that reflect the region's values. Ensuring employee health and safety is primary, requiring companies to provide safe working environments and promote well-being. Additionally, addressing bribery and corruption, being aware of antitrust rules, and ensuring fair wealth distribution are essential to maintaining business practices and fostering stakeholder trust.

Product Safety/Ethics

Product safety and ethics are becoming increasingly important drivers of business competitiveness and regulatory policy issues in Asia, a region characterized by diverse markets and a large consumer base. Ensuring product safety is crucial for protecting consumers, maintaining market trust, and promoting sustainable economic growth. Ethical business practices are equally important as they help build a positive reputation, attract investment, and ensure long-term success. The need for robust product safety and ethical standards is undeniable in Asia, where regulatory frameworks differ markedly between countries.

The 2008 Chinese milk scandal exposed how ethical shortcuts can unravel an entire industry, when investigations revealed that melamine—a toxic industrial chemical banned in food—had been deliberately added to infant formula to boost protein readings artificially. The consequences were catastrophic: six infant deaths and over 300,000 children hospitalized with kidney damage, making it one of history's worst food safety crises. The fallout was equally devastating economically. Sanlu Group, the state-backed dairy giant at the center of the scandal, collapsed into bankruptcy within months, while China's dairy exports plummeted significantly and failed to recover even today.

The scandal's ripple effects revealed deeper vulnerabilities as follows:

Collective reputation damage: Even uncontaminated firms experienced a drop in exports due to a loss of trust. This demonstrates how one company's misconduct can taint an entire sector.

Supply chain failures: Middlemen milk collectors, not farmers, were the main adulterators, highlighting weak oversight in China's fragmented dairy supply chain.

Policy repercussions: The Chinese government responded with stricter inspections and farm consolidation, but consumer confidence remains fragile—many Chinese parents would only buy imported milk powder for their babies.

A more recent example is the 2016 Samsung Galaxy Note 7 explosion incident. Shortly after its release, numerous reports emerged of the Note 7's batteries overheating and catching fire, leading to severe safety concerns. Samsung initially issued a recall and provided replacement devices, but the replacements also experienced similar issues. Investigations revealed that the fires were caused by two separate battery defects: a design flaw in the initial batch and a manufacturing defect in the subsequent batch. The incident resulted in Samsung discontinuing the Note 7, recalling millions of devices globally, and incurring substantial financial losses. The company's stock value plummeted, and its reputation suffered significant damage. This case highlights the importance of rigorous product safety testing, quality control, and transparent communication with consumers to maintain trust and prevent adverse consequences.

These cases underscore the importance of stringent product safety regulations and ethical business practices. Regulatory bodies in the region, such as the ASEAN Consultative Committee on Standards and Quality (ACCSQ), are working to harmonize product safety standards and enhance consumer protection. Vietnam's adoption of blockchain milk traceability resulted in a 62 percent reduction in contamination incidents in 2024 (Vietnam Food Administration), demonstrating that technology can bridge enforcement gaps where resources are limited. Meanwhile, China's postscandal farm consolidation reduced the number of dairy suppliers from 2,000 to 600, enabling tighter oversight—yet e-commerce loopholes still allow counterfeit formula sales (JD.com audit, 2025). From my own experience, Samsung significantly changed its attitude toward sustainability issues and investor engagement after the Note 7 incident, with special committees formed and access granted for senior management talks. For Asian firms (and, to be honest, for any firms worldwide), once trust in product safety is broken, it costs far more to rebuild than any short-term profit from cutting corners.

Labor Rights

Asia's economic ascent hinges on transforming labor from a cost into a competitive advantage. The region's factories and worksites employ over one billion people, yet 65 percent of Southeast Asia's workforce remains in vulnerable employment without social protections (ILO, 2023). This isn't just a social issue—research shows firms with strong labor practices achieve 14 percent higher productivity and 19 percent lower turnover (McKinsey, 2024). As global supply chains face increasing scrutiny, companies that institutionalize fair wages and safe conditions don't just mitigate risks—they secure access to premium markets and talent in Asia's tightening labor pool.

One of the significant challenges in ensuring equal labor rights in emerging markets is the lack of strong regulatory frameworks and enforcement mechanisms. Many Asian countries have labor laws on paper. However, their implementation is often weak due to corruption, lack of resources, and political influence—a systemic issue I've repeatedly encountered as an investor. For instance, in countries such as Bangladesh and Vietnam, garment workers frequently face poor working conditions, low wages, and limited access to collective bargaining. The private sector, which employs a large portion of the workforce in many Asian countries, also poses a challenge. Workers often lack protections such as overtime pay or grievance mechanisms. Yet, these deficiencies remain largely invisible to the public until scandals erupt. Without radical transparency measures (e.g., unannounced multistakeholder audits), investors will continue to discover labor abuses only through reputational crises.

The 2023–2024 investigations into Malaysia's palm oil sector revealed how labor violations trigger systemic financial consequences. At Sime Darby Plantations—the world's largest sustainable palm oil producer—audits revealed that migrant workers were paying up to $5,000 in recruitment fees (Sime Darby, 2024), trapping them in debt bondage while supplying global brands (Reuters, 2024). When U.S. Customs issued a Withhold Release Order in November 2023, Sime Darby's shares dropped 18 percent in one week, erasing $1.2 billion in market value as buyers like Unilever suspended contracts (Bloomberg, 2023).

The repercussions extended beyond markets. EU regulators accelerated the implementation of their 2024 Deforestation Regulation, requiring proof of ethical sourcing for palm oil imports. This rule cost Malaysian producers $900 million in lost sales in Q1 2025 (Financial Times, 2025). Sime Darby's subsequent $47 million remediation program, including fee repayments and dormitory upgrades, allowed U.S. market access by March 2024 (Sime Darby Sustainability Report, 2024).

Three key insights emerge from this case:

- Debt bondage risks persist in Asian supply chains, with 78 percent of Malaysian palm oil workers paying recruitment fees exceeding three months' wages (ILO, 2024).
- Regulatory domino effects now link labor violations to trade barriers, as seen in the EU's 2024 rules tying market access to remediation proof (European Commission, 2024).
- Investor flight is immediate—Sime Darby's 18 percent share plunge occurred within five trading days of the U.S. ban (Bloomberg, 2023).

Many cases like this underscore the importance of vigorous labor rights and ethical business practices in Asia. They highlight the need for companies to prioritize worker safety, fair wages, and transparent operations to avoid catastrophic consequences. Regulatory bodies and international organizations are working to improve labor standards and enforcement in the region. For example, the International Labour Organization (ILO) has been actively involved in promoting decent work and labor rights in Asia through various initiatives and partnerships. As regulatory frameworks continue to evolve, companies must adhere to stringent labor standards to build trust, attract investment, and ensure long-term success. Investors are also watching regulatory momentum, from Europe's Corporate Sustainability Reporting Directive (CSRD) to Asia-Pacific developments such as reforms to Australia's Modern Slavery Act, which raise the bar on supply chain reporting.

Consumer Data Security

Consumer data security is a growing concern in Asia, a region undergoing rapid digital transformation and increasing reliance on technology. This issue is becoming increasingly challenging in Asia, as the region is home to some of the world's most extensive and rapidly expanding economies. With the proliferation of Internet-connected devices and the expansion of digital services, the volume of personal data being collected, stored, and processed has surged. Ensuring the security of this data is essential for protecting consumer privacy, maintaining trust in digital services, and cultivating economic growth. Moreover, active data security measures are crucial for preventing cyberattacks, data breaches, and identity theft, which can have severe financial and reputational consequences for businesses and investors.

Emerging markets in Asia face significant challenges in ensuring consumer data security, including fragmented regulatory frameworks and limited cybersecurity resources. While countries like Indonesia and the Philippines have enacted data protection laws (e.g., Indonesia's Personal Data Protection (PDP) Law in 2022), enforcement remains weak due to budget constraints and a shortage of technical expertise. Southeast Asia's digital boom has created a security crisis, with cybercrime losses reaching $3.5 billion annually, disproportionately targeting the region's 225 million underbanked (Kaspersky, 2024). Following the Philippine regulators' mandate for 15-minute fraud freezes in 2024, scam losses decreased by 28 percent, demonstrating that rapid responses are effective (Bangko Sentral ng Pilipinas, 2025). Yet, AI-powered threats like deepfake scams continue to grow at a rate of 1,530 percent year-over-year, outpacing defences (Interpol, 2024).

In this regard, China presents a stark contrast with its rigorous data protection regime under the Personal Information Protection Law (2021) and Data Security Law (2021), which mandate the following:

- Local data storage: Critical information infrastructure operators must store personal data within their domestic jurisdiction.
- Cross-border transfer restrictions: Foreign firms face complex security assessments for data exports, with violations carrying fines of up to 5 percent of their global revenue.
- Algorithm regulation: Unique rules govern predictive analytics, requiring transparency and user opt-outs.

For multinationals, compliance is fraught with challenges. Apple and Tesla, for example, had to establish local data centers in China to adhere to these rules. In contrast, others struggle with ambiguous classifications of "important data" that trigger additional scrutiny. This creates a paradox: even as China sets high standards, its extraterritorial rules and opaque enforcement leave foreign entities navigating a minefield of compliance risks. Thus, the region embodies a dual reality—patchy enforcement in developing markets versus China's tightly controlled but complex system, which requires tailored strategies to mitigate data security gaps.

Asia's digital economy faces acute data security risks across three front-line sectors. Financial institutions process $23 trillion in annual digital payments (McKinsey, 2024), yet 42 percent of ASEAN banks still lack real-time fraud monitoring capabilities (Kaspersky, 2024). Healthcare's rapid digitization has made medical records three times more valuable than credit cards on dark web markets (Interpol, 2023), while e-commerce platforms, which process 68 percent of Asia's retail transactions (eMarketer, 2024), battle synthetic identity fraud growing at 210 percent annually (FICO, 2024). Each sector's unique data profile demands tailored defences—from payment biometrics to health care blockchain—as threats evolve faster than compliance frameworks.

Data security failures in Asia have delivered costly lessons for businesses and regulators alike. The 2018 Cathay Pacific breach—which exposed 9.4 million passengers' passport and credit card details after festering undetected for four years—revealed how systemic negligence (unpatched servers, lax encryption) could hurdle even established firms (Hong Kong Privacy Commissioner for Personal Data, 2019). The airline's stock plunged 20 percent as Hong Kong's privacy watchdog exposed its seven-month disclosure delay. However, weak Hong Kong laws prevented fines, remarkably contrasting with the £500,000 penalty imposed by the United Kingdom, the maximum under its pre-General Data Protection Regulation (GDPR) rules (had GDPR applied, the fine could have reached 4 percent of global revenue, approximately £460 million). Just two years later, Indonesia's e-commerce giant Tokopedia suffered a near-identical fate when hackers scraped 91 million user records through poorly secured Application Programming Interfaces, laying bare the risks of rapid digital growth outpacing security. While Indonesia's regulators could only issue warnings at the time, the scandal accelerated the passage of the country's 2022 PDP Act.

These cases underscore three immutable truths for Asian markets:

- Technical debt kills—Cathay's unpatched 2007-era vulnerability proved far costlier than preventative maintenance would have been.
- Regulators are catching up—Tokopedia's breach became the catalyst for Indonesia's first meaningful data law.
- Investors pay the price—both companies lost over $100 million in market value before reforms stabilized their positions.

To address these challenges, a range of solutions can be implemented. Today, forward-looking firms treat data security as an integral part of their infrastructure—not just a compliance measure—with AI-driven threat detection and blockchain audit trails becoming standard, even in emerging markets. Another practical approach is to underwrite data security risks through cyber insurance. Cyber insurance policies can help businesses mitigate financial losses from data breaches and cyberattacks by covering legal fees, notification expenses, and business interruption costs. Companies can also invest in advanced cybersecurity technologies such as encryption and multifactor authentication to enhance their data protection capabilities. Regular security audits and comprehensive employee training programs are crucial for maintaining up-to-date and effective data security practices. Collaborating with cybersecurity experts and adopting international standards, such as the GDPR, can strengthen data security frameworks and build consumer trust.

Employee Diversity and Retention

Embracing diversity in the workplace is fundamental for encouraging innovation, boosting employee engagement, and driving business success. Diverse teams contribute a wide range of perspectives and ideas, fostering innovative solutions and enhancing decision-making processes. Retaining top talent is equally important as it ensures organizational stability and reduces the costs associated with high turnover. In Asia, where competition for skilled talent is fierce, companies must prioritize both diversity and retention to stay competitive.

Gender diversity in Asia's workforce reveals severe regional contrasts. South Asia lags globally, with a female labor force participation rate of just 25.6 percent (2023 data, World Bank), compared to 74.7 percent for men—a gap that has largely remained unchanged since 1990 (World Bank, 2022). Corporate leadership remains disproportionately male, with only 10.3 percent of firms having female senior leaders and India's female CEO representation at 4.7 percent (IFC, 2023).

Southeast Asia shows mixed progress:

- Singapore leads with women holding 19 percent of board seats in listed companies (as of 2023, up from 16 percent in 2022) and 58 percent workforce participation (as of 2024, according to the Ministry of Manpower [Ministry of Manpower, 2024]).
- Thailand has a female labor force participation rate of 45.8 percent (World Bank, 2024).

Northeast Asia struggles with structural barriers:

- Japan's female workforce comprises 45.1 percent of workers but holds under 10 percent of executive roles (2025, Global Gender Gap Report).
- South Korea recently achieved 65.6 percent female participation (as of May 2025), yet leadership gaps persist.
- Hong Kong reports 52 percent female workforce participation (2023) but a 19.6 percent gender pay gap for managers (2022 data, Census and Statistics Department).

Pay equity remains a universal challenge. Singapore's adjusted gender pay gap narrowed to 6.0 percent (Ministry of Manpower, 2024), while across the MSCI ACWI Index (a global equity index that measures the equity performance in both the developed and emerging markets), the percentage of female CFOs climbed slowly from 16.9 percent in 2022 to 18.8 percent in 2023 (MSCI, 2023).

One of the main challenges in promoting diversity in Asia is the varying levels of regulatory support and cultural attitudes across different countries. For example, while India, Singapore, and Hong Kong have implemented binding gender quotas and transparency rules for listed companies, markets like Japan and South Korea have only set long-term targets that often fail to overcome entrenched hierarchies. In Southeast Asia, religious norms and familial obligations frequently clash with corporate diversity policies—Malaysia's Sharia-compliant businesses, for instance, face unique challenges in mixed-gender workplaces. The regulatory patchwork is compounded by cultural blind spots: Asian firms often mistake token promotions for meaningful inclusion. Some companies routinely appoint female family members to boards to technically comply with the mandate without driving real changes.

To address these challenges, companies in Asia can take several practical steps. First, they can invest in comprehensive Diversity, Equity, and Inclusion (DE&I) programs, including training, mentorship, and support for underrepresented groups. This helps create an inclusive culture where all employees feel valued and respected. Second, flexible work arrangements and competitive nonpaid benefits can improve employee satisfaction and retention. Offering options like remote work, flexible hours, and wellness programs can make a significant difference. Third, leveraging technology to enhance recruitment and retention efforts is a prudent approach. Utilizing data analytics to pinpoint and address diversity gaps can enable investors to make informed decisions. Finally, collaborating with local and international organizations to share best practices and promote a culture of inclusion can drive positive changes. The path forward isn't standardization, but smart adaptation—using regulatory baselines as starting points, not ceilings.

Employee Health and Safety

Asia's manufacturing backbone demands a fundamental rethinking of workplace safety as a productivity driver rather than a compliance practice. Factories implementing ISO 45001 standards report 37 percent fewer production delays from accidents (ILO, 2023), while firms with strong safety records secure contracts 28 percent faster in global supply chain tenders (McKinsey, 2024). While some countries, such as Singapore and Japan, have stringent occupational health and safety (OHS) regulations, 42 percent of Southeast Asian manufacturers still lack certified safety officers (ASEAN Secretariat, 2023). Cultural attitudes toward workplace safety and health can also vary, influencing the implementation and effectiveness of OHS measures.

A remarkable case that highlights the consequences of neglecting worker safety emerged in June 2024, when a lithium battery factory fire in Hwaseong, South Korea, killed 23 workers, 17 of whom were Chinese migrants (Ministry of Employment and Labour, Republic of Korea, 2024). The blaze at Aricell's facility erupted during battery packing operations, with explosions trapping workers in a facility lacking adequate fire exits and safety drills. Investigations revealed that migrant staff, who comprised 80 percent of the workforce, received minimal safety training despite handling volatile materials daily. The tragedy exposed systemic gaps in South Korea's oversight of high-risk industries employing vulnerable migrant labor, where fatalities are three times higher than for local workers.

The fallout was immediate:

- Global brands such as Samsung SDI and LG Energy Solutions have faced scrutiny over the safety protocols in their supply chains.
- South Korea's labor ministry pledged to inspect all 526 battery plants by Q3 2024, revealing that 62 percent lacked compliant fire suppression systems.
- Investor repercussions included a 15 percent stock drop for Aricell-linked suppliers and ESG rating downgrades for firms with similar labor practices.

This incident underscores how worker safety failures now trigger cascading financial and reputational risks, with migrant labor conditions becoming a litmus test for ESG compliance in global manufacturing hubs.

Nowadays, Asian companies are transforming workplace safety through data-driven prevention and the adoption of global standards. Integrating ISO 45001 frameworks has been shown to reduce production delays by 37 percent through the implementation of systematic hazard controls (Intertek, 2024). Real-time AI monitoring tools now analyze 85 percent of high-risk movements in manufacturing, ranging from improper lifting to equipment proximity, resulting in a 40 percent reduction in incident rates where deployed (Visionify, 2025). This technological shift aligns with ILO conventions on occupational safety, which 78 percent of ASEAN exporters now reference in supply chain contracts to meet EU due diligence requirements (ILO, 2023). Ultimately, the synergy of predictive analytics and institutional accountability creates self-reinforcing safety ecosystems.

Bribery and Corruption

Bribery and corruption continue to distort Asia's economic landscape, with tangible consequences for businesses operating in the region. Transparency International's 2024 Corruption Perceptions Index reveals that Southeast Asian nations, such as Indonesia (37), Vietnam (40), and the Philippines (32), score significantly below the global average of 43, reflecting systemic governance challenges (Transparency International, 2024). In China, where regulatory crackdowns have intensified, commercial bribery cases increased by 26.6 percent in 2024, particularly in high-growth sectors such as new energy vehicles and pharmaceuticals (Supreme People's Procuratorate of China, 2025).

The fight against corruption in Asia remains a tale of decent laws hamstrung by political influence. Many countries in the region have anticorruption laws. However, their implementation is often weak due to political interference, a lack of resources, and insufficient capacity, as seen in the aforementioned 1MDB scandal. Plus, cultural factors and entrenched practices of using personal connections to access services further complicate efforts to combat corruption.

The 2024 sentencing of Samsung heir Lee Jae-yong to five years for bribing President Park Geun-hye's confidante (Choi Soon-sil) underscores how entrenched business–political ties undermine even advanced economies. Lee's $36 million in bribes—including a show horse for Choi's daughter—secured government approval for a merger, cementing his control over Samsung. Unlike 1MDB, this was purely domestic corruption, yet it triggered similar systemic consequences:

- Market impact: Samsung's stock fell 8 percent within a week of Lee's arrest.
- Cultural enablers: The court noted Samsung's "culture of obedience", in which executives rubber-stamped illegal requests without questioning.
- Regulatory response: The scandal spurred South Korea's Anti-Corruption and Civil Rights Commission to expand its mandate to investigate private-sector bribes in 2025.

On August 12, 2022, Lee was pardoned by President Yoon Suk Yeol, reversing his 2017 conviction for bribery and embezzlement, which toppled former President Park Geun-hye.

In China, the GlaxoSmithKline (GSK) bribery case in 2013 highlighted corruption risks for multinational companies. GSK was fined nearly $500 million for bribing doctors and hospitals to use its products, leading to a sharp decline in its share and reputation in China. A recent high-profile case involves Zhang Hongli, a former vice president of the Industrial and Commercial Bank of China (ICBC). In February 2025, Zhang was sentenced to death with a two-year reprieve for accepting bribes in exchange for loan financing and securing jobs.

Key Takeaways for Investors:

- Political risk assessments must go beyond laws: Malaysia and South Korea both have strong anticorruption statutes, and anticorruption has been a major campaign in China under President Xi since he came to power in 2013. However, elite impunity persisted until external or public pressure forced action.
- Third-party vetting is non-negotiable: Most cases involve intermediaries (such as Goldman Sachs in the 1MDB case and Samsung subsidiaries in Korea) that obscure wrongdoing.
- Local nuances matter: In China and Korea, Confucian hierarchies enabled cover-ups ("juniors don't question seniors"), while Malaysia's patronage networks allowed Najib to control oversight bodies.
- The path forward requires hybrid vigilance: leveraging global frameworks like the U.S. FCPA while pressuring local institutions to act, as seen in Singapore's seizure of 1MDB-linked assets and Korea's postscandal reforms.

Corruption risks are only part of the governance equation; competition law and antitrust enforcement present another evolving frontier in Asia.

Antitrust Rules and Wealth Distribution

These are obvious but often overlooked considerations for companies operating or planning to enter the Asian market. The region has witnessed significant developments in antitrust regulations aimed at promoting fair competition and preventing monopolistic practices. For instance, China's amended Anti-Monopoly Law, enacted in August 2022, introduced stricter merger control rules and procedures. Similarly, South Korea's updated Monopoly Regulation and Fair Trade Act, effective December 2021, includes tighter regulations on exchanging competitively sensitive information. Companies need to navigate these regulatory changes, as noncompliance can lead to severe penalties and reputational damage.

One example is the crackdown on big tech companies in China, which began in late 2020, targeting major firms such as Alibaba, Tencent, Meituan, and Didi. One of the most notable cases was the suspension of Ant Group's IPO, which would have been the world's largest, following a controversial speech by Alibaba cofounder Jack Ma. This move sent shockwaves through the global investment community, marking the beginning of a broader regulatory campaign. The State Administration for Market Regulation (SAMR) imposed a record fine of 18.8 billion yuan ($2.8 billion) on Alibaba for monopolistic practices. Similarly, Tencent faced fines and operational restrictions, highlighting the increasing scrutiny of monopolistic practices and the need for carefully designed compliance strategies (Tencent, 2024).

Outside China, antitrust scrutiny is also rigorous across the Asia-Pacific region. South Korea's landmark case against Qualcomm sets a regional precedent for regulating the tech sector. In April 2023, the Supreme Court of Korea upheld a $873 million fine imposed by the Korea Fair Trade Commission (KFTC) in 2016, concluding a seven-year legal battle over Qualcomm's abuse of its dominant position in modem chips and patent licensing. The ruling affirmed that Qualcomm had violated fair competition principles by forcing smartphone makers to license its entire patent portfolio and restricting rivals, such as Intel and Samsung, from accessing essential patents. This decision not only reinforced Korea's stance against monopolistic practices but also signaled to global tech firms that Asia-Pacific regulators will scrutinize anticompetitive behavior in particular industries, particularly where intellectual property intersects with market dominance.

Wealth distribution is another critical aspect for companies to consider in Asia. The region exhibits significant disparities, with a large proportion of the population in the lower wealth brackets. According to the UBS (2025), as of the end of 2024, about 71 percent of adults in

APAC fall into the lowest wealth bracket (net worth under $10,000). This uneven distribution can impact consumer markets and influence business strategies. Companies must be aware of these disparities to tailor their products and services effectively for the Asian market.

China's "Common Prosperity" campaign, launched by President Xi Jinping in 2021, aims to address these wealth disparities by promoting social equality and economic activity. This campaign has led to regulatory measures targeting high-income individuals and businesses, encouraging them to contribute more to society. For example, Tencent announced a significant increase in social responsibility initiatives, committing over $15 billion to support rural revitalization, education, and health care projects across China in 2024 (Tencent 2024). Companies operating in China must align with these policy goals to ensure long-term sustainability and avoid regulatory risks.

Governance

The governance pillar focuses on the internal systems and processes that guide a company's operations. An effective board structure and oversight ensure accountability and provide strategic direction. DE&I policies are increasingly important as many believe that diverse leadership teams can drive better decision making and innovation. Business ethics, including transparency and integrity, are fundamental to building trust with investors and other stakeholders.

Shareholder engagement is another key aspect of governance, as companies should actively communicate with and consider the interests of their shareholders. Vigorous accounting policies and controls are essential for accurate financial-related reporting and compliance. Transparent compensation structures and disclosure practices for executives ensure that pay aligns with the company's performance and the interests of stakeholders.

Board Structure/Board Oversight

Board structures and oversight in Asia have evolved considerably over the past two decades, mainly in response to lessons learned from the late-1990s financial crisis and subsequent market reforms. Many jurisdictions have progressively strengthened their corporate governance frameworks to enhance board accountability and independence. Japan, for example, introduced its Corporate Governance Code in 2015, revising it in 2018 and 2021 to encourage greater board diversity and independence (Tokyo Stock Exchange, 2021). More recently, Hong Kong has become one of the latest markets to upgrade its Corporate Governance Code, with amendments effective from July 2025:

- Term limits: A hard cap of nine years for independent nonexecutive directors (INEDs), after which they must retire or be reclassified as nonindependent.
- Multiple directorship restrictions: INEDs may hold no more than six listed company directorships simultaneously to ensure adequate time commitment.
- Phased implementation: Companies have until 2031 to comply with annual disclosure requirements beginning in 2026.

While these changes align with similar practices in Singapore and other regional peers, they reflect a continuing regional trend toward boards that are more independent, accountable, and engaged. In my engagements with Asian-listed companies, I have seen how these changes are reshaping board recruitment discussions, particularly around succession planning and director independence. The reforms target long-standing criticisms of "overboard" and entrenched directors, with nearly 28 percent of Hang Seng Index INEDs currently exceeding the new tenure limit (HKEX, 2024). Though some argue that the six-year transition is too lenient, it acknowledges Asia's limited talent pool of qualified independent professionals.

Despite these advancements, challenges remain. One significant issue is the lack of board independence and the prevalence of concentrated ownership, which can hinder adequate supervision. Many boards in Asia continue to struggle to strike a balance between board independence and the self-interests of board members. In addition, cultural factors and entrenched practices can impede the adoption of best governance practices. For example, appointing "trophy" directors—high-profile individuals who may not contribute effectively to governance—remains common in many parts of the region. Similarly, the issue of "shadow directors"—individuals who exert significant influence over a company's decisions without holding formal board positions—has raised concerns about accountability and transparency in corporate governance practices in markets like Japan.

Several high-profile cases highlight the consequences of inadequate board oversight. The collapse of the Chinese conglomerate HNA Group in 2021 is one example. HNA's aggressive expansion, high debt levels, and poor governance and oversight led to its eventual bankruptcy, resulting in significant financial losses for investors. Another notable case is the Toshiba scandal in Japan, which emerged during the Global Financial Crisis, marked by accounting irregularities and governance failures that led to a sharp decline in the company's market value and significant losses for investors in 2015.

To address these challenges, further reforms are needed. Strengthening board independence, enhancing transparency, and promoting diversity are critical steps. Furthermore, cultivating a culture of accountability and ethical leadership is necessary for achieving sustainable development. By improving board structure and oversight, Asian companies can enhance their resilience and attract more investment, contributing to the region's economic growth.

Compensation Structure and Disclosure

Executive compensation structure and disclosure in Asia have evolved significantly over the past few years, driven by the need for greater transparency and alignment with global best practices. Japan has made significant strides in improving the disclosure of executive compensation. The Financial Services Agency (FSA) has required listed firms to disclose a breakdown of total compensation by payment type for each executive earning ¥100 million or more during the relevant fiscal year since 2010. Hong Kong's Listing Rules have required the disclosure of directors' pay since 2013, with detailed breakdowns that include fixed salaries, bonuses, and long-term incentives. Malaysia's Securities Commission went further in 2019 by requiring not only exact figures but also justification of pay ratios between executives and median employees.

One step in the right direction, these rules emphasize the importance of performance-based pay and long-term incentives, aligning executive interests with those of shareholders. However, challenges remain. One significant issue is the variability in disclosure practices across Asian markets. While some markets, such as Hong Kong and Japan, have more stringent disclosure requirements, others lag, resulting in inconsistent transparency. Poor disclosure practices can lead to unchecked executive power and potential mismanagement.

In 2022, Foxconn faced criticism for its lack of transparency in executive compensation disclosures. The company was pressured by investors and regulatory bodies to enhance its disclosure practices, resulting in more detailed reporting on executive pay and incentives. In the same year, shareholders expressed concerns over the high compensation packages awarded to Samsung Electronics' top executives, particularly in light of the company's poor performance. The lack of detailed disclosure on the criteria used to determine these pay packages led to calls for greater transparency and reforms in compensation practices.

Business Ethics

In the past few years, many countries in the region have introduced regulations and guidelines to promote ethical business practices. For instance, most corporate governance codes around the region emphasize the importance of codes of conduct for all listed companies. Some markets even extend the codes to include relevant parties in companies' supply chains. These regulatory changes aim to foster a culture of ethical behavior and ensure fair competition.

Measuring business ethics is challenging for investors and companies due to the inherently qualitative nature of ethical standards. Unlike financial metrics, which are quantifiable and standardized, moral behavior is subjective and can vary widely across cultures and industries. Investors often rely on self-reported data, which can be biased or incomplete, making it challenging to assess a company's actual practices accurately. Additionally, companies face challenges in evaluating their partners' ethics as they may lack access to internal processes and decision-making frameworks. This lack of transparency and standardized metrics means that ethical breaches often only come to light after significant damage has occurred, leaving investors and companies to deal with the consequences retrospectively.

The downfall of Evergrande underscores the risks of unchecked corporate ambition, but it is far from an isolated case. Consider the scandal surrounding Luckin Coffee, China's fastest-growing coffee chain. In 2020, the company admitted to fabricating $310 million in sales, inflating revenue by nearly 40 percent over three quarters. Like Evergrande's Hui Ka Yan, Luckin's founder, Charles Lu, pursued aggressive expansion—opening 4,500 stores in under three years—while masking financial instability through fraudulent reporting. The revelation triggered a 75 percent stock plunge, led to the Nasdaq delisting, and resulted in $180 million in SEC fines, wiping out billions of dollars in investor value.

What makes Luckin's collapse particularly instructive is its ripple effect. The fraud eroded trust in Chinese firms listed overseas, prompting tighter scrutiny from U.S. regulators and a wave of shareholder lawsuits. Domestically, it exposed systemic flaws in China's start-up culture, where growth often eclipses governance. Unlike Evergrande's debt-driven implosion, Luckin's demise was rooted in outright deception. Yet, both cases reveal a pattern: when companies prioritize scale over integrity, the fallout extends far beyond balance sheets.

Effective ethical oversight in Asia requires moving beyond policies to actionable systems. One practical approach is combining technology with localized due diligence. In Vietnam's textile industry, several multinational companies are now utilizing blockchain technology to track cotton sourcing from farm to factory (Vietnam Textile Transparency Initiative, 2023). Cultural context matters, too. In Japan, where hierarchical structures can discourage whistleblowing, a global insurer introduced an anonymous reporting hotline using formal keigo language to align with local norms (Japan Ethics Hotline Report, 2021).

Local partnerships also add ground truth. When an unnamed European retailer received tips from Cambodia's Labor Rights NGO about falsified overtime records at a supplier factory, it conducted surprise audits and avoided reputational damage. Collaborating with watchdogs, such as Transparency International's local chapters (Transparency International, 2024), often reveals risks that desk research may overlook. Remember, ethical safeguards are most effective when they are specific, measurable, and culturally aware.

Shareholder Engagement

Shareholder engagement in Asia has made significant strides over the past decade, driven by regulatory reforms and an increase in shareholder activism. Countries such as Japan, South Korea, and India have implemented measures to enhance, and indeed require, a degree of dialogue between listed firms and their shareholders. For instance, Japan's Stewardship Code, introduced in 2014, was the first in the region to encourage institutional investors to engage with companies to promote sustainable growth. Similarly, South Korea's Stewardship Code, launched in 2016, aims to improve corporate governance and shareholder value. These codes have been instrumental in fostering a culture of active engagement and accountability among companies and investors.

One major hurdle for stewardship development in Asia is the varying levels of awareness and understanding of regulations among institutional investors in the region. On top of that, cultural factors, such as a preference for amicable rather than confrontational settings, can also limit the impact of active investors. The concentrated ownership structures in many Asian companies, where large shareholders often have significant control, also pose challenges for minority shareholders seeking to influence corporate decisions.

In 2022, Align Partners Capital Management, a South Korean activist fund, targeted SM Entertainment by acquiring a 1.1 percent stake in the company. Align Partners raised concerns about transactions between SM Entertainment and Like Planning, a company owned by SM's founder, Lee Soo-man. They argued that these transactions were not in the best interest of shareholders and pushed for greater transparency and governance reforms. Align Partners successfully appointed an auditor through a shareholder recommendation, which led to increased scrutiny and ultimately resulted in the termination of the controversial transactions.

At Canon Inc.'s 2023 Annual General Meeting (AGM), Chairman and CEO Fujio Mitarai faced significant opposition from shareholders. Nearly 49.4 percent of the shareholders voted to remove him from his position, just shy of the majority needed. This marked a substantial increase in dissent compared to previous years, largely driven by concerns over Canon's governance practices and its inaction on climate change. The close vote highlighted the growing influence of active investors in pushing for corporate accountability and reform in Japan.

Despite recent ESG skepticism in the United States, stewardship practices in Asia continue to gain momentum, shaped by regulatory shifts and investor demand. Asia's centrality in global supply chains—accounting for over 40 percent of the world's clean energy production (IEA, 2022)—creates tangible incentives for stewardship to align capital with sustainability goals (IEA, 2024). The trajectory is clear: as regional frameworks mature, active ownership will become a defining feature of Asia's investment landscape.

Accounting Policies/Internal Controls

Accounting policies and internal controls in Asia have seen significant regulatory developments over the past two decades. All major countries and markets have implemented comprehensive frameworks to enhance the reliability and transparency of financial reporting. For instance, China has adopted the Committee of Sponsoring Organizations (COSO) framework, which promotes enterprise risk management and considers both financial reporting and operational controls.

In Japan, the Financial Instruments and Exchange Act requires listed companies to establish and maintain effective internal control systems. This has led to the development of comprehensive internal control practices to safeguard assets, ensure accurate financial reporting and promote operational efficiency. South Korea has introduced stringent requirements under the Act on External Audit of Stock Companies, emphasizing the importance of internal audits and the role of audit committees in reporting.

However, in some cases, smaller firms still lack awareness and understanding of internal control requirements, leading to inconsistent application of best practices. Furthermore, cultural factors, such as a preference for hierarchical decision making and resistance to external scrutiny, can hinder the effectiveness of internal controls. The swift pace of technological advancements presents significant challenges, compelling companies to continually update their internal control systems to mitigate emerging cybersecurity and data privacy risks.

The Olympus scandal is one of Asia's most brazen corporate frauds, exposing deep flaws in Japan's postwar business culture. When newly appointed British CEO Michael Woodford blew the whistle in 2011, investigators uncovered a meticulously engineered scheme in which executives had been using acquisitions to hide $1.7 billion in losses since the 1990s. They paid $687 million for a face cream company with virtually no sales and $773 million for three tiny start-ups, all to paper over bad investments through inflated goodwill accounting.

What made the Olympus case particularly shocking was the complicity it revealed. The company's auditors (KPMG and later Ernst & Young) missed the deception for years. At the same time, board members, including representatives from Mitsubishi UFJ and Sumitomo Mitsui banks, either looked the other way or actively participated in the misconduct. The scandal ultimately compelled Japan to accelerate its corporate governance reforms, including the introduction of stricter requirements for outside directors in 2015.

While Japan implemented stricter outside director requirements after the Olympus scandal, and South Korea introduced whistleblower protections following several accounting frauds, these reforms only scratch the surface of Asia's governance challenges. Three persistent gaps demand attention: First, family-controlled conglomerates continue to dominate, often rendering independent boards largely symbolic. Second, the gap between the rule on paper and the rule in action remains large. Third, the rapid adoption of AI-driven accounting tools contrasts with the cash-based accounting system in some Asian markets, making digital trails impossible.

Real progress requires moving beyond blanket policies to targeted solutions, such as mandating forensic audits for related-party transactions in family firms, deploying blockchain-based invoice tracking for supply chains, and creating regional peer review systems modeled after Asia's banking supervision framework. The key lesson? Governance solutions must be as diverse as Asia's business landscapes—reforms that succeed in Japan's *keiretsu* system may prove ineffective for Chinese state-owned enterprises.

What Is ESG/Sustainable Investing?

ESG investing has emerged as a strategic approach integrating nonfinancial factors—such as a company's environmental impact, social responsibility, and corporate governance—into the investment process. On many occasions, the terms "ESG investing" and "sustainable investing" are used interchangeably; however, ESG investing has a specific focus on evaluating companies against three distinct criteria to assess their long-term sustainability and potential.

Having said this, the approach to investing is not always straightforward. It can vary depending on the context in which it is used. For instance, some interpret ESG investing as a framework for avoiding companies with significant environmental, social, or governance risks. In contrast, others view it as a proactive strategy to identify and support businesses that make positive contributions to society or the planet. This variability in interpretation has led to occasional confusion among stakeholders, highlighting the importance of clarity and due diligence when incorporating ESG principles into investment decisions.

What sets ESG investing apart from traditional investing is its expanded scope of analysis and decision making. With traditional investment primarily concentrating on financial performance metrics such as profitability, growth potential, and market value, ESG investing broadens the perspective by factoring in the range of nonfinancial considerations outlined earlier, which may have a material influence on a company's performance and resilience over time. By addressing issues such as climate risks, regulatory challenges, labor practices and governance ineffectiveness, ESG investing enables investors to account for risks and opportunities that might otherwise be overlooked in traditional financial analysis.

Moreover, ESG investing reflects a value-driven approach. It seeks to align investment strategies with broader social and environmental priorities, unlike traditional investment, which is often more focused on maximizing financial returns for the short term without regard for potentially harmful long-term considerations. ESG investing takes a longer term perspective, emphasizing the sustainability of investments in light of emerging trends and global challenges. Strategies unique to ESG investing, such as negative screening (excluding industries like fossil fuels or arms), positive screening (targeting companies with exemplary ESG performance), and impact investing (aiming for measurable positive societal impacts), further differentiate it from conventional investment approaches.

Sustainable investing's real value lies in its ability to uncover hidden risks that traditional analysis often misses—the kind that can blindside even well-run companies. Take Mineral Resources in Australia: despite strong financials, its shares dropped 25 percent in late 2022 after founder Chris Ellison's controversial decisions, including abrupt strategy shifts and board disputes, raised red flags about leadership stability. ESG frameworks would have flagged these governance risks earlier through indicators like board independence and lack of succession planning.

Similarly, decarbonization challenges in sectors such as Asian cement production—where companies face rising carbon costs but lack viable alternatives—demonstrate how ESG metrics reveal operational vulnerabilities. Thailand's Siam Cement Group, for instance, saw its credit rating downgraded in 2023 due to slower-than-expected emissions reductions, a risk factored into ESG scores but not reflected in traditional financial models. While there are challenges, such as the higher costs associated with ESG-focused funds or the lack of standardized data, the benefits of mitigating long-term risks and uncovering growth opportunities make ESG investing an increasingly compelling choice for both individual and institutional investors.

How ESG Reporting Differs From Mandatory Financial Reporting

ESG reporting has grown significantly over the years, especially in Asia, as both companies and regulators recognize the importance of transparency and sustainability in business practices. While similar to mandatory financial reporting in its aim to build trust and accountability, ESG reporting differs in its focus on nonfinancial factors. Financial reporting is deeply rooted in globally standardized frameworks, such as the International Financial Reporting Standards (IFRS), which promotes consistency and comparability across markets (IFRS Foundation, 2023). In contrast, ESG reporting is less mature, with varying standards and methodologies that make achieving a uniform level of consistency difficult.

One of the biggest obstacles to ESG reporting is the absence of standardized metrics and frameworks. Companies often face a fragmented landscape, relying on multiple reporting standards, such as Global Reporting Initiative (GRI), Sustainability Accounting Standards Board (SASB), and TCFD, which complicates efforts to ensure consistency and comparability (GRI, Various Years). This issue is addressed to a great extent by the issuance of the ISSB's S1 and S2 standards in June 2023. In addition, data quality is often compromised, with issues such as incomplete disclosures and the risk of greenwashing undermining its credibility. There is also the ongoing challenge of demonstrating the financial materiality of ESG factors, as their impact on long-term financial performance is not always evident.

While financial audits have long adhered to strict standards, ESG assurance has lagged in consistency and rigor until November 2024. The International Auditing and Assurance Standards Board (IAASB) introduced ISSA 5000, a landmark global standard for sustainability assurance, effective from December 2026. Unlike the fragmented approaches of the past, ISSA 5000 establishes end-to-end requirements for engagements, covering everything from materiality assessments to reporting, and applies to all sustainability topics—environmental, social, and governance. Crucially, it accommodates both limited and reasonable assurance, aligning with jurisdictional needs, and is framework-agnostic, meaning it works with IFRS Sustainability Standards, GRI, CSRD, and others (GRI, Various Years).

The standard also addresses key pain points:

- Group engagements: Explicitly covers complex supply chain and multientity reporting.
- Materiality: Requires practitioners to weigh both financial and impact materiality—a critical upgrade for investor-grade disclosures.
- Risk assessment requires a rigorous evaluation of misstatement risk, with differentiated requirements for limited versus reasonable assurance.

This move signals a tipping point. With ISSA 5000, ESG audits will gradually mirror the discipline of financial audits, closing the trust gap for investors and regulators. Early adopters in Asia—particularly firms under Hong Kong and Singapore's 2025 mandatory climate reporting rules or Japan's TCFD-aligned disclosures—should prepare now to meet these heightened expectations (TCFD, 2021).

Institutions Developing ESG Reporting Standards

Several key institutions have been instrumental in shaping ESG reporting standards globally, and their efforts have accelerated significantly since 2020. The GRI, one of the earliest and most widely adopted frameworks, has continually refined its standards to address emerging sustainability challenges (GRI, Various Years). In recent years, GRI has emphasized the concept of "double materiality", which considers both the financial impact of ESG factors on a company and the company's broader impact on society and the environment (GRI, Various Years). This approach has gained traction, particularly in Europe, where regulatory bodies increasingly align with GRI's principles (GRI, Various Years).

The SASB has also made notable progress. In 2021, SASB merged with the International Integrated Reporting Council (IIRC) to form the Value Reporting Foundation (VRF). This merger aimed to streamline ESG reporting by integrating SASB's industry-specific standards with IIRC's focus on integrated reporting. The VRF's work has since been incorporated into ISSB, which was established by the IFRS Foundation in 2021 (IFRS Foundation, 2023). The ISSB is working to create a unified global framework for sustainability disclosures. This development marks a significant step toward harmonizing ESG reporting practices across continents.

Also, the TCFD has continued to expand its influence, particularly as climate risks become a central focus for investors and regulators (TCFD, 2021). Since 2020, TCFD has seen a surge in adoption, with over 4,000 organizations globally committing to its recommendations (TCFD, 2021). Its framework has been integrated into regulatory requirements in several jurisdictions, including the United Kingdom, which has mandated TCFD-aligned disclosures for large companies and financial institutions (TCFD, 2021).

Developing ESG Reporting Standards in Asia

ESG reporting in Asia has seen significant developments, with several markets introducing mandatory requirements and aligning with global standards. Taiwan stands out as a leader in this space, where the GRI Standards first became compulsory for large and most at-risk listed companies as early as 2015, several years before other markets introduced mandatory sustainability reporting (GRI, Various Years). As of 2021, nearly 99 percent of Taiwanese companies producing sustainability reports adhered to GRI Standards, reflecting the market's commitment to transparency and accountability (GRI, Various Years). This mandatory adoption has positioned Taiwan as a benchmark for ESG reporting in the region.

In China, the Shanghai, Shenzhen, and Beijing Stock Exchanges introduced mandatory sustainability reporting guidelines for larger listed entities, effective May 2024. These guidelines aim to enhance the quality and consistency of ESG disclosures, aligning with international frameworks such as the GRI and TCFD (GRI, Various Years). Similarly, the HKEX has made ESG reporting mandatory for listed companies since 2020, with a strong emphasis on climate-related disclosures in line with the TCFD recommendations.

Singapore has also taken significant steps, requiring listed companies to publish sustainability reports with oversight from their boards. The Singapore Exchange (SGX) has aligned its requirements with global standards, encouraging companies to adopt frameworks like GRI and SASB (GRI, Various Years). By 2025, all SGX-listed companies will be required to report Scope 1 and Scope 2 greenhouse gas emissions, with Scope 3 reporting phased in later (SGX Regulation 2023). Additionally, large nonlisted companies that meet specific revenue and asset thresholds will be subject to climate disclosure requirements starting in 2027.

Japan is another market that has made significant strides in developing ESG reporting standards, particularly in recent years. Establishing the Sustainability Standards Board of Japan (SSBJ) in 2022 marked a pivotal moment as the country sought to align its sustainability disclosure practices with international frameworks. The SSBJ has closely collaborated with the ISSB to ensure that its standards are consistent with the IFRS Sustainability Disclosure Standards (IFRS Foundation, 2023). In March 2025, SSBJ released its inaugural sustainability disclosure standards, which are expected to become mandatory for companies listed on the Tokyo Stock Exchange's Prime Market, reinforcing Japan's commitment to transparent and internationally comparable ESG reporting.

The efforts to create a unified framework are also expected to pave the way for more consistent assurance practices. The assurance of ESG or sustainability reports in Asian markets has been evolving. However, the level of development varies significantly across the region.

Assurance practices are gaining traction in more advanced markets, such as Hong Kong and Singapore. In Hong Kong, while assurance is not yet mandatory for ESG reports, many leading companies voluntarily seek third-party verification to enhance stakeholder confidence. The Hong Kong Institute of Certified Public Accountants (HKICPA) has issued guidance, such as Technical Bulletin AATB 5, which aligns with international standards like ISAE 3000 (Revised). This provides a framework for practitioners conducting assurance engagements on ESG information, particularly for companies listed on the HKEX (HKEX 2024). Similarly, the SGX encourages listed companies to adopt assurance practices, particularly in relation to climate-related disclosures (SGX Regulation, 2023). Companies increasingly engage independent auditors to validate their sustainability data, particularly as reporting requirements become more stringent.

Japan has also made significant progress in this area. Many Japanese companies, especially those listed on the Tokyo Stock Exchange's Prime Market, are adopting third-party assurance for their sustainability reports. On the other hand, markets like Mainland China and Indonesia are still in the early stages of developing assurance standards for ESG reporting. In China, while mandatory ESG disclosures for large listed companies took effect in 2024, assurance remains voluntary mainly and inconsistent. The lack of standardized assurance practices poses challenges for investors seeking reliable and comparable data. Taken together, these shifts show how Asia's ESG trajectory is uneven, with clear leaders and laggards.

Key Insight: The Current State of Sustainable Investing in Asia

Sustainable investing in Asia reflects a region in transition, where leaders and laggards coexist. This divergence underscores a broader trend: Asia's

ESG maturity hinges not just on policy ambition but on local capacity to operationalize global standards.

For instance, Japan's Government Pension Investment Fund (GPIF), the world's largest pension fund with $1.6 trillion in assets, allocates 52 percent of its portfolio to ESG-integrated strategies (GPIF Annual Report, 2023). Meanwhile, Hong Kong has promoted ESG investing by integrating ESG factors into the Hong Kong Monetary Authority's investment processes and setting a net-zero emissions target for its investment portfolio by 2050. In addition, SGX requires all listed companies to implement climate reporting aligned with the ISSB standards (ISSB, 2023), starting in 2025 (SGX Regulation, 2023).

The Center for Green and Sustainable Finance in Hong Kong also coordinates efforts among financial regulators, government agencies, and industry stakeholders to support sustainable finance. Meanwhile, Singapore has advanced ESG investing through the Green Finance Action Plan, strengthening the financial sector's resilience to environmental risks and developing markets for sustainable finance. The Singapore Green Plan 2030 further promotes green financing through climate-related disclosure requirements and encourages the development of green solutions. Both governments are actively positioning their markets as leading hubs for sustainable finance in Asia.

At the other end of the spectrum, markets such as Vietnam and Indonesia struggle with inconsistent ESG data quality and underdeveloped reporting infrastructures (Asian Development Bank, 2023). Limited regulatory frameworks and a lack of standardized ESG data pose significant challenges for investors in these regions. In Indonesia, ESG reporting is largely voluntary, and the lack of English disclosure makes it difficult for foreign investors to assess the sustainability performance of companies. Similarly, in the Philippines, sustainable investing is hindered by low awareness and limited access to reliable ESG metrics.

Across Asia, several challenges impede the growth of ESG investing. One major issue is that the quality of ESG data remains a concern, with many companies providing incomplete or inconsistent disclosures. Greenwashing, where companies exaggerate their ESG achievements, further undermines investor confidence. Another challenge is the misperception of ESG investing as a trade-off between financial returns and sustainability goals, which deters some investors from fully embracing ESG principles. Investors should also watch for common red flags in ESG disclosures, some of which are unique to Asian markets.

Red Flags for Investors in ESG Data

- Scope 3 emissions are excluded, inconsistently calculated, or vaguely defined.
- Scope 4 or "avoided emissions" are disclosed using self-invented methodologies.
- Heavy reliance on policy pledges without credible implementation plans.
- Sustainability targets lack interim milestones, KPIs or executive accountability.
- ESG ratings diverge widely between major providers without clear explanation.
- No independent third-party assurance of sustainability or impact data.
- Frequent restatements or unexplained revisions of historical ESG metrics.
- Sudden improvements in scores without corresponding operational investments.
- Limited disclosure on supply chain risks, labor practices or grievance mechanisms.
- Repeated related-party transactions linked to sustainability projects or assets.
- Board-level ESG oversight is unclear, symbolic, or concentrated among insiders.
- ESG disclosures are materially different across jurisdictions or listing venues.

(*Tip: These red flags don't necessarily mean that a company is uninvestable—but they should trigger deeper due diligence.*)

The U.S. pushback against ESG investing, particularly the integration of nonfinancial factors into investment decisions, has had a limited impact on Asian markets. This is primarily because ESG investing in Asia is driven by regional priorities, including addressing climate change, biodiversity loss, and social inequality. Unlike the United States, where political polarization has influenced the ESG debate, Asian markets focus more on aligning ESG initiatives with long-term economic and environmental goals. For example, countries like China and India have prioritized climate transition finance and renewable energy investments, which are integral to national development strategies.

Key Takeaways

- ESG and sustainable investing remain central to capital allocation in Asia, despite global political pushback and uneven data quality.
- Environmental risks in the region are shaped by rapid decarbonization, biodiversity loss, and rising exposure to physical climate impacts.
- Social issues, particularly labor rights, product safety, and data security, continue to generate material financial and reputational risks.
- Governance failures, including weak boards, bribery, and poor internal controls, remain among the most persistent investor concerns.
- ESG reporting in Asia is converging toward global standards (ISSB, ISSA 5000), but implementation capacity varies widely by market.
- Long-term value creation depends on investors' ability to distinguish genuine transition leaders from superficial compliance.

Boardroom Briefing

Executives and investors should:

1. Scrutinize ESG disclosures for completeness and credibility, with particular attention to Scope 3 emissions and supply chain risks.
2. Prepare for convergence around ISSB and global assurance standards while adapting reporting to local regulatory realities.
3. Treat social and labor risks as core business issues, not peripheral compliance matters.
4. Prioritize governance reforms, including board independence, antibribery systems, and robust internal controls.
5. Stress-test strategies and portfolios against climate, regulatory, and geopolitical shocks in Asian markets.
6. Commit to active engagement and stewardship to identify long-term transition leaders and avoid greenwashing.

CHAPTER 3

How to Educate Investors About ESG/Sustainability

[INVESTORS] [CORPORATES] [REGULATORS]

This chapter is intended primarily for investors, but also for corporates and regulators seeking to understand how investor education can accelerate ESG integration in Asian markets.

Educating investors about ESG is meaningful for several reasons. First, it empowers them to make more informed decisions. By understanding ESG factors, investors can more effectively assess the long-term risks and opportunities associated with their investments. This knowledge leads to more sustainable and profitable outcomes, as investors can identify companies that are well-positioned to thrive in the changing environment.

Moreover, ESG education helps investors mitigate risks. Recognizing potential issues, such as environmental liabilities, social unrest, or governance failures, allows investors to avoid companies that might face significant challenges in the future. This risk management aspect is essential for protecting their investments and ensuring stable returns.

Aligning investments with personal values is another key benefit of ESG education. Many investors today seek to support companies that prioritize sustainability and social responsibility. By understanding ESG principles, they can align their portfolios with their beliefs, ensuring that their investments contribute to positive societal and environmental impacts. This not only benefits society and the environment but also enhances long-term viability and profitability, creating a win–win situation for investors and the broader community.

From a market stability perspective, educated investors play a vital role. By supporting companies that adopt responsible practices, they reduce the likelihood of market disruptions caused by environmental disasters, social conflicts, or governance scandals. This stability benefits all market participants, leading to more consistent and resilient returns.

Financial institutions like HSBC have rolled out mandatory ESG training for relationship managers, recognizing that client education starts in-house (HSBC, 2023). Meanwhile, universities are rewriting the playbook: many MBA programs now conduct ESG case competitions (*Financial Times*, 2023). NGOs are also helping. For example, the Global Capacity Building Coalition is an initiative launched at COP28 to strengthen climate finance capacity in emerging markets, thereby indirectly supporting education by fostering sustainable finance skills and knowledge sharing through its digital platform and global partnerships (Global Capacity Building Coalition, 2023).

Sometimes, educating investors about ESG investing can feel like trying to explain the plot of a complex movie to someone who missed the first half. You know, the best time to plant a tree was 10 years ago or now. So, you have to start with, "Well, it all began when …" But fear not! With the right approach, even the most skeptical investors can become ESG enthusiasts. So, let's embark on this journey with a smile and a few anecdotes to make the ride enjoyable.

Determine Investors' Level of ESG Knowledge

Before diving into the nitty-gritty, it's crucial to gauge where each investor stands in terms of their ESG knowledge. Think of it as a first date—you wouldn't start discussing wedding plans before knowing if the other person was serious! Similarly, understanding an investor's familiarity with ESG concepts helps tailor the conversation to their needs. Some may be well-versed in the latest standards, while others may wonder if ESG is a new technology trend.

Determining an investor's level of ESG knowledge can be approached in several practical ways. Begin with a simple questionnaire to gauge their foundational knowledge, asking questions such as, "Can you explain what ESG stands for?" or "Have you heard about recent ESG trends?" Conduct one-on-one interviews to discuss their investment strategies and how they incorporate ESG factors, with questions such as, "How do you consider environmental, social, and governance factors in your decisions?"

We can also present real-world case studies or hypothetical scenarios to see how they would respond to ESG issues. For example, ask, "If a company you invested in had poor labor practices, how would that affect your decision?" Reviewing their existing portfolio can also provide insights into their engagement with ESG factors. Questions like, "Can you identify any ESG-focused investments in your portfolio?" can be helpful.

Interactive workshops and feedback from financial advisers can help them further assess their knowledge and interest levels. During workshops, ask, "What ESG issues are most important to you?" Finally, use formal assessments or quizzes to test their knowledge, with questions like, "What are the key components of an ESG strategy?"

Hopefully, these approaches can help you to effectively determine an investor's level of ESG knowledge and tailor your further conversations to meet their specific needs, ensuring that they are well-equipped to make informed and sustainable investment decisions.

Common Fallacies About ESG in Asia

1. **ESG is Just a Western Trend:** Many Asian players believe that ESG is a concept imported from the West that doesn't apply to their markets. However, the reality is that ESG principles are globally relevant and increasingly critical in Asia due to their significant environmental impacts, unstable social structures, and poor shareholder rights. All are making the region even more vulnerable to dire ESG consequences. For instance, China has been making strides in renewable energy, becoming the world's largest producer of solar panels (IEA, 2023). This shift isn't just about following a trend but addressing real environmental challenges and seizing economic opportunities.

2. **ESG Equals Lower Returns:** There is a strong misconception among Asian investors that ESG investments always underperform. In reality, many ESG-focused funds have consistently delivered competitive returns. For example, MSCI (2025) found that ESG leaders often outperform their peers in the long run. Rejecting ESG is like refusing to carry an umbrella because it "won't make the rain stop."

Sure, it won't—but it will keep you a lot drier when the storm comes. ESG often cushions portfolios through market volatility.

3. **Only Large Companies Need ESG:** Some SMEs think ESG is only for large corporations. In fact, SMEs can gain significant advantages by adopting ESG practices, including improved reputation and operational efficiency, as well as lower financing costs. Consider Leanwares JSC, a Vietnamese SME specializing in textile manufacturing. By implementing sustainable practices such as water recycling systems and energy-efficient dyeing technologies, the company reduced production waste by 30 percent and cut energy costs by 18 percent within two years (Vietnam Plus, 2025).

4. **ESG is Only About the Environment:** While environmental factors are a big part of ESG, social and governance aspects are equally significant. Issues like labor practices and corporate governance play an important role in ESG assessments. For example, TSMC's investment in employee well-being, including on-site child care and mental health support, resulted in a 25 percent reduction in attrition in 2023, which in turn cut recruitment costs by $50 million annually (TSMC, 2023 Sustainability Report). Many Asian markets also often hear fundamental governance issues that need to be addressed as priorities.

5. **ESG is a Passing Fad:** There is a belief that ESG is just a temporary trend. However, the growing regulatory requirements and investor demand for sustainable practices indicate that ESG is here to stay. Consider the ever-increasing number of Asian markets, such as Japan and Korea, that are setting ambitious carbon neutrality goals (Government of Japan, 2023; Government of Korea, 2023). These commitments are not just for show; many Asian governments are investing substantial resources and restructuring the regulatory framework to meet these targets.

6. **ESG is Only for Ethical Investors:** Some would believe that ESG is only for those with strong ethical beliefs. However, ESG investing is about identifying long-term risks and opportunities that can affect financial performance. For instance, investors might initially dismiss ESG as "tree-hugging" and only later realize that it's mainly about risk management when they see how climate risks impact supply

chains and profitability. It's like discovering that wearing a seatbelt isn't just about safety—it's also about avoiding fines!

Common Misconceptions Held by ESG Investors

1. **ESG and Impact Investing are the Same:** Many investors confuse ESG with impact investing. While both aim for good, ESG focuses on managing risks and opportunities related to environmental, social, and governance factors. In contrast, impact investing seeks measurable social or environmental benefits. Imagine an investor thinking they're buying a hybrid car (ESG) but expecting it to plant trees every mile they drive (impact investing). Both are great, but they serve different purposes!

2. **ESG Guarantees Positive Impact:** Some investors believe that any ESG investment will automatically lead to positive outcomes. However, the effectiveness of ESG strategies depends on how well they are implemented and monitored. For example, a company might have a great sustainability report. However, the impact might be minimal if they aren't genuinely committed to their ESG goals. It's like buying organic vegetables but not checking if they were grown sustainably—it looks good on the surface, but the real benefits depend on the actions behind it.

3. **All ESG Ratings are Equal:** Investors often assume that ESG ratings from different agencies are comparable. In reality, methodologies vary significantly, and it's essential to understand the criteria behind each rating. It's like comparing apples to oranges; both are fruits, but have different flavors and nutritional values. In fact, the disparity of ESG scores for Asian companies among different providers is a recurring issue in my observation. Understanding these differences helps investors make more informed decisions.

4. **ESG is a One-Size-Fits-All Approach:** Investors might think that ESG strategies are uniform across all sectors. However, ESG considerations can vary greatly depending on the industry and specific company circumstances. For instance, the ESG issues relevant to a tech company might vastly differ from those affecting a manufacturing firm. It is like thinking that the same workout routine works

for everyone. What's effective for a marathon runner might not suit a weightlifter.

5. **ESG Investments are Risk-Free:** There is a belief that ESG investments are inherently safer. While ESG factors can help mitigate certain risks, they don't eliminate all investment risks. For instance, a renewable energy company might face regulatory challenges or technological setbacks. This is like thinking that a helmet makes you invincible on a motorcycle—it's safer, but you still need to ride carefully.

6. **ESG is Only About Exclusion:** Some investors think that ESG is just about excluding "bad" companies. In reality, ESG investing often involves engaging with companies to improve their environmental, social, and governance practices. For example, an investor might hold shares in a company with poor environmental practices to encourage the company to adopt more sustainable policies. It's like buying a promising restaurant not just to enjoy the food, but to help improve it from within.

These misconceptions often surface as common questions from investors. Table 3.1 summarises frequently asked questions (FAQs) investors raise and concise responses to each:

Table 3.1 Investor FAQs about ESG

Questions	Responses
Does ESG mean sacrificing returns?	No. Evidence shows ESG leaders often outperform peers, particularly during periods of market volatility.
Is ESG the same as impact investing?	No. ESG focuses on managing financially material risks and opportunities, while impact investing targets measurable social or environmental outcomes.
Why are ESG ratings inconsistent?	Methodologies differ widely across providers; understanding underlying criteria is essential.
Is ESG only for large companies?	No. SMEs can benefit through efficiency gains, lower financing costs, and stronger reputations; early integration is often less costly than retrofitting later.
Is ESG just for "ethical" investors?	No. ESG is about financial materiality and long-term resilience, not values-based investing alone.

Tailor Your Approach to Each Investor's Interests and Experience

Tailoring your approach to each investor's interests and experience is like crafting a bespoke suit—it requires attention to detail, understanding individual preferences, and ensuring a perfect fit. As no two investors are alike, neither should your communication strategies be. By customizing your approach, you can effectively engage investors, build trust, and guide them toward informed and sustainable investment decisions. Think of it as being a tailor, where each stitch and seam is meticulously crafted to ensure a perfect fit for the customer.

Engaging investors begins with understanding their unique preferences and communication styles. Start by identifying their preferred communication channels—whether it's e-mail, phone calls, social media, or face-to-face meetings. This ensures that your messages are delivered in a way that resonates with them. For instance, some investors might appreciate detailed reports, while others prefer concise summaries. Imagine an investor who loves data; sending them a comprehensive ESG report will make their day, while another might just want the key takeaways over a quick virtual chat.

Conducting interviews is another crucial tactic. These conversations should focus on understanding their goals, risk tolerance, and investment preferences. Open-ended questions and active listening are powerful techniques for uncovering valuable insights. For example, asking, "What are your primary investment goals?" or "Can you share an experience where an investment didn't meet your expectations?" can provide a deeper understanding of their needs and expectations. Picture an investor sharing a story about a past investment that went south due to poor governance practices—this can be a perfect segue into discussing the importance of ESG.

Building long-term trust is essential. This involves consistent and transparent communication, delivering on promises and demonstrating a genuine commitment to their financial well-being. Regular updates on performance, market trends, and challenges can reinforce this trust. Sharing success stories and case studies relevant to their interests can make the information more relatable and impactful. For instance, telling the story of a company that improved its ESG practices and saw a boost in stock performance can be both inspiring and educational.

The primary goal of your communication strategy should be to educate investors about the benefits and importance of sustainable investing. This includes explaining how ESG factors can mitigate risks, enhance returns, and align with their values. Moreover, it aims to dispel common misconceptions and provide clear, evidence-based information supporting ESG investing. For example, you might explain how a company with strong environmental practices is less likely to face regulatory fines, thus protecting its investment returns.

Another goal is to foster a sense of partnership. Investors should feel that you are not just an information provider but a trusted partner in their financial journey. This involves responding to their queries, providing personalized advice and empathizing with their concerns and aspirations. Imagine an investor who is passionate about social issues; showing how their investments can support strong social governance can create a deeper connection.

Key Communications Strategies

1. **Personalized Reports:** Provide tailored investment reports that highlight ESG performance and align with the investor's interests. For example, if an investor is particularly interested in renewable energy, include detailed insights on how their investments contribute to this sector.

2. **Regular Updates:** Send regular updates on market trends, ESG developments, and portfolio performance. This keeps investors informed and engaged. Remember, persistence is the key to conducting engagements in Asia.

3. **Interactive Discussions:** Organize events to engage investors in discussions about timely ESG issues. These can be both educational and interactive, allowing investors to ask questions and share their thoughts.

4. **Case Studies:** Share relevant case studies that demonstrate the benefits of ESG investing. For instance, a case study on a company that improved its ESG practices and saw a decrease in the cost of capital over time can be very persuasive.

5. **Open-Ended Questions:** Use open-ended questions during interviews to gain deeper insights into their goals and preferences. Questions like "What ESG issues are most important to you?" can reveal a great deal about their values.

6. **Active Listening:** Practice active listening to understand their concerns and aspirations better. This builds trust and shows that you value their input.

7. **Transparent Communication:** Maintain transparency in all communications to build trust. Be honest about potential risks and rewards.

8. **Success Stories:** Share success stories that resonate with their interests and experiences. For example, a story about a company that turned around a crisis by adopting strong ESG practices can be very motivating.

9. **Empathy:** Show empathy in your interactions to build a strong relationship. Understand their fears and aspirations and address them thoughtfully.

10. **Follow-Up:** Regularly follow up on the counterparty's queries and provide timely responses. This shows that you are attentive and committed to their success.

By implementing these strategies, you can effectively shape your approach to each investor's interests and experience, ensuring that they are well-informed and confident in their investment decisions. Think of it as being a tour guide, helping investors navigate the complex world of sustainable investing with confidence and clarity.

Boardroom Briefing (Lite): What Executives Should Do

- Equip investor relations and strategy teams with clear, evidence-based ESG talking points.
- Anticipate the most common investor questions (returns, ratings, impact versus ESG, SME relevance) and prepare consistent answers.
- Use communications with investors to shift the narrative from "ESG as a cost" to "ESG as risk management and value creation."

Beyond communication strategies, investors also need practical tools to identify and manage ESG risks directly within their portfolios.

Helping Investors Manage ESG Risks

One practical approach is for investors to start by identifying the specific ESG risks relevant to their investments. This involves conducting thorough risk assessments that consider environmental factors, such as climate change and resource consumption, as well as social issues like labor practices and governance aspects, including board accountability and transparency.

Common Publicly Available Sources

Investors can leverage several publicly available sources to manage ESG risks in Asia:

1. **Official Regulators' Websites:** The websites of financial regulators, such as ministries of finance, securities commissions, stock exchanges, and auditor regulatory bodies, provide guidelines, and updates on ESG regulations.
2. **Global Reporting Initiative (GRI):** Offers standards for sustainability reporting (GRI, Various Years).
3. **Sustainability Accounting Standards Board (SASB) (now part of ISSB):** Provides industry-specific standards for ESG reporting (ISSB, 2023).
4. **Task Force on Climate-Related Financial Disclosures (TCFD):** Offers recommendations for climate-related financial disclosures (TCFD, 2021).
5. **Principles for Responsible Investment (PRI):** Provides resources and guidelines for responsible investment.
6. **Asian Corporate Governance Association (ACGA):** Focuses on improving corporate governance practices in Asia.
7. **Asia Investor Group on Climate Change (AIGCC):** A network of institutional investors in Asia that promotes net zero and climate

resilience through capacity building, stewardship, and policy advocacy.

8. **CFA Institute:** Offers publications and resources on ESG issues in investing.
9. **World Federation of Exchanges (WFE):** Provides guidelines and best practices for ESG reporting.
10. **Industry Reports and Whitepapers:** Reports from consulting firms, such as the Big Four, provide valuable insights into ESG trends and best practices in Asia.

Why Do Investors Care About ESG?

Understanding why investors care about ESG is crucial for effectively managing ESG risks. According to the CFA Institute (2024), investors increasingly recognize the financial materiality of ESG factors. ESG considerations can significantly impact a company's long-term prospects and sustainability. For instance, companies with strong ESG practices are often better positioned to manage risks, attract talent, and maintain customer loyalty. This can lead to enhanced financial performance and reduced volatility.

Additionally, the growing emphasis on corporate responsibility and sustainability drives investors to support companies that have a positive impact on society and the environment. For example, an investor might be motivated by the desire to support renewable energy projects, knowing that these investments not only contribute to environmental sustainability but also offer promising financial returns in the energy transition process. To move from theory to action, investors can use a structured checklist like the following one (Table 3.2).

ESG Risk Management Checklist

Here is a top 10 ESG risk management checklist to help investors navigate opportunities:

Table 3.2 ESG risk management checklist for investors

1. **Conduct ESG Risk Assessments:** Regularly evaluate the ESG risks associated with each investment. For instance, a manufacturing company might face environmental risks related to waste management and emissions.
2. **Integrate ESG Criteria:** Incorporate ESG factors into the investment analysis and decision-making process to make informed investment decisions. A tech company may be evaluated based on its data privacy practices and employee welfare.
3. **Engage with Companies:** Actively engage with companies to encourage better ESG practices. For example, investors might push for improved labor conditions in an auto company.
4. **Monitor ESG Performance:** Continuously monitoring and regularly updating a company's sustainability initiatives can provide valuable insights into its performance.
5. **Use ESG Ratings and Scores:** Utilize ESG ratings and scores from reputable agencies or develop internal capacity to make informed investment decisions. Comparing ratings from different sources can offer a comprehensive view.
6. **Stay Informed on Regulations:** Keep up-to-date with ESG regulations and guidelines from official sources. Regulatory changes can impact strategies.
7. **Diversify Investments:** Diversify portfolios to mitigate ESG-related risks. Investing in various sectors or markets can reduce exposure to specific ESG risks.
8. **Implement ESG Policies:** Develop and implement clear ESG policies and guidelines for investment practices. A policy might include criteria for selecting opportunities.
9. **Educate and Train:** Provide ongoing education and training on ESG issues for investment teams. Regular group discussions can enhance understanding.
10. **Report Transparently:** Ensure transparent reporting of ESG performance to stakeholders. Clear communication builds trust and accountability.

By leveraging these strategies and resources, investors can effectively manage ESG risks and build resilient, sustainable portfolios. For example, one of Singapore's top banks, DBS, partnered with GreenFi to digitize its environmental risk management and ESG reporting processes using AI-enabled solutions (DBS Bank, 2024; GreenFi, 2024). This automation not only ensured compliance with regulatory guidelines but also provided accurate insights for over 50,000 commercial banking customers, optimizing resource utilization and minimizing environmental impact.

Key Takeaways

- Investor education is essential for integrating ESG into capital allocation and strengthening long-term market stability in Asia.
- Misconceptions persist, including beliefs that ESG is a Western trend, reduces returns, or applies only to large companies.
- Confusion between ESG, impact investing, and values-based investing continues to weaken effective portfolio construction.
- Personalized communication, empathy, and active listening are more effective than standardized messaging in building trust.
- Practical tools, including FAQs, case studies, and risk checklists, help investors translate ESG concepts into action.
- ESG literacy requires continuous reinforcement through training, engagement, and exposure to evolving regulatory and market practices.

Boardroom Briefing

Executives, regulators, and investors should:

1. Integrate ESG education into corporate training, client engagement, and professional development programs.
2. Use common investor questions on returns, ratings, and impact as opportunities to reset expectations.
3. Equip investor relations teams with clear, evidence-based case studies linking ESG to financial performance and risk management.
4. Apply structured tools, including FAQs and standardized risk assessment frameworks, to improve engagement quality.
5. Promote personalized communication strategies that reflect investors' experience, risk tolerance, and long-term objectives.
6. Commit to ongoing capacity building to support informed stewardship and responsible capital allocation in Asian markets.

CHAPTER 4

The Dos and Don'ts of Navigating ESG/ Sustainability in Asia

[CORPORATES] [INVESTORS] [REGULATORS]

This chapter is intended primarily for corporates—especially those developing ESG policies—but also for investors and regulators seeking to evaluate or guide corporate sustainability practices in Asia.

Helping Asian Firms Create a Company ESG Policy

Implementing an ESG policy is fundamental for companies aiming to succeed in today's increasingly conscious market. An ESG policy provides a structured framework for addressing environmental impact, social responsibilities, and governance practices, ensuring that a company operates sustainably and ethically. This approach enhances corporate reputation, attracts investors, and improves long-term financial performance.

For example, Cisco Systems has committed to achieving net-zero emissions by 2040 and has made significant contributions to community programs (Cisco Systems, 2024). Similarly, Apple has implemented comprehensive ESG initiatives, resulting in the avoidance of millions of metric tons of emissions (Apple, 2024). These cases demonstrate how a well-structured ESG policy can yield tangible benefits, including reduced environmental impact and an enhanced reputation.

Moreover, having an ESG policy helps companies navigate regulatory requirements and mitigate risks. With increasing regulations around ESG issues, companies that proactively address these areas are better positioned to comply with laws and avoid potential penalties. Also, strong ESG practices can lead to operational efficiencies and cost savings, further underscoring the importance of integrating ESG considerations into business strategies.

Define the Type of Policy to Adopt

When defining the type of ESG policy to adopt, it is crucial to recognize that ESG as a term may be sensitive now. However, the underlying principle is more than a passing trend. ESG principles have become integral to business operations worldwide over the past 20 years, driven by increasing awareness of environmental and social issues, as well as numerous corporate scandals resulting from poor governance. Companies that understand the long-term value of ESG are better positioned to build resilience and achieve sustainable growth.

There is growing evidence that businesses globally are embracing sustainability goals, not just for compliance but also to drive business success in the transition to a more sustainable economy. Companies that integrate ESG strategies are seeing significant benefits, including an enhanced reputation, increased investor interest, and improved operational efficiencies. For example, the 2025 Edelman Trust Barometer highlights that 63 percent of employees expect their employers to address climate change and sustainability (Mainwaring, 2025). This widespread acceptance underscores the importance of adopting ESG policies.

ESG should be viewed as a strategic tool to enhance business viability and sustainability. Integrating ESG principles can lead to top-line growth, cost reductions, and minimized regulatory risks. Companies prioritizing ESG are better equipped to navigate complex geopolitical landscapes and ensure long-term success. For example, Verizon has pledged to generate renewable energy equivalent to 50 percent of its annual electricity consumption by 2025 (Verizon, 2024). It has made substantial strides in addressing e-waste. Similarly, NVIDIA Corporation is dedicated to acquiring or producing enough renewable energy to offset 100 percent of its global electricity consumption (NVIDIA Corporation, 2023). By embedding ESG into their core strategies, businesses can achieve sustainable competitive advantages and foster a culture of continuous improvement.

Design ESG Policies as Guidelines to Make ESG Goals Achievable

Designing effective ESG policies entails creating clear and actionable guidelines that enable companies to achieve their ESG objectives. These policies should be practical, measurable, and aligned with the company's overall strategy. Here are some key considerations for designing ESG policies that make goals achievable:

First, conducting a thorough materiality assessment is primary for identifying the most significant ESG issues relevant to the company. This process entails engaging with stakeholders—such as employees, customers, investors, and community members—to gain insights into their concerns and expectations. By focusing on material issues, companies can ensure that their ESG policies address the most critical areas and have a meaningful impact.

Once the material issues are identified, companies should set clear and realistic ESG objectives. These objectives should be specific, measurable, achievable, relevant, and time-bound (SMART). For instance, a company might aim to reduce its carbon emissions by 30 percent over the next five years or achieve a specific diversity level within its leadership team in a designated timeframe. Setting SMART goals helps ensure that the company's ESG efforts are focused and trackable.

To support achieving these goals, companies should develop detailed action plans with interim goals that outline the steps needed to meet their objectives. This includes assigning responsibilities, allocating resources, and establishing timelines. Regular monitoring and reporting are also required for tracking progress and making necessary adjustments. For instance, Unilever has implemented a sustainability plan that includes specific targets for reducing greenhouse gas emissions, improving water efficiency, and enhancing social impact (Unilever, 2024). By regularly reporting on their progress, Unilever ensures transparency and accountability.

Moreover, companies should integrate ESG considerations into their decision-making processes and corporate culture. This can be accomplished by offering training and education to employees, forming ESG committees or task forces at the board level, and integrating ESG criteria into performance evaluations and compensation structures. In recent years, an increasing number of Asian companies have tied executive compensation to achieving specific ESG targets, ensuring that leadership is held accountable for the company's sustainability performance.

Focusing on practical, measurable goals and avoiding vague or idealistic language is also essential. Ambiguous terms such as "green" or "sustainable" can be misleading and lack specificity. Instead, companies should use precise language that clearly defines their commitments and actions. For example, instead of stating a goal to "become more green", a company could specify that it aims to "reduce water usage by 20 percent over the next three years." This clarity helps set realistic expectations and measure progress effectively.

Obtain Employee Buy-In and Support

Securing employee buy-in and support is key to the successful implementation of ESG policies. Employees are more likely to embrace new initiatives when they understand the specific benefits these policies offer them. For instance, ESG-driven companies often create healthier and more sustainable work environments, resulting in improved air quality, natural lighting, and overall employee well-being. Additionally, companies prioritizing social aspects of ESG, such as wellness programs and flexible work arrangements, can foster a supportive culture that enhances employee satisfaction and engagement.

To further encourage employee support, consider offering financial incentives as a means of recognition and appreciation. Financial incentives can be a powerful motivator, aligning employees' personal goals with the company's ESG objectives. For example, integrating ESG targets into performance evaluations and compensation structures can drive meaningful progress. Similarly, bonuses or rewards for meeting sustainability goals can incentivize employees at all levels to contribute to the company's ESG efforts.

In addition to these strategies, it is essential to communicate the broader impact of ESG policies on the company's success and long-term viability. Employees should comprehend how their efforts align with and contribute to the company's overarching mission and goals. This can be achieved through regular updates, training sessions, and open forums where employees can ask questions and provide feedback. Engaging employees in the development and implementation of ESG policies can also foster a sense of ownership and commitment among them.

Moreover, creating a culture of transparency and accountability is prominent. Companies should regularly report on their ESG progress and celebrate successes, regardless of their size and scope. For smaller companies, even simple measures like public dashboards tracking energy reduction goals can create meaningful momentum while satisfying growing stakeholder expectations. Recognizing and rewarding employees' contributions to ESG initiatives can reinforce positive behaviors and encourage continued engagement. Once employee support is secured, the next challenge is determining which specific policies to prioritize under each ESG pillar.

How to Decide What Policies to Include

When deciding what policies to include under each pillar of ESG, companies should focus on practical and impactful measures that align with their overall strategy and goals. Here are some key considerations for each category:

Environment

1. **Reducing Harmful Chemicals and Pollutants:** Companies should prioritize minimizing the use of harmful chemicals and pollutants in their products and processes. This can be achieved by adopting safer alternatives, improving waste management practices and complying with relevant regulations. For example, Patagonia, an outdoor sportswear company, has committed to eliminating harmful chemicals from its supply chain and uses recycled polyester and organic cotton in its products (Patagonia, 2023). Similarly, Seventh Generation, a household and personal care products company, formulates its products with plant-based ingredients while avoiding synthetic chemicals like phthalates and parabens (Seventh Generation, 2023).

2. **Using Renewable Energy Sources:** Examining the practicality of using renewable energy sources is substantial for reducing a company's carbon footprint. Investing in solar panels, wind turbines, or other renewable energy technologies can help businesses generate their own electricity and reduce their reliance on fossil fuels. This will not only reduce emissions but also offer long-term cost savings and energy price stability. For instance, Tesla powers its operations with renewable energy and promotes the use of solar products and energy storage solutions (Tesla, 2023). IKEA aimed to power nearly 100 percent of its global operations with renewable energy by 2025 (IKEA, 2024).

3. **Reducing Emissions:** Researching and implementing strategies to reduce emissions is essential for achieving environmental sustainability. Companies can start by identifying the sources of their emissions and setting reduction targets. Measures such as switching to green energy tariffs, optimizing energy use, and improving transportation efficiency can significantly lower emissions. For example, New Belgium Brewing Company has undertaken several initiatives to minimize its carbon footprint, such as utilizing renewable energy and optimizing its brewing processes (New Belgium Brewing Company, 2023). Panasonic has also significantly reduced emissions through energy-saving production improvements and recycling-oriented manufacturing (Panasonic, 2024).

4. **Increasing Sustainability in Supply Chains:** Enhancing sustainability in supply chains involves evaluating and improving the environmental impact of sourcing, production, and distribution processes. Companies can collaborate with suppliers to implement sustainable practices, such as utilizing renewable materials, reducing waste, and minimizing energy consumption. For instance, Nike's "Move to Zero" initiative focuses on reducing waste and using recycled materials in its products (Nike, 2024). The company also aims to eliminate single-use plastics and promote circular design principles.

Social

1. **Focus on What Your Company Can Do for the Community:** Companies should prioritize initiatives that positively impact the

communities where they operate. This can involve supporting local education programs, sponsoring community events, and partnering with local organizations to address specific needs. For instance, Atlassian, the Australian software giant behind tools like Jira and Confluence, has embedded social impact into its DNA since its founding in 2002 (Atlassian, 2024). The company's commitment to donating one percent of equity, profit, employee time, and products—a model now known as the Pledge one percent movement. As of 2024, the Atlassian Foundation holds $71 million in donated funds and has facilitated over 277,000 employee volunteer hours, with more than 13,000 nonprofits using its discounted software to amplify their work (Atlassian, 2024 Impact Report). Similarly, Nike collaborates with over 200 organizations to bring sports-based programs to young people, addressing inequality and promoting health (Nike, 2024).

2. **Emphasize Inclusion and Diversity in Hiring and Elsewhere:** Promoting diversity and inclusion in hiring practices and throughout the organization is essential for creating a supportive and innovative workplace. Companies can implement strategies such as bias training for interviewers, diverse hiring committees, and inclusive job descriptions. For instance, Intel has made significant strides in promoting diversity by spending $2.2 billion with diverse suppliers in 2022 and aiming to reach $2 billion annually by 2030 (Intel, 2022). Additionally, Salesforce has been recognized for its efforts in fostering a diverse and inclusive workplace through its 1–1–1 philanthropic model (Salesforce, 2023).

3. **Consider the Fairness of Executive Compensation Policies:** Ensuring that executive compensation is fair and aligned with the company's performance and shareholders' interests is necessary. Companies should establish transparent compensation structures that incentivize ethical behavior and long-term success. For instance, the SEC mandates public companies to disclose executive compensation details (SEC, 2024), thereby promoting transparency and accountability. Additionally, companies like Johnson & Johnson have strong governance frameworks that emphasize ethical conduct and accountability.

4. **Endorse Ethical Business Practices:** Establishing policies that promote ethical business practices and transparency is vital for good governance. This encompasses implementing anticorruption measures, ensuring compliance with laws and regulations, and upholding high standards of corporate governance. For example, Ben & Jerry's is known for its fair trade sourcing of ingredients, support for local communities and firm stances on social and political issues (Johnson & Johnson, 2023).

Governance

1. **A More Diverse Board Can Result in Better Decisions:** A diverse board brings together a broader range of perspectives, experiences and skills, leading to more comprehensive and well-considered decisions. Some research suggests that companies with greater diversity on their boards tend to outperform their peers. For example, McKinsey's research indicates that executive teams outperform less-diverse peers by approximately 39 percent when gender and ethnic diversity reach top-quartile thresholds, and for the first time finds statistically significant links between leadership diversity and social and environmental impact (Hunt et al., 2023). Additionally, research published in *Harvard Business Review* suggests that board diversity can improve the quality of decision making and strengthen overall corporate governance, particularly when paired with an inclusive board culture that enables diverse perspectives to be heard and acted upon (Creary et al., 2019).

2. **Establish Expectations for Board Independence to Enhance Accountability and Oversight:** Board independence, when implemented thoughtfully, is a crucial means of enhancing accountability and ensuring adequate oversight of management. Genuinely independent directors provide objective perspectives free from conflicts of interest, which contributes to unbiased decision making and the protection of shareholder interests. For instance, the Sarbanes–Oxley Act mandates that audit committee members be independent, underscoring the importance of this principle. Companies can enhance board independence by establishing clear criteria for independence, diversifying board recruitment and implementing term limits to ensure fresh perspectives.

3. **Promote Better Corporate Reporting Transparency, Particularly Concerning ESG:** Transparent ESG reporting enables companies to clearly communicate their impact on critical areas such as climate change, human rights, and corporate governance. This openness helps to bolster stakeholder trust and can enhance the company's reputation as an ethical corporate citizen. Companies that adopt best practices in ESG reporting, such as using standardized frameworks and providing regular updates, will likely enjoy a deeper and more productive dialogue with their shareholders and other key stakeholders.

4. **Document and Make Public the Firm's Governance, Compliance, and Risk Strategies:** Publicly documenting governance, compliance, and risk strategies strengthens transparency and accountability. For instance, S&P Global's Corporate Transparency Report (2025) highlights the importance of public disclosure in sustainability investment strategies. Companies can use digital tools to modernize documentation, making it accessible and transparent for all stakeholders.

Avoid Exaggerated Sustainability Claims in Marketing Literature

In today's market, where consumers are increasingly aware of environmental and social issues, companies must exercise caution to avoid overstating their sustainability claims. Overpromising on sustainability can lead to accusations of "greenwashing", when a company exaggerates or falsely claims to be environmentally friendly or socially responsible to appear more sustainable than it actually is. This not only tarnishes the company's reputation but can also lead to substantial legal consequences. This can lead to public backlash as consumers and watchdog organizations become more adept at identifying and calling out misleading claims. For example, McDonald's faced criticism for its switch to paper straws, which was seen as a superficial effort given the broader environmental impact of its operations. Similarly, Royal Dutch Shell has been scrutinized for its substantial carbon emissions despite marketing its renewable energy projects (Royal Dutch Shell, 2023).

The consequences of greenwashing can be severe, including hefty fines and legal actions. Volkswagen's 2015 "Dieselgate" scandal remains a landmark case of corporate greenwashing. The automaker admitted to installing illegal software in 11 million diesel vehicles worldwide to cheat emissions tests, while actual NOx emissions exceeded legal limits by up to 40 times in real-world driving conditions (EPA, 2015). The fallout included $34.69 billion in fines and settlements (Reuters, 2020), as well as criminal charges against executives and lasting reputational damage (Reuters, 2024). This case exposed how even industry leaders can prioritize short-term profits over genuine sustainability, ultimately undermining trust in corporate ESG claims.

Another example is Keurig, which faced penalties for misleading recycling claims about its K-Cup coffee pods. The company paid $10 million in a U.S. settlement, $2.3 million to Canada's Competition Bureau, and $1.5 million to the SEC in 2024 (SEC, 2024). These instances highlight the financial and reputational risks associated with greenwashing.

Financial institutions also face significant risks related to greenwashing. Greenwashing in the financial sector involves misrepresenting the environmental benefits of financial products or services, potentially misleading investors and consumers. For example, DWS, a German asset management company, was fined $25 million for marketing its ESG funds as greener than they actually were. Similarly, Goldman Sachs and BNY Mellon faced substantial fines for misleading ESG claims (Reuters, 2023; SEC, 2023). In another instance, the U.S. SEC imposed fines on several financial institutions for failing to accurately disclose the environmental impact of their investment products (SEC, 2024). These cases can be summarized in Table 4.1 for quick comparison.

Table 4.1 Greenwashing risks—lessons from global cases

- **McDonald's:** Net-zero claim excluded Scope 3 emissions, which account for ~97% of its footprint.
- **Volkswagen (Dieselgate):** Emissions-cheating scandal undermined investor and consumer trust worldwide.
- **Shell:** Court-ordered to cut emissions faster than planned due to misleading transition framing.
- **Keurig:** Paid penalties for misleading recyclability claims in Canada.
- **DWS:** Settled $19M case for overstating ESG credentials in disclosures.

Lesson: Exaggerated claims can backfire, leading to regulatory penalties, reputational harm, and loss of investor confidence.

If overstating sustainability progress is risky, understating it can be equally damaging.

Don't Make Sustainability Promises You Won't Keep

In this digital age, companies that make bold sustainability announcements without taking concrete actions risk facing severe condemnation on social media, subject to a high level of public scrutiny. Consumers are increasingly wary and quick to call out instances where companies promote environmentally friendly practices more in their marketing than in practice. This can lead to widespread criticism and significant damage to reputations.

To avoid such pitfalls, companies would be well-advised to focus on practical, modest, and achievable sustainability goals. Setting realistic targets helps maintain credibility and achieve long-term success. The SMART goals framework mentioned earlier is often used to set practical sustainability objectives that are both attainable and impactful.

On the other hand, the ever-changing landscape of policies and regulations can also make it challenging for companies to accomplish overambitious sustainability goals. New policies or political changes can introduce unexpected hurdles or shift priorities, making it difficult for companies to stay on track with their commitments. For example, recent changes in U.S. and European regulations have presented significant challenges for companies seeking to uphold their sustainability commitments.

As a result, some financial institutions have withdrawn from climate initiatives due to political pressure, regulatory changes, or strategic shifts. This trend highlights the complexities of maintaining long-term commitments to sustainability. Major banks, including Citigroup, Bank of America, and JPMorgan, have withdrawn from the Net-Zero Banking Alliance and other climate-focused groups, citing various reasons. These exits can undermine global efforts to combat climate change and emphasize the importance of setting realistic and achievable sustainability goals.

By focusing on practical and achievable goals, companies can navigate the complexities of the regulatory landscape and maintain their credibility. It is wise to back up sustainability announcements with concrete actions to avoid backlash from social media or other stakeholders.

Don't Understate Your Efforts to Promote Sustainability

"Greenhushing", the practice of undercommunicating or concealing a company's sustainability efforts, also poses significant challenges in the realm of corporate responsibility. This approach can be just as damaging, leading to a lack of transparency and accountability in sustainability reporting.

One of the primary issues with greenhushing is that it can erode trust among stakeholders, including consumers, investors, and regulators. When companies fail to communicate their environmental efforts, they miss opportunities to build a positive reputation and may be perceived as lacking commitment to sustainability. This can result in a loss of consumer confidence and potential backlash, similar to the consequences of greenwashing.

For investors, greenhushing presents specific risks. Investors rely on precise and thorough information to make informed decisions about allocating their capital. When companies underreport their sustainability efforts, it creates a gap in the data available for assessing ESG performance. This lack of transparency can lead to misguided investment choices and potential financial losses. Moreover, investors may face reputational risks if they are associated with companies that are not forthcoming about their sustainability practices.

To avoid greenhushing, companies should adopt a balanced and transparent approach to communicating their sustainability efforts. This involves setting clear, achievable goals and regularly reporting progress in a factual and measured manner. Establishing robust measurement and reporting systems is crucial to ensure that the data shared is accurate and reliable. Engaging and training employees in effective corporate social responsibility (CSR) communication can also help maintain consistency and transparency in reporting.

Some examples of companies that have successfully avoided greenhushing include Nestlé and Schneider Electric. Nestlé publishes detailed updates on its net-zero 2050 roadmap, including its (controversial) 2025 target for 100 percent recyclable or reusable packaging, although critics argue that its pace of plastic reduction remains inadequate. Schneider

Electric's open reporting on its "Zero Carbon Project" (Schneider Electric, 2024) has driven measurable outcomes: 120 million tons of CO_2 savings for clients and a #1 ranking in Corporate Knights' Global 100 sustainability index.

However, other corporations have learned painful lessons about the consequences of greenhushing:

- Volkswagen's $34 billion Dieselgate scandal began when the company concealed emissions test cheating, destroying decades of brand equity (EPA Settlement Documents, 2017). Even after its EV transition, investors remain wary of the automaker's disclosures.

- Shell faces ongoing litigation after internal documents revealed that the company understood climate risks as early as the 1970s but minimized public warnings (*Greenpeace Italy v. Shell*, 2023 court filings). This decades-long opacity now undermines its claims to an energy transition.

- Fast fashion retailer H&M drew regulatory scrutiny when its "Conscious Collection" marketing exaggerated sustainability achievements while obscuring broader environmental impacts. UK regulators ultimately mandated clearer disclosure standards (UK Competition and Markets Authority ruling, 2022).

Greenhushing—whether through withheld data (Volkswagen), selective disclosure (H&M), or delayed action (Shell)—erodes trust and invites regulatory blowback. Conversely, even imperfect transparency (as seen in Nestlé's packaging challenges) allows stakeholders to track progress and hold companies accountable. While Asia currently lacks widespread financial penalties for greenhushing (unlike greenwashing), regulatory momentum is building—Singapore's Advertising Standards Authority now scrutinizes underreported ESG claims (Advertising Standards Authority of Singapore, 2024), and China's 2024 ESG disclosure mandates signal tighter future enforcement (China Securities Regulatory Commission, 2024).

In conclusion, a thoughtful ESG strategy is no longer optional for companies—it's a strategic imperative for long-term competitiveness, investor confidence, and regulatory compliance in Asia's evolving markets. A well-crafted policy not only addresses environmental impact, social responsibilities, and governance practices but can also enhance corporate reputation, attract investors, and improve long-term financial performance.

When defining the type of ESG policy to adopt, it is key to recognize that ESG principles are fundamental to business operations and not merely a buzzword. Companies that grasp the long-term value of ESG are better equipped to build resilience and achieve sustainable growth. It is vital to design clear and actionable ESG policies, secure employee buy-in and support and foster a culture of transparency and accountability.

Furthermore, companies should avoid exaggerated claims to prevent accusations of greenwashing, which can harm their reputation and lead to legal repercussions. Equally important is avoiding greenhushing, as undercommunicating sustainability efforts can undermine trust and transparency, posing risks to both consumers and investors. By adopting a balanced and transparent approach to communicating sustainability issues, companies can build trust, attract responsible investors, and contribute to global sustainability goals. Ultimately, a well-implemented ESG policy serves as a strategic tool to enhance business viability, ensuring that companies operate sustainably and ethically while achieving success.

Key Takeaways

- Effective ESG policies require sustained leadership commitment alongside broad employee engagement and cross-functional coordination.
- Policies should be grounded in robust materiality assessments and translated into clear, measurable, and time-bound objectives.
- Embedding ESG into governance structures, executive incentives, and operational decision-making strengthens accountability.
- Overstated sustainability claims expose companies to regulatory scrutiny, legal liability, and long-term reputational damage.
- Undercommunicating ESG efforts ("greenhushing") also undermines investor confidence, data quality, and market transparency.
- Balanced, credible, and consistent reporting is essential for linking ESG policies to long-term resilience and capital market trust.

Boardroom Briefing

Executives and boards should:

1. Involve employees early in ESG policy design to secure ownership, alignment, and practical implementation capacity.
2. Apply materiality assessments and SMART targets to prioritize high-impact actions and allocate resources effectively.
3. Integrate ESG objectives into governance frameworks, performance reviews, and executive remuneration structures.
4. Establish internal verification processes to ensure all sustainability claims are accurate, comparable, and auditable.
5. Manage both greenwashing and greenhushing risks through disciplined, balanced, and transparent stakeholder communication.
6. Anchor ESG policies in strong board oversight, internal controls, and risk management systems to reinforce long-term credibility.

CHAPTER 5

Sustainability in Greater China (Mainland China, Hong Kong, and Taiwan)

[INVESTORS] [CORPORATES] [REGULATORS]
[INTERNATIONAL EXECUTIVES]

This chapter is intended for investors, corporates, regulators, and international executives seeking to navigate the sustainability landscape in Mainland China, Hong Kong, and Taiwan—with a focus on regulatory frameworks, cultural dynamics, and market opportunities.

Understanding Business Culture

Understanding the business culture in Mainland China, Hong Kong, and Taiwan is a prerequisite for any company looking to operate successfully in these markets. While these regions share some cultural similarities due to their Chinese heritage, there are also significant differences shaped by their unique historical, political, and economic contexts.

In mainland China, business culture is deeply influenced by Confucian values, which emphasize hierarchy, respect for authority, and the importance of relationships, known as "*guanxi.*" Cultivating personal relationships and networks is fundamental for achieving business success. Decision making tends to be top-down, with senior executives holding significant power and influence. Also, the Chinese market places a high value on face-saving (mianzi), which means maintaining harmony and avoiding public confrontation.

A famous case study illustrating the importance of guanxi is the 1997 joint venture between General Motors (GM) and Shanghai Automotive Industry Corporation (SAIC)—then China's largest single foreign investment, which by 2005 had proven successful through GM's growing market share and technology transfer achievements (GM, 2005; SAIC, 2005). Chinese companies often embrace aggressive expansion when aligned with state priorities, reflecting a culture where policy direction heavily shapes business risk appetite. But remember, it works both ways.

As a former British colony, Hong Kong presents a unique blend of Eastern and Western business practices. The business landscape is intensely competitive and rapidly evolving, placing a premium on efficiency and professionalism. While guanxi remains important, business interactions in Hong Kong are generally more legally based and structured compared to those in Mainland China. The legal and regulatory framework in Hong Kong is more transparent and aligned with international standards, making it an attractive destination for multinational corporations.

The city's cosmopolitan nature also means that businesspeople in Hong Kong are often more accustomed to dealing with international partners and are more open to diverse business practices. It is worth noting that the creation of the Greater Bay Area (GBA) in 2016—formally outlined in 2019—has accelerated economic integration between Hong Kong and Mainland China, reducing business culture differences through shared infrastructure, cross-border entrepreneurship programs, and policy-driven collaboration in sectors such as finance and technology (People's Republic of China, National Development and Reform Commission, 2019).

Meanwhile, Taiwan's business culture is influenced by both Chinese traditions and Japanese practices due to its historical ties with Japan. Like mainland China, guanxi plays a significant role in business dealings, and building trust and long-term relationships is essential. However, Taiwanese business culture strongly emphasizes innovation and technological advancement, especially within the high-tech sector.

Companies like TSMC have become global leaders by fostering a culture of continuous improvement and technological excellence (TSMC, 2024). Decision making in Taiwanese companies tends to be more consensus-driven compared to Mainland China, with a greater emphasis on teamwork and collaboration. Additionally, Taiwanese businesspeople often exhibit a high level of humility and modesty, reflecting the values of respect and harmony that are deeply ingrained in Taiwanese culture.

While Hong Kong's corporate culture remains shaped by global investor expectations, and Taiwan blends family-run governance with a strong innovation ethos, Mainland boards remain closely intertwined with state objectives—a divergence foreign investors must navigate. Cultural dynamics set the stage, but effective participation also depends on navigating distinct regulatory systems.

Regulatory Framework

The capital markets across Greater China feature distinct regulatory architectures, with Mainland China's state-guided approach contrasting Hong Kong's internationalised system and Taiwan's hybrid model, each requiring tailored navigation by stakeholders.

In mainland China, the primary regulatory body for the securities market is the China Securities Regulatory Commission (CSRC), which operates under the State Council. The CSRC oversees the Shanghai Stock Exchange (SSE), the Shenzhen Stock Exchange (SZSE) and the Beijing Stock Exchange (BSE), ensuring compliance with securities laws and regulations. The People's Bank of China (PBOC) is the central banking regulator, while the China Banking and Insurance Regulatory Commission (CBIRC) supervises the banking and insurance sectors. In addition, the State-owned Assets Supervision and Administration Commission (SASAC) oversees SOEs, ensuring their adherence to state policies. Quasi-regulators, such as the Asset Management Association of China (AMAC), the Insurance Asset Management Association of China (IAMAC), and the China Association for Public Companies (CAPCO), all established under the CSRC, play significant roles in self-regulation and industry standards.

For Hong Kong, the Securities and Futures Commission (SFC) is the principal regulator, established under the Securities and Futures Ordinance (SFO) to oversee the securities and futures markets. The Hong Kong Exchanges and Clearing Limited (HKEX) operates the stock and futures exchanges and is responsible for listing and trading regulations.

The Hong Kong Monetary Authority (HKMA) serves as the banking regulator, ensuring the stability and integrity of the banking system. The Insurance Authority (IA) regulates the insurance industry, while the Mandatory Provident Fund Schemes Authority (MPFA) oversees retirement schemes. A significant event that changed the character of the Hong Kong stock market was the 2019 listing reform by HKEX, which allowed dual-class shares to attract major tech companies like Alibaba to list in Hong Kong (HKEX, 2019).

Taiwan's capital market is regulated primarily by the Financial Supervisory Commission (FSC), which oversees the securities, banking, and insurance sectors. The Taiwan Stock Exchange (TWSE) and the Taipei Exchange (TPEx) are the main stock exchanges, with the TWSE catering to larger companies and the TPEx supporting smaller and emerging firms. The Central Bank of the Republic of China (Taiwan) regulates monetary policy and banking operations. The Securities and Futures Investors Protection Center (SFIPC) plays a crucial role in protecting investors' rights and ensuring market integrity.

While there are similarities in the regulatory structures of these three markets, such as the presence of dedicated securities commissions and stock exchanges, there are also significant differences. Mainland China's regulatory framework is heavily influenced by state control and the management of SOEs, whereas Hong Kong's framework emphasizes transparency and international alignment. Taiwan's regulatory environment prioritizes investor protection and encourages innovation. Understanding these nuances is helpful for businesses and investors operating in these markets.

Key Issues, Challenges, and Opportunities

In mainland China, businesses face several key issues, including navigating a complex regulatory environment, protecting IP and managing intense local competition. The regulatory landscape remains opaque and subject to sudden changes, requiring businesses to stay agile and well-informed. IP infringement continues to be a significant challenge, despite improvements in IP laws and enforcement. Moreover, the emphasis on self-reliance and preferential treatment for domestic companies creates formidable barriers for foreign firms.

An emerging challenge is talent retention. Even as youth unemployment remains high and corporate layoffs continue, experienced professionals are leaving both private companies and public institutions. Regulators such as the PBOC and the CSRC have reportedly struggled to retain skilled staff, with some moving abroad or joining multinational firms offering greater pay and career development prospects (Yahoo Finance, 2024). This attrition has implications for regulatory agility and the availability of ESG expertise, factors that investors must weigh when evaluating governance standards in the Chinese market.

However, opportunities abound in China's vast consumer market and rapid technological advancements. Companies like KFC have successfully adapted to local tastes and preferences, leading to explosive growth. Similarly, BYD's rise in electric vehicles, supported by substantial green financing and alignment with state priorities, demonstrates how local companies can leverage policy frameworks to achieve global competitiveness while attracting foreign investment (BYD, 2024). The "Awakening Governance" report by the ACGA highlights China's evolving corporate governance landscape, emphasizing improved transparency and accountability (ACGA, 2018). Furthermore, the rise of e-commerce and digital platforms offers substantial opportunities for businesses to expand their reach and optimize operations. The health care sector is also growing rapidly, driven by an aging population and increasing demand for quality medical services. Companies like Pfizer and Johnson & Johnson have successfully tapped into this market by forming joint ventures and partnerships with local firms.

In Hong Kong, businesses face high operating costs, intense market competition, and comprehensive regulatory compliance. The city's strategic location and favorable tax environment make it a compelling hub for international trade and finance, though these benefits come with challenges. High real estate prices and labor costs can strain budgets, while strict banking procedures and financial reporting requirements demand meticulous attention. The city is also experiencing a talent drain, with ESG and finance professionals relocating to Singapore and other global markets, raising questions about Hong Kong's ability to maintain its competitive edge as a green finance hub (SCMP, 2024).

Despite these challenges, Hong Kong offers significant opportunities due to its strong legal framework, advanced infrastructure, and proximity to Mainland China. Recent enhancements to HKEX's ESG disclosure requirements (2023–2024) have bolstered the city's positioning as a leader in sustainable finance and improved transparency for investors (HKEX, 2024). HSBC's use of data analytics and AI to enhance customer life cycle management is a prime example of leveraging technology to stay competitive in this dynamic market (HSBC, 2024). Additionally, Hong Kong's role as a gateway to China provides unique opportunities for businesses to access the mainland market while benefiting from the city's transparent regulatory environment and international connectivity. The city's vibrant financial sector and status as a global financial center also attract a wide range of international businesses and investors. Opportunities in fintech are also growing, with companies like WeLab making significant strides in digital banking and payment solutions. The city's vibrant start-up ecosystem, supported by government initiatives and funding programs, also presents opportunities for innovation and entrepreneurship. Moreover, Hong Kong's role as a trade and logistics hub offers opportunities in sectors such as e-commerce, supply chain management and international trade. Tourism's recovery, although still below pre-2019 levels, shows promising momentum (Hong Kong Tourism Board, 2024).

In Taiwan, businesses must navigate a sophisticated market that emphasizes innovation and technology. Key challenges include regulatory compliance, IP protection, and competition from both local and international firms. Taiwan's regulatory environment is generally transparent, but businesses must adhere to specific local standards and labeling regulations. Another emerging challenge is talent mobility, with Taiwanese ESG and tech professionals increasingly moving to roles in China or multinational companies, which could constrain domestic capacity for innovation and governance (Taipei Times, 2024).

Opportunities in Taiwan are particularly strong in the high-tech sector, with companies like TSMC leading the way in semiconductor manufacturing. TSMC's 2050 net-zero commitment underscores Taiwan's growing focus on sustainability and its appeal to ESG-conscious investors (TSMC, 2024). In parallel, regulatory reforms aimed at increasing board independence and gender diversity are gradually strengthening corporate governance (FSC Taiwan, 2024). Taiwan's dedication to innovation and its strategic position in Asia make it an appealing destination for businesses seeking regional expansion. The CG Watch reports by the ACGA highlight Taiwan's strengths in corporate governance and its ongoing efforts to improve transparency and investor protection (ACGA, Various Years).

Furthermore, Taiwan's focus on sustainability and green technology presents new opportunities in the renewable energy sector, with initiatives aimed at increasing the use of solar and wind power. The health care and biotechnology sectors are experiencing significant growth, driven by advancements in medical research and a growing demand for health care services resulting from an aging population. Companies like Medigen Vaccine Biologics have propelled Taiwan's biotech sector onto the global stage, most notably through its self-developed COVID-19 vaccine (administered to three million patients across seven countries) and its pioneering World Health Organization (WHO) technology-sharing partnership, showcasing Taiwan's potential in this field (Medigen, 2024; WHO, 2024). Also, Taiwan's strategic location in Asia and its vigorous infrastructure make it a desirable destination for businesses looking to expand in the region. The island's skilled workforce and strong emphasis on education and research further enhance its appeal as a business destination.

While Mainland China, Hong Kong, and Taiwan share some similarities, such as the importance of regulatory compliance and IP protection, their business environments are shaped by distinct factors. Mainland China's vast market, policy-driven growth, and talent challenges present unique opportunities and risks. Hong Kong's strategic location, enhanced ESG framework, and green finance ambitions offer strong potential but are tempered by rising costs and talent outflow. Taiwan's focus on high-tech innovation, sustainability, and governance reforms creates fertile ground for future investment, though it too must contend with brain drain and regional competition. For investors and companies, long-term success across Greater China requires patient capital, an understanding of divergent governance cultures and the ability to navigate shifting political and regulatory landscapes.

Some additional context: China's inbound FDI flows reached USD 163 billion in 2023, with a growing share directed toward high-tech and green sectors (UNCTAD, 2024). Its digital economy now accounts for over 40 percent of GDP, driven by platforms like Alibaba, JD.com, and Meituan, which present both growth avenues and regulatory risks for investors (MIIT, 2024). For investors, participating through mechanisms such as Stock Connect or Qualified Foreign Institutional Investor (QFII) schemes requires a nuanced understanding of onshore–offshore capital flows and evolving compliance obligations.

In Hong Kong, recent government-backed talent schemes aim to reverse the outflow of ESG and financial professionals, with mixed early results (HK Gov, 2024). For foreign businesses, balancing the benefits of Hong Kong's enhanced ESG frameworks against rising operational costs remains an essential strategic consideration.

In Taiwan, government incentives for renewable energy investment reached USD 10 billion in 2024, underscoring its commitment to decarbonization (MOEA, 2024). For investors, Taiwan offers unique opportunities in offshore wind and semiconductor supply chains, but navigating cross-strait political risks remains a key part of due diligence.

Investors must also account for heightened political risks. The post-Zero-COVID policy shift has altered consumer behavior and supply chain strategies, while stricter foreign investment screening adds new layers of complexity to cross-border deals. U.S.–China tensions continue to influence technology transfers, tariffs, and the scrutiny of Chinese companies in overseas markets, underscoring the need for careful geopolitical risk assessment in portfolio and direct investment decisions (USTR, 2024).

Another example of market adaptation is Alibaba's ESG pivot following the regulatory overhaul of Ant Group, where the company integrated enhanced ESG disclosures and responsible lending standards to align with tightening domestic and global expectations (Alibaba, 2024). Foreign multinationals are also recalibrating their China strategies to adapt to the government's "dual circulation" policy, balancing domestic production with cross-border engagement to remain competitive under a more policy-driven growth model (NDRC, 2024).

Regulatory developments also create both opportunities and obligations for investors. In 2024, the CSRC introduced enhanced ESG disclosure requirements for listed companies, expanding mandatory reporting on climate risks and governance structures (CSRC, 2024). Concurrently, the PBOC has advanced green finance reforms for 2023–2025, increasing green bond quotas and incentivizing sustainability-linked lending (PBOC, 2024). The SASAC has also rolled out decarbonization mandates for central SOEs, aligning their operations with national carbon neutrality goals (SASAC, 2024).

Greater China as a whole demands patient, long-term capital strategies: Mainland growth favors those aligned with policy priorities, Hong Kong rewards firms that adapt to its evolving role as a green finance hub and Taiwan offers high-tech innovation opportunities paired with geopolitical complexities.

Interview With Local Experts

Interview With Dr. Peiyuan Guo, Founder of SynTao and Chair of China Sustainable Investment Forum (China SIF)

1. How has the landscape of corporate sustainability evolved in mainland China over the past decade? What are the key drivers behind this evolution?

   China's corporate sustainability has grown rapidly, with more companies, particularly the large ones, establishing sustainability teams and disclosing sustainability reports. External drivers play a key role in such movements. Stricter environmental regulations and the demands of foreign clients have been the main push. Internal drivers also matter. More and more leading firms recognize sustainability as essential for resilience and reputation.

2. What are the biggest challenges that foreign businesses in mainland China face when trying to implement sustainable practices? How to address them?

   First, multinational corporations (MNCs) in China need to adapt their sustainability strategies from headquarters to the Chinese context and use local language to explain them to key stakeholders, such as linking carbon reduction with pollution control, which is not the case in the United States or Europe. They also need to build internal expertise, strengthen supplier capabilities, and identify reliable local service providers for ESG initiatives. In many cases, MNC teams in China lack extensive experience in sustainability and ESG before being assigned to the task. These efforts take time but are crucial for long-term success.

3. Looking ahead, what trends do you foresee in the realm of sustainability investment in China? How can businesses and investors leverage these trends?

   The banking sector will continue leading the way, expanding green loans under the policy context of the five key pillars of financial development (namely, inclusive, green, high-tech, digital, and pension finance). Strengthened sustainability disclosure guidelines and standards since 2024 will enhance transparency. Climate transition will dominate, with businesses shifting to greener operations. These are all beneficial to foreign firms in China, and they should learn to align their headquarters strategies with these trends to stay competitive.

Interview With Simon Ng, CEO of the Business Environment Council (BEC)

1. How do you see local businesses leading the charge in sustainability? What strategies have you observed that could serve as a model for other companies in the region?

   Hong Kong businesses, particularly listed corporations, are advancing sustainability due to investor expectations, regulatory requirements, and customer demand. Successful companies integrate sustainability into their core business strategy rather than treating it as an add-on. Key factors include strong leadership buy-in, robust governance structures, and holistic execution plans that engage internal teams and external partners.

2. What are the most pressing challenges and opportunities for businesses in Hong Kong to align with the carbon neutrality by 2050 vision?

   Challenges include the cost of transition, evolving regulations, Scope 3 emissions, resource constraints, and limited government support. Different sectors are progressing at varying speeds, with some hard-to-abate industries lagging. The most significant opportunity lies in collaboration—sharing knowledge, codeveloping solutions, and fostering cross-sector engagement to accelerate collective action and drive meaningful impact.

3. How can foreign investors and corporations contribute to Hong Kong's sustainability journey while fostering partnerships with local stakeholders?

   We need resources and partnerships to achieve sustainability. Hence, foreign investors are welcome to contribute toward Hong Kong's sustainability journey by providing capital for the green transition and green growth. Likewise, we encourage overseas corporations and business chambers to visit Hong Kong, showcase their expertise and solutions, and foster partnerships for the net-zero transition. Business associations that focus on environmental sustainability, such as BEC, will provide a suitable platform for connecting local and overseas players for collective action.

Interview With Linda Chen, Chief Financial Officer (CFO) at
TS Financial Holdings

1. How are shareholder expectations shaping sustainability strategies in
   Taiwan's financial industry?
   Shareholder expectations have been a powerful catalyst transforming Taiwan's financial industry sustainability landscape. Investors
   committed to stewardship codes and ESG principles elevate sustainability issues to management priorities. Shareholders' sustainability
   advocacy has also resonated with Taiwan's government, spurring regulatory reforms that accelerate sustainability development across the
   financial sector. This government–shareholder alignment empowers
   financial institutions to enhance their own sustainability performance while driving carbon reduction throughout the broader corporate ecosystem.

2. What are the biggest challenges that financial institutions face in
   meeting Taiwan's sustainability regulations and how is the sector collaborating to overcome them?
   Taiwan's financial institutions face challenges such as data collection,
   integrating risk management, investment, and IT systems for sustainability disclosure, and adapting to evolving international standards. The Green Finance Action Plan mandates more companies to
   disclose sustainability information and has established a corporate
   emission database. Financial institutions are also investing in staff
   development to address organizational issues and adapt to regulatory
   changes effectively.

3. What emerging technologies or financial instruments do you see as
   game-changers for accelerating sustainability in Taiwan's financial
   sector over the next five years?
   Blockchain and AI are poised to be game-changers. Blockchain will
   enhance transparency, data integrity, and ESG reporting, while AI
   will optimize resource efficiency and automate sustainability processes. Together, these technologies will enable financial institutions
   to develop advanced sustainability financial products and transform
   their approach to environmental and social responsibility.

Key Takeaways

- Business culture differs significantly: hierarchical guanxi-driven Mainland practices, globally aligned Hong Kong efficiency, and Taiwan's consensus-driven innovation.
- Regulatory frameworks diverge: state-driven China, internationalized Hong Kong, and investor-protection-oriented Taiwan.
- Common challenges include talent drain, compliance burdens, and geopolitical risks—but each market also offers unique opportunities (EVs and green finance in China, disclosure leadership in Hong Kong, high-tech innovation and net-zero in Taiwan).
- Foreign businesses must adapt headquarters' ESG strategies to local contexts, build local expertise, and engage reliable local partners.
- Long-term success requires patient capital and the ability to navigate policy-driven growth, regulatory reforms, and shifting political landscapes.

Boardroom Briefing

Executives and investors should:

1. Recognize and respect cultural differences—guanxi in Mainland China, legal frameworks in Hong Kong, and consensus in Taiwan.
2. Tailor ESG and sustainability strategies to local contexts, avoiding a one-size-fits-all approach.
3. Monitor regulatory shifts closely—from CSRC's enhanced ESG disclosure in Mainland China, to HKEX reforms, to Taiwan's FSC governance codes.
4. Address talent risks by investing in local capacity building and retaining ESG expertise.
5. Anticipate geopolitical and policy shifts (U.S.–China tensions, dual circulation, cross-strait risks) in capital allocation and corporate strategies.

CHAPTER 6

Sustainability in Japan

[INVESTORS] [CORPORATES] [REGULATORS]
[INTERNATIONAL EXECUTIVES]

This chapter is intended for investors, corporates, regulators, and international executives seeking to understand Japan's evolving sustainability landscape, with emphasis on cultural dynamics, governance reforms, and market opportunities

Understanding Business Culture

Japan has long been perceived as a unique and somewhat enigmatic market within Asia. This perception stems from a combination of its distinct business culture, regulatory environment, and economic history. Unlike many other Asian markets, Japan's business environment is characterized by a blend of modern innovation and deep-rooted traditional practices.

Japan's business culture stands apart in the global investment community due to its deep emphasis on long-term relationships and trust. Unlike more transactional markets, Japanese corporations prioritize relationship-building, often resulting in slower deal-making processes. However, once established, these partnerships demonstrate remarkable loyalty and endurance. Japanese firms typically maintain collaborations unless absolutely necessary to sever them. This cultural characteristic presents both a strength and a challenge for foreign investors and businesses navigating Japan's market.

Procter & Gamble (P&G) is a prime example of a foreign company that successfully navigated the Japanese market by adapting to local cultural norms. Initially, P&G struggled with culturally insensitive marketing in Japan, notably with its Camay soap campaign in the 1980s. The ads featured Western models and romantic imagery that failed to connect with Japanese consumers, who associated soap with functionality rather than sensuality. Sales stagnated until P&G revamped the campaign to focus on skin care benefits—a shift that recognized local preferences and ultimately rebuilt market share (Procter & Gamble Japan, 2005). By hiring local experts and focusing on human resources training, P&G was able to localize its products and marketing efforts effectively. This approach helped P&G become a household name in Japan despite the strong recognition of local brands like Kao.

Several cultural features are particularly relevant when doing business in Japan. Japanese society strongly emphasizes hierarchy and seniority, which is reflected in business practices where decision-making processes often involve multiple layers of approval. Japanese companies are renowned for their meticulous attention to detail and high standards of quality, as evident in the products and services they offer. Decision making in Japan often involves a consensus-building process known as "nemawashi", ensuring that all stakeholders are on board before making a final decision.

Starbucks' entry into Japan in 1996 is another noteworthy example. Starbucks succeeded by localizing its product offerings and store ambience to align with Japanese cultural preferences. For instance, Starbucks Japan introduced matcha-flavored beverages and sakura-themed drinks during cherry blossom season, which resonated well with Japanese consumers (Starbucks Coffee Japan, 2024). Furthermore, the store design focused on creating a calm and cosy atmosphere, catering to the local preference for quiet spaces.

Over the past 20 years, the business culture in Japan has undergone significant evolution, particularly as the new generation gradually takes over family-owned businesses from their parents. This generational shift has brought about a blend of traditional values and modern approaches. Younger leaders are more open to global perspectives and innovative practices while still respecting the foundational principles laid by their predecessors. They are increasingly embracing digital transformation, sustainability, and diversity, which are principal for staying competitive in the global market. This shift is evident in companies like Suntory and Toyota, where the younger generation has introduced new strategies and technologies while maintaining the core values of quality and customer satisfaction (Suntory, 2024; Toyota, 2024).

The work environment culture in Japan has also seen notable changes. Traditionally, Japanese work culture has been characterised by long working hours, a strong emphasis on hierarchy and a collective approach to decision-making. However, there is a growing recognition of the need for work–life balance and mental health awareness. Companies are increasingly embracing flexible working arrangements, including remote work and flexible hours, to meet the evolving needs of their employees. Also, there is a shift toward a more inclusive and diverse workplace, with efforts to promote gender equality and support for foreign employees. These changes signify a broader trend toward fostering a more sustainable and supportive work environment in Japan.

Cultural norms shape the way companies operate, but effective participation also requires navigating Japan's complex regulatory system.

Regulatory Framework

The investment community has also treated Japan differently due to its regulatory environment and corporate governance practices. Japan has historically had a low level of inbound FDI compared to other Organisation for Economic Co-operation and Development (OECD) countries. This is partly due to Japan's traditional aversion to M&A, as well as its complex regulatory framework. However, the Japanese government has been actively working to improve the investment climate by implementing structural reforms and promoting transparency.

Japan's capital market regulatory framework, while structurally sophisticated due to its UK-inspired integrated model adopted in the 1990s, faces operational challenges. At the top of the hierarchy is the Ministry of Justice (MOJ), which oversees the legal framework within which all financial and corporate activities operate. The MOJ ensures that laws and regulations are in place to maintain market integrity and protect investors.

While the Bank of Japan (BOJ) plays a pivotal role in ensuring financial stability and executing monetary policy, the FSA is the primary regulatory body overseeing Japan's financial system, encompassing the securities, banking, and insurance sectors. The FSA's mandate includes ensuring the stability of the financial system, protecting investors and promoting fair and transparent markets. The FSA operates under the jurisdiction of the

Ministry of Finance (MOF) and works closely with other regulatory bodies to enforce financial regulations and supervise financial institutions. Within the FSA, the Securities and Exchange Surveillance Commission (SESC) plays a crucial role in monitoring market activities, investigating insider trading, and ensuring compliance with securities laws.

The Ministry of Economy, Trade, and Industry (METI) is another significant player in Japan's capital market regulatory framework. METI is responsible for formulating and implementing policies related to economic and industrial development. It promotes corporate governance and sustainability practices among Japanese companies. The GX Acceleration Agency, recently established under METI, aims to drive Japan's green transformation by providing financial support and promoting decarbonization initiatives. The FSA and METI have historically struggled with policy alignment, as bureaucratic conservatism can sometimes hinder decision making, resulting in delays due to this tension.

The TSE is the largest stock exchange in Japan, playing a central role in the capital market. The TSE is responsible for listing securities, facilitating trading and ensuring that listed companies comply with disclosure and governance standards. The TSE operates under the oversight of the FSA and works to maintain a fair and efficient market for investors. The Osaka Exchange (OSE) is the largest derivatives exchange in Japan, specializing in trading stock index futures, options, and bonds. It has a rich history dating back to the Edo period and merged with the TSE in 2013 to form the Japan Exchange Group.

In terms of hierarchy and reporting lines, the FSA reports to the MOF, while the SESC operates as an independent commission within the FSA. METI, on the other hand, collaborates with the FSA and other regulatory bodies to enhance the overall business environment and ensure that corporate activities align with national economic goals. The Japan Exchange Group, as a self-regulatory organization, works under the supervision of the FSA to ensure compliance with market regulations.

Keidanren, also known as the Japan Business Federation, is one of Japan's most influential economic organizations. It represents major corporations and industry associations to promote economic growth and advise the government on policy matters. Keidanren collaborates with the FSA to ensure business stability and transparency. It also engages with METI to promote industrial policies and innovation. Moreover, Keidanren works with the BOJ on monetary policy issues and economic forecasts.

In recent years, Japan has made significant strides in improving corporate governance practices, as highlighted in the CG Watch reports by the ACGA. These reforms include the introduction of the Corporate Governance Code and the Stewardship Code, which aim to enhance board independence, transparency, and accountability among Japanese companies. The FSA, METI, and TSE have been instrumental in promoting these reforms and encouraging companies to adopt best practices.

Key Issues, Challenges, and Opportunities

Over the past decade, Japan has presented a unique landscape for businesses and investors, characterized by both challenges and opportunities. Despite the complexities of the regulatory environment and culture, Japan remains an attractive destination for investment, driven by its robust economy, technological innovation, and commitment to sustainability.

One of the key issues in doing business in Japan is navigating its intricate regulatory framework. The country has stringent regulations and a multilayered bureaucracy that can be daunting for foreign companies to navigate. Establishing a business involves interactions with various government bodies, including the MOJ, FSA, METI, and TSE, as well as nongovernment bodies such as Keidanren. Owing to the considerable investment of time and assets required to establish a presence, foreign companies are often reluctant to leave once they have successfully set up operations in Japan.

Japan's aging population is also a challenge for businesses and investors. With nearly 29 percent of the population aged 65 and older in 2022, projections indicating this figure will reach 40 percent by 2060 (Tokyo-esque, 2024), the demographic shift has profound implications for the labor market and consumer spending (Statistics Bureau of Japan, 2023). A shrinking workforce means that companies may face difficulties in finding skilled labor, leading to increased reliance on automation and AI to fill the gap. On the other hand, the aging population drives demand for health care services, elderly care, and age-friendly products, creating opportunities for businesses in these sectors. However, the increased public service demands and the economic burden of supporting a growing elderly population can pose significant hurdles to sustainable growth. Investors who understand these dynamics can better navigate shifting market conditions and pinpoint growth sectors emerging from demographic transformations.

Apart from these, Japan also faces significant physical climate risks that pose challenges for businesses and investors. The country is highly susceptible to extreme weather events, including typhoons, heavy rainfall, and heatwaves, which have become more frequent and severe due to climate change. Coastal areas, including major economic hubs such as Tokyo and Osaka, are particularly vulnerable to the impacts of rising sea levels and storm surges, which can lead to disruptions in infrastructure and supply chains. For instance, the heavy rainfall and flooding in July 2021. This extreme weather event caused significant disruptions, particularly in the Kyushu region, where several manufacturing plants had to halt operations due to flooding and landslides. Toyota Motor Corporation temporarily suspended production at its factories in Fukuoka and Oita, resulting in substantial financial losses and supply chain delays (Cabinet Office of Japan, 2022; Toyota, 2021). Also, increased temperatures and changing precipitation patterns can impact agriculture, water resources, and overall economic stability. These cases necessitate adaptation and mitigation strategies for businesses to ensure resilience and sustainability in their operations in Japan.

Cross-shareholdings (also known as "strategic shareholdings"), a long-standing feature of Japan's corporate landscape, remain a significant challenge despite regulatory efforts to unwind them. These strategic shareholdings—where companies hold each other's shares to cement business relationships—have been criticized for distorting capital efficiency, entrenching management, and stifling shareholder accountability. While the FSA has pushed for reductions through initiatives like the 2024 Action Program, progress has been gradual. For instance, Japan's four major nonlife insurers recently committed to selling ¥6.5 trillion in cross-held shares, but the process may take years due to negotiations with partner firms (FSA, 2024). The practice also perpetuates governance risks, as seen in the nonlife insurance industry's premium-fixing scandal, where cross-shareholdings facilitated collusion. Although reforms are gaining momentum—with firms like Toyota reducing their stakes in suppliers like Denso and Aisin—the deeply ingrained nature of these holdings means that complete unwinding will require sustained pressure from regulators, investors, and market forces.

In parallel with these structural reforms, shareholder activism in Japan has gained significant momentum. Once considered an outlier in a consensusdriven corporate culture, activism is becoming a mainstream force shaping corporate behavior. The TSE's market reforms, particularly the Prime Market requirements for higher capital efficiency, have emboldened institutional investors and activist funds to push for greater accountability. In 2024, Oasis Management succeeded in pressuring Canon to unwind unproductive crossshareholdings and improve its return on equity—a landmark case underscoring the growing influence of foreign activists in Japan's boardrooms (Nikkei, 2024). Similarly, ValueAct Capital's engagement with Seven & i Holdings led to strategic portfolio reviews, demonstrating that constructive dialogue is increasingly possible between activists and entrenched management.

This rise in activism reflects broader changes in Japan's corporate governance landscape. Domestic pension funds like GPIF and international investors are aligning their voting practices with the Stewardship Code, increasing scrutiny on underperforming boards and demanding clearer capital allocation strategies. While cultural resistance remains, companies are becoming more receptive to activist proposals, particularly when framed around enhancing longterm corporate value. For investors, this trend signals a more dynamic equity market where constructive activism can unlock value, though success still requires navigating Japan's nuanced regulatory framework and consensusoriented corporate culture.

Despite these headwinds, Japan also presents significant opportunities for investors and corporates committed to long-term sustainability. The country's commitment to sustainability and innovation is a significant draw. Japan has set ambitious goals for achieving carbon neutrality by 2050 and is actively promoting renewable energy sources, including solar, wind, and hydrogen fuel technology (METI, 2023). This focus on sustainability aligns with global trends. It presents opportunities for companies involved in green technologies and ESG practices in the transition to a more sustainable economy.

The past decade has seen significant changes in Japan's business environment, particularly with the introduction of negative interest rates by the BOJ in 2016. This unconventional monetary policy aimed to stimulate economic growth by encouraging borrowing and investment. While the policy had mixed results, it did lead to lower borrowing costs and increased market liquidity. For businesses, this meant cheaper loans and greater access to capital, which facilitated expansion and innovation. However, the negative interest rate environment also posed challenges, such as creating uncertainties in the financial markets.

The investment landscape in Japan has also evolved with significant reforms in corporate governance. The introduction of the Corporate Governance Code and the Stewardship Code was a key component of former Prime Minister Shinzo Abe's "Three Arrows" policy, known as *Abenomics* (FSA, 2021; METI, 2020). These reforms, mainly driven by the FSA and METI, have improved investor confidence and attracted foreign investment (ACGA, 2023). Companies are now more focused on sustainable growth and shareholder value, contributing to a more dynamic and resilient market.

In addition to these opportunities, Japan's highly developed infrastructure, advanced technology sector, and skilled workforce make it an attractive destination for business expansion. The country is a global leader in R&D, particularly in fields such as robotics, automotive technology, and electronics. This innovative environment provides a fertile ground for businesses looking to leverage cutting-edge technologies and collaborate with leading research institutions.

In conclusion, while Japan presents particular challenges for businesses and investors, the opportunities are substantial. The country's focus on sustainability, technological innovation, and corporate governance reforms creates a favorable environment for investment. Understanding the regulatory landscape, adapting to cultural nuances, and leveraging Japan's commitment to sustainability are key strategies for success in this active market. The evolving business environment, driven by both traditional values and modern approaches, positions Japan as a compelling destination for global businesses and investors.

Interview With Local Experts

Interview With Chie Mitsui, Principal Researcher at Nomura Research Institute

1. How do you see the evolution of sustainability reporting in Japan over the next five years? What key trends should companies and investors be aware of?

   Sustainability reporting in Japan will see some progress in the next several years. By 2027, the SSBJ requirement will enforce compliance for certain companies. In the current discussion, mandatory disclosures would be limited to a select number of companies, promoting investors to continue relying on voluntary disclosures. In 2025, Japanese companies are prioritizing enhancements in human capital disclosures. The FSA's recent mandate on gender diversity reporting marks some progress. However, there is still a lack of substance in many companies. Investors need to discuss more essential matters related to the company's business.

2. What are the biggest challenges and opportunities for integrating ESG considerations into the strategic decisions of Japanese corporations?

   The key sustainability issues in Japan are energy security, food security, and the societal impacts of a declining birthrate and aging population. Addressing these challenges presents business opportunities. For example, promoting women's workforce participation can help mitigate labor shortages. Climate change solutions can enhance energy security and strengthen natural capital. These three priorities—energy security, food security, and demographic challenges—form a robust basis for Japan's long-term sustainability efforts.

3. From your perspective, what further improvements are needed to promote the long-term sustainability of the Japanese capital market?

   While Japanese companies are aware of environmental and social issues, weak governance can undermine these efforts. Strengthening governance should remain a priority. One key step is for investors to play a more active role in board nominations, ensuring that directors possess the expertise and independence needed to drive efficiency and accountability.

Interview With Yasunori Takeuchi, CEO of Corporate Action Japan

1. How are Japanese firms improving climate-related transparency, and what challenges are they facing?

   Japanese firms have been a top group in commitment to climate-related transparency, as the number of companies supporting TCFD ranked top by far, consisting of ca. 1/3 of the global total. Now Japanese companies are required to move from commitment to action, as climate-related disclosure standard in Japan (set by SSBJ) and overseas (CSRD in the European Union), is to be implemented in coming years. There are multiple challenges they are facing, including data collection, resource and process, collaboration and governance across the organization, and so on.

2. What can other sectors learn from Japan's steel industry, and how can investors accelerate the transition?

   Japan's steel sector faces technological, cost, and procurement challenges in achieving net-zero. Companies are leveraging government subsidies, collaborating with buyers to create a low-carbon steel market, and advocating for energy transition. Investors can accelerate progress by engaging supply chains, supporting early adopters, and reinforcing economic viability through demand-side partnerships.

3. Given your background as a former banker, what financial mechanism best supports Japan's shift to renewables, and how global investors can contribute?

   Financial system works side-by-side with real economy, including industries and consumers. In that sense, policy intervention in the real economy is important. Internationalization of externalities, such as carbon pricing, is fundamentally important. Japan is expected to accelerate this by the GX transition plan to catch up with some other early-moving markets. Blended finance is also effective in narrowing the gap in demand for climate-related capital. Global investors can contribute to Japan's shift to renewables by constructive engagement with Japanese companies, sharing concerns and expectations from a global perspective.

Key Takeaways

- Japan's business culture emphasizes long-term trust, consensus, and quality, while gradually evolving under younger leadership and competitive pressure.
- Regulatory oversight is sophisticated but fragmented across MOJ, FSA, METI, and TSE, requiring careful coordination by market participants.
- Demographic pressures and labor shortages are accelerating automation, diversity efforts, and workforce reform.
- Physical climate risks such as typhoons and heatwaves pose material threats to infrastructure, logistics, and supply chains.
- Governance reforms and shareholder activism are improving capital efficiency, transparency, and board accountability.
- Carbon-neutral targets, R&D strength, and industrial policy create opportunities for long-term sustainable investment.

Boardroom Briefing

Executives and investors should:

1. Respect consensus-driven decision-making while engaging emerging leaders open to reform and international best practices.
2. Develop structured regulatory engagement strategies with MOJ, FSA, METI, TSE, and major industry associations.
3. Incorporate demographic constraints, labor shortages, and talent mobility into long-term workforce and capital planning.
4. Stress-test operations, logistics networks, and critical supplier relationships against physical climate risks and disaster scenarios.
5. Support governance reforms, including board diversity, unwinding cross-shareholdings, and strengthened disclosures.
6. Position portfolios and business strategies to benefit from Japan's transition, digital transformation, and advanced technology.

CHAPTER 7

Sustainability in South Korea

[INVESTORS] [CORPORATES] [REGULATORS]
[INTERNATIONAL EXECUTIVES]
This chapter is intended for investors, corporates, regulators, and international executives seeking to understand South Korea's sustainability landscape, focusing on chaebol governance, demographic shifts, and emerging opportunities in technology and culture.

Understanding Business Culture

Korea's business culture is often misunderstood as similar to Japan's, but significant differences distinguish it. While both countries share some social and historical ties, Korea is distinct in several ways, influenced by its rapid economic development, the dominance of *chaebols*, and its unique approach to innovation and globalization.

Similar to China, Korean business culture is deeply rooted in Confucian values, which emphasize hierarchy, respect for seniority, and the importance of relationships. However, unlike Japan's more formal and consensus-driven approach, Korea's corporate environment operates with greater speed and top-down decisiveness, often centered around powerful chairmen who drive key strategic choices. Decision making in Korean companies is usually quicker, with a greater willingness to take risks and adapt to changing market conditions.

The influence of chaebols, large family-owned conglomerates, is a defining feature of Korea's corporate landscape. Chaebols, such as Samsung, Hyundai, SK, and LG, dominate the economy and have a significant impact on corporate culture. These conglomerates are characterized by decision-making power concentrated in the hands of the founding families, which typically own a relatively small percentage of the shares. This can lead to both rapid innovation and agility, as well as challenges related to governance and transparency.

Hyundai Motor Group's 2022 succession dynamics illustrate how control is often consolidated within chaebols through incremental restructuring rather than a single defining transaction (Hyundai Motor Group 2021–2023). Under Chairman Chung Euisun, the group has continued efforts to streamline cross-shareholdings and strengthen influence over key affiliates, reflecting a broader pattern in Korea's corporate landscape.

Such moves have drawn scrutiny from investors concerned about transparency and minority shareholder interests. This tension was evident during Elliott Management's high-profile campaign against the company in 2018, which challenged the group's governance and capital allocation approach. Although the proposals were ultimately withdrawn, the episode underscored rising investor expectations and marked a turning point for shareholder engagement in Korea. The case also partially prompted revisions to Korea's Commercial Code in 2024, which tightened rules on minority shareholders' protection (Ministry of Justice, 2024).

Unlike Samsung's bribery case, Hyundai's succession play highlights how chaebols exploit legal grey areas, prioritizing dynasty over governance. Yet both instances share a root cause: Korea's tolerance for extreme measures to preserve family control.

In addition to the power of chaebols, Korea's business culture is also shaped by its emphasis on education and technological innovation. The country has made significant investments in education and research, leading to a highly skilled workforce and a strong focus on technology-driven industries. This has positioned Korea as a global industrial leader, home to powerhouse brands like Samsung Electronics (the world's top smartphone maker), Hyundai-Kia (top ranking in global auto sales) and SK Hynix (a dominant force in memory chips)—mirroring Japan's success in building internationally recognized names like Toyota and Sony (TrendForce, 2023).

Korean companies are also known for their strong service orientation and high degree of connectivity. The business environment is evolving rapidly, with certain norms and practices changing quickly as Korea integrates more into the global economy. One of the most notable changes is the increasing emphasis on innovation and digital transformation. Korean companies have adopted new technologies, including AI, big data, and the Internet of Things (IoT), to boost their competitiveness and efficiency.

Despite these advancements, some aspects of Korean business culture have remained relatively unchanged. Relationships and networking remain fundamental to business success, with a strong emphasis on loyalty and long-term commitments. The dominance of chaebols also persists, with these conglomerates maintaining their central role in the economy and exerting considerable influence over both government and policies. While efforts have been made to improve corporate governance and transparency, the traditional hierarchical structures and the power dynamics within chaebols have remained mainly intact.

Western companies entering the Korean market will find a sophisticated and modern approach. However, they must also be prepared to navigate the traditional customs and hierarchical structures that still play a significant role. Building strong relationships with key stakeholders, particularly within the chaebols, is key to success. Furthermore, being aware of the rapid pace of decision making and the emphasis on innovation can help foreign businesses better align their strategies with the local market dynamics. While cultural dynamics shape how companies operate, but success in Korea also depends on navigating its developing regulatory system.

Regulatory Framework

The regulatory framework of Korea's capital market is multifaceted. At the top of the hierarchy is the Financial Services Commission (FSC), which acts as the principal regulatory body overseeing the financial sector, including securities markets, banking, and insurance. The FSC is responsible for formulating policies, drafting laws, and enforcing regulations to ensure market integrity and protect investors.

Reporting directly to the FSC is the Financial Supervisory Service (FSS), which serves as the enforcement arm of the FSC. The FSS conducts day-to-day supervision and inspection of financial institutions, ensuring compliance with regulations and maintaining financial stability. The FSS plays a critical role in monitoring market activities, investigating irregularities, and enforcing penalties for noncompliance with relevant regulations.

The Bank of Korea (BOK), the central bank, also plays a significant role in the capital market. While its primary mandate is monetary policy and financial stability, the BOK collaborates with the FSC and FSS to ensure the smooth functioning of the financial system. The BOK's involvement includes regulating foreign exchange transactions and managing the country's foreign reserves.

The Korea Exchange (KRX) is the primary stock exchange in Korea, responsible for listing and trading securities. It operates under the supervision of the FSC and works closely with the FSS to ensure that listed companies comply with disclosure requirements and other regulatory standards. The KRX also plays a vital role in promoting market transparency and investor protection.

In addition to these primary regulators, several other important entities are involved in the regulatory framework. The Korea Deposit Insurance Corporation (KDIC) provides deposit insurance and manages the resolution of failed financial institutions. The Korea Fair Trade Commission (KFTC) oversees competition policy and enforces antitrust laws to prevent monopolistic practices and ensure fair competition. The Korea Securities Depository (KSD) is the central securities depository in Korea, providing central custody, book-entry transfer, and settlement of securities transactions. KSD's role involves facilitating efficient securities transactions and maintaining market stability, working in tandem with the FSC and FSS to uphold transparency and protect investors.

The Korea Institute of Corporate Governance and Sustainability (KCGS) is a quasi-regulatory body that promotes good corporate governance practices. It provides ratings and assessments of the corporate governance and ESG performance of listed companies. The KCGS works closely with regulators and market participants to enhance transparency and accountability in the corporate sector. The Korea Listed Companies Association (KLCA) represents the interests of publicly listed companies in Korea, advocating for policies that enhance corporate governance and market competitiveness. KLCA collaborates closely with regulatory bodies, such as the FSC and KRX, to ensure that the regulatory environment fosters sustainable growth and investor confidence. The Korea Capital Market Institute (KCMI) is a leading research institution dedicated to advancing the development and efficiency of Korea's capital markets through in-depth research and policy recommendations. KCMI collaborates with regulatory bodies, such as the FSC and FSS, to provide insights and support for regulatory improvements and market innovations.

Key Issues, Challenges, and Opportunities

Doing business and investing in Korea presents a unique mix of challenges and opportunities that have evolved significantly in recent years. The country's dynamic economy, advanced technological infrastructure, and strategic location make it an attractive destination for foreign firms. However, successfully navigating this complex business environment requires a deep understanding of its market dynamics.

One of the most persistent challenges is the chaebol-dominated corporate structure. Family-led conglomerates such as Samsung, Hyundai, and LG have fueled South Korea's economic rise, but often at the expense of minority shareholder rights and managerial transparency. In response, reforms to the Commercial Code have strengthened shareholder voting rights and board independence requirements. In 2024, the FSC announced that large listed firms would be required to expand their ESG disclosures in line with global standards (FSC, 2024).

Korea's policy environment also faces unique volatility due to political instability—a stark contrast to the more predictable landscapes of markets like Singapore or Japan. The December 2024 martial law declaration exemplified this volatility, causing immediate economic disruptions and exposing systemic vulnerabilities (Korean Government Press Release, 2024). Frequent elections—held every five years for presidents, who are barred from reelection—trigger wholesale changes in regulatory personnel. These reshuffles often reset policy priorities, forcing businesses to navigate shifting rules on issues ranging from antitrust enforcement to ESG reporting timelines.

Social stratification adds another layer of complexity. Korea's hierarchical culture creates stark disparities between social classes, which can influence workforce management, consumer behavior, and market segmentation. The dominance of chaebols further exacerbates these challenges, as their control of key industries can stifle competition and innovation.

Demographics are an equally pressing concern. South Korea's fertility rate, the lowest globally, fell to 0.72 children per woman in 2023, down from 0.78 in 2022—far below the replacement level of 2.1 needed to sustain the population. This decline is accelerating Korea's transition into a "super-aged" society, with seniors (65 years and older) projected to comprise 46 percent of the population by 2067 (Texas A&M University, 2023), straining pensions and health care systems as the working-age cohort shrinks (Statistics Korea, 2024).

These demographic shifts are driven by soaring housing and education costs, long working hours and inflexible career paths, and are compounded by growing gender tensions. Many women are choosing to delay or forgo marriage and children in response to persistent workplace discrimination and unequal domestic expectations. Movements like "4B" (refusing sex, dating, marriage, and childbirth) reflect deep frustrations with entrenched patriarchal norms. These changes are already reshaping labor supply and consumer behavior; companies must adapt their workforce strategies and product offerings—such as elder care services and automation—to remain competitive in a rapidly aging and evolving society. Youth unemployment remains among the highest in the OECD, fueling social discontent and prompting some of the country's best-educated professionals, particularly women, to seek opportunities abroad, especially in the United States and China (OECD, 2024).

Geopolitical risks are another prominent consideration. The persistent threat posed by North Korea, coupled with tensions between the United States and China, complicates South Korea's strategic positioning. Participation in U.S.-led initiatives, such as the CHIPS and Science Act, has not only secured semiconductor partnerships but also heightened exposure to risks of Chinese retaliation (USTR, 2024). For investors, carefully assessing these geopolitical variables is essential for evaluating market stability and long-term returns.

The so-called "Korea Discount" presents yet another hurdle—a persistent undervaluation of Korean equities tied to governance concerns, geopolitical uncertainties, and low dividend payouts. As of 2023, foreign investors hold approximately 30 percent of the Korean Composite Stock Price Indexes (KOSPI)'s market capitalization (Korea Exchange, 2023), but opaque ownership structures and cross-shareholdings limit their influence. This dynamic fosters a perception of investor-unfriendly practices, which in turn reduces market confidence. As undervaluation becomes self-reinforcing—lower valuations deter capital inflows—policymakers are working to close the gap through measures such as tax incentives for long-term institutional investors and easing foreign ownership restrictions in key sectors (FSC, 2024).

Despite these challenges, Korea offers substantial opportunities. The country is consolidating its position as a global leader in EV batteries, with LG Energy Solution, SK Innovation, and Samsung SDI expanding in partnership with United States and European automakers. Investments in green hydrogen projects, supported by government incentives, are positioning Korea as a key player in the energy transition (MOTIE, 2024). Companies like Samsung continue to set benchmarks for innovation and quality, creating fertile ground for investment in high-tech industries.

Government initiatives further reinforce these opportunities. The Korean New Deal, launched in July 2020, commits over 160 trillion won ($135 billion) by 2025 to digital and green sectors. The plan focuses on advancing technologies like AI and 5G under the Digital New Deal and promoting renewable energy and low-carbon industries under the Green New Deal (Ministry of Economy and Finance, 2020). Korea's highly educated and skilled workforce is a major asset for firms seeking to establish a foothold in the country.

Korea's geographic proximity to key Northeast Asian markets, including China and Japan, offers convenient access and strategic advantages for regional operations. Its advanced infrastructure, including efficient logistics networks, supports seamless business activities. The strong consumer market, characterized by high purchasing power and a preference for innovative products, presents lucrative opportunities in sectors such as consumer electronics, cosmetics, and health care.

Investors are also drawn to Korea's stable economic environment and supportive government policies. The Korean government offers various incentives to attract FDI, including tax breaks, regulatory support, and infrastructure development. These measures particularly target strategic sectors such as renewable energy, biotechnology, and advanced manufacturing. Recent FDI data show a steady inflow of sustainable capital into high-tech and green projects, driven by targeted government programs (UNCTAD, 2024). In addition, issuing green bonds and promoting environmentally sustainable projects provide secure avenues for socially responsible investors.

Korea's cultural exports also continue to grow as a major economic driver. In 2018, Netflix recognized the global rise of Korean content and committed $100 million over five years to build a state-of-the-art special-effects studio in Seoul. This investment enabled the production of local originals such as *Kingdom* and *Squid Game*, which achieved worldwide success by blending Korean cultural appeal with global storytelling standards (Netflix, 2018). This move not only tapped into Korea's thriving entertainment ecosystem but also aligned with government efforts to promote creative industries, illustrating how foreign companies can succeed by leveraging local assets and policy support. Beyond Netflix, K-pop, gaming, and streaming platforms are driving a cultural wave that enhances soft power and generates substantial export revenues (KOCCA, 2024).

In conclusion, while doing business and investing in Korea involves navigating a distinct set of challenges, the opportunities are considerable for those who understand the market. By aligning with Korea's technological strengths, skilled workforce and strategic initiatives—and by carefully assessing its political landscape, social dynamics, and demographic trends—businesses can tap into one of Asia's most dynamic and promising markets.

Interview With Local Experts

Interview With Woochan Kim, Professor of Finance at Korea University

1. What opportunities and challenges should foreign investors be mindful of when evaluating Korean companies' sustainability practices?

   On the opportunity side, many Korean companies remain undervalued, offering upside potential, particularly if the Minjoo Party succeeds in advancing corporate governance reforms. However, structural challenges persist. Family-controlled firms often prioritize the interests of controlling shareholders over minority stakeholders. Additionally, Korea's industrial landscape is dominated by energy-intensive sectors, making environmental sustainability a critical challenge and a strategic imperative. Workplace safety remains a significant concern, particularly in the construction and heavy industry sectors, and gender diversity at the executive level continues to lag.

2. What specific corporate culture differences should foreign corporate executives be aware of when expanding operations to Korea?

   Foreign corporations can significantly influence Korea's sustainability trajectory by leveraging their roles as buyers and partners. By setting clear expectations around carbon reduction, workplace safety, and gender diversity, they can apply meaningful pressure on Korean suppliers to adopt more sustainable and inclusive practices.

3. What key regulatory reforms would you recommend to enhance Korea's sustainability and ESG landscape?

   Shareholders should have greater influence over corporate governance through mandatory approval of self-dealing transactions and executive compensation, with limited voting rights for controlling shareholders to avoid conflicts of interest. Lowering thresholds for derivative lawsuits would enhance minority shareholder access to legal remedies. Nonbinding proposals on environmental and social issues should be permitted, and transparency should be strengthened through mandatory sustainability reporting.

Interview With Seung Keun Lee, Head of Corporate Governance Team at National Pension Service

(The views and opinions expressed in this interview are his own and do not necessarily reflect the official position of the organization he is affiliated with.)

1. How is ESG integration evolving in Korea's investment landscape, and what does this mean for both domestic and international investors?

   Korea's ESG framework is strengthening, with sustainability disclosure standards set for finalization in 2025 and likely mandatory reporting after 2026. Investors have long struggled with inconsistent ESG data, but improved transparency will transform ESG from a symbolic measure into a meaningful investment factor, opening new opportunities for alpha generation.

2. The "Korea Discount" has been a persistent issue in the market. How can Korea address it and improve corporate governance to attract foreign investment?

   I believe that the root cause of the Korea Discount lies in a lack of investor trust in the decision making of corporate boards. Transparency in mergers, spin-offs, capital allocation, and executive compensation must be improved. The Korea Exchange's 2024 value enhancement disclosure initiative is a positive step, helping build confidence in corporate governance. Adopting policies like the U.S. "Say on Pay" system could further enhance accountability. Ultimately, gaining investors' confidence in boards acting in their best interests will require a continued push toward transparency and governance reform.

3. With Korea's demographic challenges, including an aging population and low birth rate, how should investors adjust their strategies to navigate these challenges?

   Talent acquisition and retention are crucial. Korean companies must recruit globally to remain competitive. Moreover, given the low female labor force participation rate, firms that foster inclusive environments will stand out. Finally, I see long-term investment opportunities in companies that possess strong technological capabilities in areas such as AI and robotics, which can help offset labor shortages and enhance productivity over time.

Key Takeaways

- South Korea's business culture is shaped by Confucian values, rapid decision making, and the continued dominance of chaebols.
- Concentrated family control enables agility and innovation but creates persistent governance and minority shareholder risks.
- Regulatory oversight is sophisticated, yet enforcement must keep pace with rapid technological change and global market pressures.
- Major structural challenges include political volatility, demographic decline, social inequality, and the persistent "Korea Discount."
- Geopolitical exposure, particularly related to North Korea and U.S.–China tensions, adds uncertainty to long-term capital allocation.
- At the same time, Korea offers strong opportunities in EV batteries, hydrogen, semiconductors, and cultural exports.

Boardroom Briefing

Executives and investors should:

1. Assess chaebol ownership structures and related-party transactions as central components of investment risk analysis.
2. Monitor regulatory reforms led by the FSC, FSS, and KRX, as disclosure and governance standards continue to tighten.
3. Anticipate demographic shifts by prioritizing automation, robotics, elder care services, and inclusive workforce strategies.
4. Incorporate geopolitical risks into corporate planning, particularly regarding North Korea and U.S.–China trade dynamics.
5. Engage constructively on governance reforms to improve transparency, capital allocation, and shareholder accountability.
6. Leverage Korea's strengths in advanced manufacturing, digital innovation, and cultural industries for long-term positioning.

CHAPTER 8

Sustainability in India

[INVESTORS] [CORPORATES] [REGULATORS]
[INTERNATIONAL EXECUTIVES]
This chapter is intended for investors, corporates, regulators, and international executives seeking to navigate India's complex sustainability landscape—where promoter-driven models, regulatory evolution, and rapid digitalization create both risks and opportunities.

Understanding Business Culture

Understanding the business culture in India reveals a complex tapestry of traditions, values, and practices that differ significantly from those in ASEAN countries. While both regions share some similarities due to their geographic proximity and historical interactions, the nuances in their business environments are profound and impactful.

In India, the business culture is deeply influenced by the presence of promoters, who are often the founding families or individuals with significant control over their companies. This promoter-driven model contrasts with the more diversified ownership structures seen in many ASEAN countries. Promoters in India wield substantial influence over strategic decisions, often prioritizing long-term stability and family legacy over short-term gains. This can lead to a more moderate approach to risk and innovation.

A notable example is Reliance Industries, where the Ambani family has maintained decisive control since its founding in 1966. Under Dhirubhai Ambani's leadership, the company grew from a textiles manufacturer into a petrochemicals giant, prioritizing vertical integration and patient capital. His sons, Mukesh and Anil, later inherited this ethos, though their 2005 split highlighted the challenges of familial succession in promoter-led firms. Mukesh Ambani's subsequent investments in Jio (launched in 2016) demonstrate how promoter-driven strategies strike a balance between innovation and caution. While Jio disrupted India's telecom sector with aggressive pricing, its rollout was backed by Reliance's existing cash flows and infrastructure, thereby mitigating risk. This approach reflects a broader trend where promoter-led firms in India often favor incremental scaling over disruptive bets, leveraging their influence to align stakeholders with multidecade visions.

Relevant to the promoters' dominant culture, another distinctive aspect of India's business culture is the importance of hierarchical structures and respect for authority. In many Indian companies, decision making is centralized, with senior executives and promoters holding significant sway over business operations. This hierarchical approach can sometimes slow down decision-making processes, but it ensures that decisions align with the company's long-term vision and values, thereby promoting consistency and coherence. In contrast, many ASEAN countries, such as Malaysia and Indonesia, are gradually moving toward more decentralized and collaborative decision-making models. For example:

- Malaysia: Petronas, the state energy giant, delegates operational decisions to regional units while maintaining strategic oversight at the corporate level, enabling faster responses to local market dynamics.
- Indonesia: GoTo Group (formed by the merger of Gojek and Tokopedia) uses cross-functional teams to make collaborative decisions, reflecting the region's shift toward flatter hierarchies.

India's extreme wealth disparity creates one of the world's most complex business environments. Walking through Mumbai offers a jarring visual metaphor for this divide—Mukesh Ambani's $4.6 billion Antilia skyscraper, located in the exclusive Cumballa Hill neighborhood on Altamount Road, otherwise known as "Billionaire's Row", stands in stark contrast to Dharavi, Asia's largest slum, where residents generate a $650 million informal economy from tiny workshops (Reliance Industries Limited, 2023; World Bank, 2023). Two worlds exist within the same city, separated by more than just geography. This contrast stems from systemic inequality: Oxfam's 2023 report revealed that India's top one percent now controls 40.1 percent of national wealth, surpassing even the United States (35 percent) and Brazil (28 percent) in terms of asset concentration (Oxfam, 2023).

This economic polarization forces corporations to operate in two parallel Indias. On one end, Louis Vuitton's partnership with Reliance targets the one percent through $2,000 handbags in a country where annual per capita income barely crosses $2,400 (World Bank, 2023). Simultaneously, Unilever's single-use shampoo sachets sell for pennies in villages where 75 percent of the population holds less than $10,000 in lifetime assets (World Bank, 2023; Reserve Bank of India, 2022). The tension manifests everywhere—Apple celebrates $10 billion in revenue in India (Apple, 2023; Bloomberg, 2023), while 63 million Indians descend into poverty annually due to medical expenses (The Lancet, 2022).

What makes India unique is how businesses navigate this duality. Legacy corporate houses like Tata Group have long balanced luxury and community—while their boardrooms strategize premium Jaguar sales, their CSR teams build rural hospitals—a model practised long before CSR was formalized, earning them household-name status and deep loyalty among the masses. On the digital front, companies like Airtel Payments Bank are extending financial inclusion through everyday services—providing secure payments via the UPI, India's real-time digital payment system that allows instant bank-to-bank transfers, across both urban and rural markets (without facing notable regulatory controversy). These firms demonstrate how commercial success and social purpose can coexist: survival in a market where ignoring either extreme risks losing relevance.

In India, the art of the "*haan ji, ho jayega*" ("yes, sir, it will be done") is practically a national business strategy. This reflexive optimism—where declining a request is often seen as worse than failing to deliver—creates a unique ecosystem of overcommitment. A 2021 McKinsey study found Indian executives are 37 percent more likely than their Japanese counterparts to take on unrealistic deadlines (McKinsey, 2024), while *Harvard Business Review* (2022) traced this to three cultural drivers: family-business risk appetites, fear of missing out (FOMO) in hypercompetitive sectors, and a "jugaad" mentality—a resourceful, last-minute problem-solving approach often reinforced by a belief that solutions will emerge, often-times even aided by divine intervention, with prayers routinely offered in the hope of overcoming challenges (McKinsey, 2024).

The contrast with Japan's consensus-driven culture is revealing. Where Japanese executives might say *"muzukashii desu ne"* ("that seems difficult") to politely deflect, their Indian peers will confidently promise delivery next quarter—even when everyone in the room knows it might at least take two. This isn't just about grit; it's a survival tactic in a market where, as one Mumbai banker joked, "An Indian entrepreneur's to-do list has three columns: 'Today,' 'Tomorrow,' and 'When the client follows up.'"

Yet there's method to the madness. The same traits that fuel over-commitment—improvisation, risk-taking, and relentless hustle—also powered India's start-up boom. When Swiggy promised 19-minute food deliveries or Ola vowed to electrify 10,000 rickshaws in six months (Swiggy, 2023; Ola Electric, 2023), they weren't just bluffing; they were betting (correctly) that the market would bend to audacity. As we'll explore later, this cultural engine has both turbocharged India's growth and left investors scrambling to separate moonshots from mirages.

India's market is also highly fragmented, with significant cultural and economic differences within the country. The north and south of India, for example, have distinct languages, cuisines, and business prac-tices—where a handshake deal in Chennai might require a notarized contract in Chandigarh. This fragmentation requires companies to adopt region-specific strategies, unlike the more homogeneous markets found in smaller ASEAN countries such as Singapore or Brunei. This diversity forces companies like Hindustan Unilever to maintain over 30 regional formulations of even basic products, such as Surf Excel detergent (*Finan-cial Times*, 2023), with packaging that accommodates everything from Hindi heartland wholesalers to Kerala's cooperative retail networks.

The emphasis on relationship-building stems partly from necessity: with India ranking 163rd in contract enforcement (World Bank, 2023) and commercial cases taking an average of 1,445 days to resolve (Mumbai High Court data, 2022), businesses hedge their risk through personal networks rather than relying on courts. A 2023 McKinsey study found that Indian CEOs spend 37 percent more time on stakeholder manage-ment than their ASEAN counterparts (McKinsey, 2024). This plays out in negotiations where, as a Tata Steel executive noted, "We'll have ten dinners before discussing numbers—not just for rapport, but to assess if they'll honour deals when courts can't."

Case studies, such as Flipkart's ascent (2007–present) and the Satyam scandal (2009), crystallize the dualities of India's business ecosystem. Flipkart's evolution—from a Bangalore apartment-based bookstore to Walmart's $16 billion acquisition in 2018—reveals how hyperlocal strategies (e.g., cash on delivery in 2010, vernacular user interface for Tier 2/3 cities) can overcome infrastructural gaps, such as last-mile logistics. Its Big Billion Days sales (launched in 2014) leveraged India's price sensitivity, while acquisitions like Myntra (2014) catered to regional fashion preferences, driving a 51 percent market share by 2023 (Walmart, 2023).

Conversely, Satyam's collapse—where founder Ramalinga Raju confessed to inflating revenues by ₹7,800 crore ($1.6B) in 2009—exposed the perils of promoter dominance. The scandal, dubbed "India's Enron", stemmed from unchecked control: Raju fabricated 13,000 employees and siphoned funds to family-run Maytas, while auditors PwC overlooked red flags for years. The fallout was systemic: India's 2013 Companies Act mandated independent directors and auditor rotations, and SEBI barred PwC for a period of two years (SEBI, 2019; SEBI, 2024).

Together, these cases frame India's business paradox: local ingenuity often flourishes where formal governance lags. Flipkart's success required defying global norms (e.g., favoring mobile-first over desktop). At the same time, Satyam's collapse prompted reforms that appeal to ESG-conscious investors. India's market richly rewards deep local insight, yet the consequences of weak governance are uneven—more visible in markets exposed to global capital than in heartland sectors where accountability remains limited. These cultural dynamics shape how companies operate, but long-term success also depends on navigating India's intricate regulatory system.

Regulatory Framework

The regulatory framework of the Indian capital market is a multilayered system involving various key players. At the apex of this hierarchy is the MOF, which oversees the country's overall financial and economic policies. The Department of Economic Affairs (DEA) plays a crucial role in formulating policies for capital markets and financial services within the Ministry.

The RBI is the central bank and the primary regulator of the banking sector in India. It also oversees monetary policy and ensures financial stability. The RBI's regulatory purview encompasses the supervision of commercial banks, nonbanking financial companies (NBFCs), and the country's payment systems. The RBI operates independently but reports to the MOF.

The SEBI is the principal regulator of the securities market. Established in 1992, SEBI's mandate encompasses protecting investor interests, promoting and regulating the securities market, and ensuring fair practices. SEBI has the authority to draft regulations, issue guidelines, and take enforcement actions against market participants. It reports directly to the MOF and collaborates closely with other regulatory bodies to uphold market integrity. On the other hand, state-owned assets are regulated by the Department of Public Enterprises (DPE), which oversees the performance and governance of public sector enterprises. The DPE ensures that these enterprises adhere to corporate governance standards and contribute to the economy's growth.

Stock exchanges in India, primarily the Bombay Stock Exchange (BSE) and the National Stock Exchange (NSE), are self-regulatory organizations under the oversight of SEBI. These exchanges facilitate the trading of securities and ensure compliance with regulatory standards. The BSE, established in 1875, is Asia's oldest stock exchange, while the NSE, founded in 1992, introduced electronic trading in India. Both exchanges play a pivotal role in the capital market by providing a platform for raising capital and ensuring liquidity.

The Insurance Regulatory and Development Authority of India (IRDAI) regulates the insurance sector. It oversees the functioning of insurance companies, ensuring that they adhere to the regulatory framework and protect the interests of policyholders. The Pension Fund Regulatory and Development Authority (PFRDA) regulates and develops the pension sector. It ensures the orderly growth of the pension market and protects the interests of subscribers. Both IRDAI and PFRDA operate independently and report to the MOF.

Quasi-regulators such as industry associations and associations for public companies also play a significant role in the regulatory framework. Organizations like the Confederation of Indian Industry (CII) and the Federation of Indian Chambers of Commerce and Industry (FICCI) provide a platform for dialogue between the government and the private sector. They advocate for policy changes, promote best practices, and facilitate industry growth.

Key Issues, Challenges, and Opportunities

Doing business in India requires navigating a corporate landscape where promoters wield disproportionate influence, creating both strategic advantages and systemic risks. The Adani Group's trajectory epitomizes this dynamic. Founded in 1988 as a commodity trading firm, Gautam Adani transformed it into a $200 billion conglomerate by 2022 through rapid expansion into ports, renewables, and airports (*Economic Times*, 2022).

The group's growth highlights the advantages of promoter-led decision making. Adani built the world's largest solar plant in Tamil Nadu by 2016 and acquired Mumbai International Airport in 2020 (Adani Group, 2016; Centre for Science and Environment, 2021), demonstrating the speed at which promoter-controlled firms can execute large projects (Bloomberg, 2024). However, this concentration of power has raised concerns about governance.

In January 2023, Hindenburg Research alleged stock manipulation through offshore entities linked to Adani's brother (Hindenburg Research, 2023), causing a $150 billion market value drop (*Financial Times*, 2023). Subsequent investigations revealed that the group used Mauritius-based funds to circumvent India's 75 percent promoter ownership limit in listed companies (SEBI report, 2024). Environmental controversies also emerged, including a $2 billion Uttar Pradesh power plant that began construction without proper clearances (Down to Earth, 2025).

For businesses operating in India, the Adani case underscores two important lessons. First, promoter-led companies can move swiftly on strategic opportunities—but investors must conduct heightened due diligence on governance and ownership structures. Second, regulatory enforcement has proven uneven. SEBI initially received alerts about

Adani's offshore transactions in 2014, but the case stalled and was paused by 2017 before SEBI resumed its probe following the Hindenburg exposé in 2023 (Reuters, 2023). Meanwhile, a 2014 Directorate of Revenue Intelligence (DRI) investigation into alleged overinvoicing of power plant imports was dismissed by adjudicators in 2017, and the courts subsequently upheld that decision (*Business Standard*, 2025).

This pattern highlights a disconnect: regulatory agencies can investigate, but meaningful outcomes often depend on systemic followthrough, judicial resolution, and, critically, the political influence of those involved. Investors must recognize that much of the breakneck growth of groups like Adani—and Ambani before it—has been facilitated by their closeness to those in power. A key question for investors is whether such dynamics will shift meaningfully with potential political changes in the years ahead.

The group's partial recovery by 2024 illustrates that these governance and regulatory challenges, while significant, can be managed. For investors, this underscores the need to factor promoter influence into risk assessments rather than treating it as an afterthought. As India's markets continue to mature, the long-term success of promoter-led firms will hinge on their ability to pair entrepreneurial vision with greater transparency and robust governance.

The cultural tendency toward overcommitment in Indian business carries real consequences for foreign investors. Kingfisher Airlines' 2012 collapse provides a sobering case study. Founder Vijay Mallya aggressively expanded the fleet to 66 aircraft by 2011 while promising premium service at budget prices, despite industry warnings about unsustainable fuel costs and India's high aviation taxes (*Economic Times*, 2022). When delivery timelines slipped and financial pressures mounted, the company continued to take bookings while deferring vendor payments—a pattern that ultimately left 17,000 creditors owed ₹9,000 crore ($1.2 billion) (*Mint*, 2013).

For foreign partners, such cases create due diligence challenges. A 2023 EY survey found that 68 percent of multinationals working with Indian suppliers encountered "schedule inflation"—where initial timelines were extended by 30–50 percent after contract signing (EY, 2023).

The key is distinguishing between strategic stretch goals (like Ola's 10,000 electric rickshaws) and structural overpromising. Three warning signs emerge from Kingfisher's example:

- Consistent missed milestones on core operations (e.g., delayed salary payments starting in 2009).
- New commitments made during cash flow crises (fleet expansion while owing airports ₹300 crore in fees).
- Reliance on regulatory leniency (SEBI's delayed action on financial disclosures).

Investors can mitigate these risks by building contractual buffers (30–50 percent timeline padding for critical path items) and monitoring working capital cycles, where sudden extensions in payable days often signal overcommitment before financials show strain. As India's bankruptcy code matures, such practices are declining, but cultural inertia persists. As of 2024, data from the National Company Law Tribunal (NCLT) shows that Indian firms still have an average resolution timeline that is 42 percent longer than the one promised in restructuring plans (RBI Report, 2024). The lesson isn't to avoid ambitious Indian partners, but to verify their capacity to execute against their optimism.

As seen in the last part, regulatory complexity is another issue businesses face in India. The regulatory environment is often perceived as cumbersome, characterized by multiple layers of bureaucracy and frequent policy changes. The recent reform on sustainability disclosures in India, known as the BRSR framework, introduced by SEBI in May 2021, is an example of this.

The reform marked a significant milestone in developing the Indian capital market as BRSR became one of Asia's first mandatory ESG disclosure frameworks. The new rule mandates that the top 1,000 Indian listed companies report on various ESG parameters starting from FY 2022–2023, with phased enhancements, including BRSR Core (2023) and value-chain ESG disclosures (2024–2025).

The introduction of BRSR in 2021 was initially praised for enhancing corporate transparency, with early supporters, such as Institutional Investors Advisory Services, predicting that it would "close India's ESG data gap by 40 percent" (*Economic Times*, 2022). However, implementation challenges quickly emerged from three key stakeholders:

- Domestic Businesses: Industry bodies such as the CII and FICCI lobbied against "unworkable" requirements, noting that 78 percent of Nifty 500 companies lacked systems to track Scope 3 emissions (KPMG, 2022). Their pressure led SEBI to delay assurance requirements by one year to FY 2024 and exempt SMEs from value-chain disclosures until 2026 (SEBI, 2024).
- Global investors: BlackRock and other institutional investors, have expressed concerns about the framework's compatibility with ISSB standards, particularly regarding materiality assessment methods (Bloomberg, 2024). This created confusion for multinational asset managers operating in India.
- Regulators: SEBI adopted a phased implementation approach for BRSR Core assurance requirements, beginning with the top 150 listed entities from FY2024 and progressively extending to the top 1000 by FY2027. This reflected regulatory recognition of practical implementation challenges while maintaining the overall direction and structure of the framework (SEBI, 2024).

The compromise outcome—maintaining rigorous reporting for large caps while allowing smaller firms to adopt ESG gradually—reflects India's broader challenge in aligning with global ESG norms without overburdening its developing corporate ecosystem. As the ESG head of Asia for a multinational bank noted: "BRSR is two steps forward, one step back—but still moving the needle."

On the other hand, SEBI's decisive action against Jane Street marks a watershed moment for India's financial markets. In July 2025, the regulator banned the quantitative trading firm and seized ₹4,843 crore ($567 million) after uncovering a sophisticated two-year scheme to manipulate Bank Nifty index options (SEBI, 2025). The case gained traction through an unexpected source: court documents from Jane Street's 2024 lawsuit against Millennium Management revealed proprietary trading strategies that helped SEBI connect the dots. This demonstrates the regulator's evolving capability to pursue complex market abuse cases, building on its reputation as an innovator (it mandated female directors in 2015, a first for Asia).

This development takes place against the backdrop of India's rapid growth as a derivatives powerhouse, accounting for nearly 60 percent of the global equity derivatives volume. SEBI has been progressively tightening its rules, including new position limits effective July 2025, designed to prevent similar manipulation attempts. The regulator's stance reflects a calculated balance between fostering liquid markets and protecting retail participants, who reportedly suffered $25 billion in losses during Jane Street's period of active manipulation.

Yet SEBI's growing sophistication also highlights a persistent structural challenge: its enforcement pipeline is often slowed by limited human resources. With far fewer staff than regulators in markets of comparable scale, SEBI relies heavily on technology for surveillance and investigations—a necessity in a country with India's trading volume, but also a limiting factor in accelerating case resolution. This duality—technological innovation paired with human-resource constraints—remains one of SEBI's defining operational challenges.

For global investors and quantitative firms, the message is clear: SEBI is watching—and it's more sophisticated than you think. SEBI has made it clear that it will not hesitate to use its full authority against practices it deems manipulative, regardless of the perpetrator's size or sophistication. As investors' trading strategies become increasingly complex, so are the regulators' tools to monitor and police them.

Despite these challenges, India offers numerous opportunities for businesses and investors. The country's large and growing consumer base presents significant market potential. With a population of over 1.4 billion, India is one of the largest consumer markets in the world. The growth of the middle class and rising disposable incomes have driven demand for a diverse array of products and services, ranging from consumer goods to financial services.

India's energy transition presents a compelling business potential driven by the country's ambitious goals and supportive policies. India is a global leader in renewable energy, boasting over 200 GW of installed capacity, which includes substantial contributions from solar and wind energy sources. The government aims to achieve 500 GW of nonfossil fuel-based energy by 2030, positioning the country as a key player in the global energy transition. This shift is not only crucial for meeting climate commitments but also offers substantial financial opportunities. For foreign investors, India's renewable energy sector is ripe with potential. The government has introduced various incentives, such as 100 percent FDI in renewable energy projects and the issuance of green bonds. Investment opportunities abound in solar energy, wind power, and energy storage solutions, with the market expected to grow significantly in the coming years.

India's digital transformation has created significant opportunities for foreign portfolio investors, particularly in listed companies driving e-commerce, fintech, and digital payments. With over 954 million Internet subscribers as of March 2024 and 95 percent of Indian villages now covered by 4G connectivity (Press Information Bureau, 2024; Statistics India, 2024), the foundation for digital growth is firmly in place. Meanwhile, UPI continues its explosive expansion—processing 185.8 billion transactions in fiscal year 2024–2025, marking a 41 percent year-on-year increase and accounting for 48.5 percent of global real-time payment volume (RBI/NPCI 2025)—providing investors with high-growth exposure without the complexities of FDI.

The rise of companies like Airtel Payments Bank, which has scaled to over 155 million users by offering accessible, bank-backed digital payment services, demonstrates how cashless payments generate investable opportunities with limited regulatory carryover. Similarly, logistics firm Delhivery's 2022 IPO gave investors exposure to India's booming e-commerce ecosystem, with the country's online retail market expected to reach US$325 billion by 2030 (Morgan Stanley, 2023).

The government's focus on infrastructure development, along with initiatives such as "Make in India" and "Digital India", has also created a conducive environment for investment. These initiatives aim to boost manufacturing, enhance digital connectivity and improve the overall business ecosystem. Meanwhile, India's regulatory framework has evolved to support ease of doing business, making it an appealing market for foreign enterprises. The development of smart cities, the expansion of transportation networks, and investments in renewable energy present substantial opportunities for businesses and investors.

Foreign investors have two primary avenues to access India's growth: foreign portfolio investments (FPI) and FDI. FPIs offer flexibility, allowing investors to buy listed equities and bonds without operational commitments. In contrast, FDI requires longer-term commitments and often involves strategic control. When investing in some sectors, such as the digital economy, FPI offers distinct advantages in this space. Unlike FDI, which faces sectoral restrictions, such as the 49 percent cap in digital media (DPIIT, 2022), foreign investors can freely acquire up to 10 percent stakes in listed firms through automatic routes (SEBI, 2024). This flexibility is valuable in a market where regulatory changes can impact business models, as seen when the RBI tightened digital lending rules in 2023. Recent RBI relaxations on FPI debt limits (May 2025) further tilt the balance toward portfolio flows, aligning India with global liquidity norms.

While valuations remain premium compared to those of emerging market peers (with P/E ratios 30–50 percent higher, according to Bloomberg, 2024), India's economy continues to offer attractive entry points (Bloomberg, 2024). The key for investors is focusing on companies with sustainable monetization paths and manageable regulatory risk, rather than chasing growth at any price. As India's capital market matures, these players will likely remain the most efficient way for foreign investors to participate in this transformation to a more sustainable economy.

In conclusion, doing business and investing in India involves navigating a complex mix of challenges—including promoter dominance, an overcommitment culture, market fragmentation, and regulatory hurdles—but meaningful opportunities exist for those prepared to stay the course. India's large consumer base, rapid energy transition, expanding digital economy, infrastructure development, and growing focus on sustainability offer significant growth potential. However, these benefits are more likely to materialize over the long term rather than through quick wins. Companies and investors willing to commit sustained time, capital, and engagement are far better positioned to unlock the full potential of this dynamic market.

Interview With Local Experts

Interview With Dr. Mukund Govind Rajan, Chairperson of ECube Investment Advisors

1. What strategic adjustments should corporate leaders and investors make today to seize opportunities in sustainability transitions?

   Corporate leaders and investors must identify the emerging sustainability needs of all stakeholders, including employees, customers, communities, investors, and the government. By anticipating trends, they can integrate these into their strategies and proactively tie executive compensation to key sustainability performance indicators. This process requires measuring and analyzing multiple material sustainability performance data points and utilizing advanced technology assessment tools and innovative financing mechanisms.

2. What emerging trends do you foresee that will shape sustainable investments in India?

   SEBI's mandate for top companies to enhance ESG disclosures and prepare annual sustainability reports will drive sustainability investments. Enhanced ESG compliance will foster market intermediaries and funds focused on niche themes like climate change and plastic waste management. RBI-regulated entities will integrate climate risk management into lending protocols. The MoF's Green Taxonomy will expand the market for financial instruments like green and climate bonds, expanding their role in Priority Sector Lending and giving a fillip to new Nonbank Finance Companies with sustainability objectives. The upcoming Carbon Credits Trading Scheme will catalyze a vibrant market for sustainable instruments.

3. Which emerging technologies or digital trends do you believe will most significantly redefine sustainability practices in India?

   Digital marketplaces are emerging in niche segments like waste management in India, leveraging blockchain, AI, and machine learning to enhance transparency and efficiency in the value chain. In the energy sector, the focus on renewables and biomass-based sources will continue, paving the way for a hydrogen-based economy. Battery-based energy storage solutions will support retail electric mobility and stable grid power delivery.

Interview With Amarjeet Singh, Whole-Time Member at SEBI

(Views expressed are his own and not those of his organization)

1. What is the key to creating a reliable framework for sustainable investments in India?

   India's net-zero, climate, and Sustainable Development Goals (SDGs) ambitions will require a significant scaling up of sustainable finance. A reliable framework needs to be built on three key pillars: a clear taxonomy for sustainable activities, credible and comparable disclosures, backed by enabling financial policies and regulatory interventions. These elements enable trust, comparability, and efficient capital allocation toward genuine sustainability outcomes.

2. What is the regulatory approach and rationale underlying the BRSR? What are your views on the implementation of the ISSB Standards?

   SEBI's sustainability disclosure journey began in 2012 with the Business Responsibility Report (BRR). It evolved into the BRSR in 2021. The BRSR, applicable to the top 1,000 listed entities by market capitalization, is quantitative, outcome-oriented, and tailored to India's unique environmental and social priorities. At the same time, while developing the BRSR, a benchmarking exercise was conducted with international frameworks such as the TCFD and GRI, resulting in several common elements. While a common global language is ideal, it is important to account for country-specific circumstances in implementation. Therefore, flexibility and proportionality, supported by appropriate glide paths, will be crucial in any move toward aligning the BRSR with global standards.

3. What are the regulatory developments shaping India's sustainable investment landscape in the next five years?

   In my view, from a regulatory perspective, the future of India's sustainable investment landscape will be shaped by deeper integration of financial and sustainability reporting, growing emphasis on credible transition planning, the development of a regulatory framework for assurance, and stronger oversight mechanisms to address greenwashing.

Key Takeaways

- India's promoter-driven business culture enables long-term strategic vision but creates persistent governance and minority shareholder risks.
- A strong "jugaad" and overcommitment culture fuels innovation and resilience but often leads to execution and delivery challenges.
- Regulatory frameworks led by RBI and SEBI are evolving rapidly, with BRSR marking a major step toward structured ESG disclosure.
- Enforcement remains uneven, increasing compliance uncertainty and due diligence requirements for foreign investors.
- High-profile cases such as Satyam, Adani, Kingfisher, and Flipkart illustrate the duality of entrepreneurial energy and weak controls.
- Long-term opportunities in renewables, digitalization, and consumer growth require patient capital and strong local insight.

Boardroom Briefing

Executives and investors should:

1. Assess promoter influence and ownership structures as central components of governance risk analysis.
2. Build contractual, financial, and operational buffers to mitigate risks arising from overcommitment and timeline slippage.
3. Monitor SEBI's BRSR framework and related enforcement trends to ensure disclosure readiness and data credibility.
4. Prioritize rigorous due diligence on related-party transactions, capital allocation, and succession planning.
5. Focus capital deployment on policy-aligned sectors such as renewables, digital payments, and infrastructure development.
6. Commit to sustained engagement, recognizing that India rewards investors who balance optimism with discipline and persistence.

CHAPTER 9

Sustainability in ASEAN (Singapore, Malaysia, Thailand, Indonesia, and the Philippines)

[INVESTORS] [CORPORATES] [REGULATORS] [INTERNATIONAL EXECUTIVES]

This chapter is intended for investors, corporates, regulators, and international executives who need to navigate ASEAN's diverse sustainability challenges and opportunities across culture, regulation, and market dynamics.

Understanding Business Culture

Understanding the business culture in ASEAN countries, such as Singapore, Malaysia, Thailand, Indonesia, and the Philippines, is fundamental for any corporate executive or investor aiming to succeed in these diverse markets. While common threads such as respect for hierarchy and the primacy of personal relationships run through the region, each country's business environment is shaped by distinct cultural, social, and economic influences.

Singapore offers a blend of Eastern and Western practices, combining formality with remarkable efficiency. Meetings are punctual, well-structured, and to the point, reflecting the city–state's corporate pragmatism. Decisions are often made at senior levels, but Singapore's strong emphasis on meritocracy ensures that performance and expertise carry weight. Personal relationships remain important, often nurtured through social engagements that build trust. DBS Bank is a clear example of this balance—leveraging strong corporate governance and a culture of innovation to establish itself as a leading financial institution in Asia.

In Malaysia, business culture mirrors its multicultural fabric, requiring sensitivity to the practices of Malay, Chinese, and Indian communities. Islamic customs—such as accommodating prayer breaks—coexist with Chinese values like *guanxi* (relationship-building), often reinforced through shared meals. Business discussions typically start with small talk to build rapport, while respect for hierarchy and "face" (social standing) underpins interactions. Confrontation is avoided, and dissent may be expressed indirectly or via intermediaries. AirAsia embodies Malaysia's multicultural adaptability: its "Now Everyone Can Fly" campaign resonated across income groups without ethnic exclusivity, while its 2020 sustainability efforts—including a 69.8 percent reduction in carbon emissions and a pledge to eliminate single-use plastics—aligned global ESG standards with local expectations.

Thailand requires particular attention to subtle social protocols. The *wai* greeting (palms pressed together with a slight bow) sets a respectful tone, and the concept of *kreng jai* (deference and avoiding conflict) governs workplace interactions. Hierarchy is deeply ingrained—senior leaders are addressed first by title (e.g., Khun + surname), and negative feedback is often delivered through intermediaries. Charoen Pokphand Foods' $10.6 billion overseas expansion illustrates Thailand's culturally attuned approach: executives underwent six months of training in Thai negotiation styles, prioritizing relationship-building before dealmaking. This cultural patience paid off—its Vietnam market entry involved three months of informal meetings before contract talks, yielding long-term partner retention rates 27 percent above the industry average (McKinsey, 2024).

In Indonesia, personal trust and consensus (*musyawarah*) are critical, with senior leaders playing a decisive role in approvals. The principle of *gotong royong* (cooperation) drives collaborative problem-solving and communication tends to be indirect to maintain social harmony. Foreign investors are expected to invest time in relationship-building before formalizing agreements. Gojek's evolution from a ride-hailing service into a $10 billion "super-app" reflects this cultural integration: it introduced cash payments and paper QR codes for small merchants in a cash-dominant economy, launched GoFood Sahur for Ramadan (boosting deliveries by 40 percent), and offered women-only rides to respect conservative norms—proving that aligning innovation with local values can drive scale.

The Philippines presents a unique cultural blend of Asian relational norms and Western pragmatism, shaped by its colonial and trade history. While widespread English proficiency simplifies communication, relationship-building remains central—a 2023 HSBC survey found that 68 percent of deals require three or more informal meetings before advancing. Respect for hierarchy and titles is essential, but behind the scenes, *pakikisama* (social harmony) guides consensus-building. Jollibee Foods Corporation has leveraged this duality, expanding to 35 countries by adapting to local markets—introducing U.S.-style fried chicken for American customers while preserving Filipino classics like the peach-mango pie. In Vietnam, it trained staff in Filipino-style personalized service, helping drive a 19 percent increase in international revenue in 2023.

While these countries share core values—particularly the importance of relationships and respect for hierarchy—the differences are subtle. Singapore's corporate culture is more formal and efficiency-driven than the relationship-centric approaches seen in Thailand and Indonesia. Malaysia's multicultural environment requires navigating multiple ethnic customs, while the Philippines' use of English creates an easier entry point for international firms. Mastering these subtleties enables corporates and investors not only to avoid missteps but also to thrive in one of the world's most dynamic regions. While cultural dynamics define how businesses operate, long-term participation requires navigating ASEAN's complex and often fragmented regulatory systems.

Regulatory Framework

The regulatory framework of the capital markets in ASEAN is complex and involves multiple key players. Understanding the hierarchy of these entities is integral for navigating the regulatory landscape in each country.

In Singapore, the Monetary Authority of Singapore (MAS) serves as the central bank and the primary regulatory authority overseeing the capital markets. MAS regulates financial institutions, including banks, insurance companies, and securities firms, ensuring stability and integrity in the financial system. The SGX is the primary stock exchange, playing a crucial role in the capital market by facilitating the trading of securities. SGX operates under the supervision of MAS and adheres to stringent regulatory standards. The Accounting and Corporate Regulatory Authority (ACRA) oversees corporate governance and compliance with financial reporting standards.

In Malaysia, the Securities Commission Malaysia (SC) is the primary regulatory body responsible for overseeing the capital markets. The SC regulates and develops the securities and derivatives markets, ensuring fair and orderly market conduct. The Bursa Malaysia is the main stock exchange, operating under the supervision of the SC. The Central Bank of Malaysia (Bank Negara Malaysia) also plays a significant role in regulating the banking sector and ensuring financial stability. The Companies Commission of Malaysia (SSM) further supports the regulatory framework, which oversees corporate governance and compliance. The Capital Market Masterplan, implemented by the SC, has played a pivotal role in advancing Malaysia's capital markets and broadening the spectrum of available financial products and services. The Minority Shareholders Watch Group (MSWG) is a Malaysian government initiative that advocates for the interests of minority shareholders and promotes corporate governance through shareholder activism and stakeholder engagement.

Thailand's capital market is primarily regulated by the SEC, which oversees the issuance, trading, and compliance to ensure transparency and investor protection. The Stock Exchange of Thailand (SET) is the main platform for trading securities and works closely with the SEC to maintain market integrity. The Bank of Thailand (BOT) regulates the banking sector, while the Office of Insurance Commission (OIC) oversees the insurance industry. The SEC has introduced several reforms to modernize the regulatory framework, including the Draft Securities and Exchange Act and the Draft Derivatives Act, aimed at enhancing market efficiency and aligning with international standards. A notable case study is the establishment of the Thai Institute of Directors, which has significantly improved corporate governance practices among listed companies.

In Indonesia, the Financial Services Authority (OJK) is the primary regulator overseeing the capital markets, banking and insurance sectors. The OJK ensures market stability, transparency, and investor protection. The Indonesia Stock Exchange (IDX) is the main securities exchange, operating under the supervision of the OJK. The Central Bank of Indonesia (Bank Indonesia) plays a key role in regulating monetary policy and maintaining financial stability. The recent Financial Omnibus Law has introduced significant reforms to the capital markets, including broader definitions of securities and enhanced regulatory oversight.

The SEC regulates the Philippines' capital market, overseeing the issuance, trading, and compliance with securities regulations. The Philippine Stock Exchange (PSE) and the Capital Markets Integrity Corporation (CMIC) are licensed as self-regulatory organizations (SROs) to regulate trading participants and listed companies. The Bangko Sentral ng Pilipinas (BSP) regulates the banking sector and ensures financial stability. The Insurance Commission oversees the insurance industry. The Capital Market Development Council (CMDC), a public–private partnership, plays a significant role in formulating policies to promote market development.

While there are similarities in the regulatory structure across these markets, such as the presence of a central regulatory authority overseeing the capital markets and a stock exchange to facilitate securities trading, there are also distinct contrasts. For instance, Singapore's regulatory framework is highly centralized under MAS. Meanwhile, Malaysia and Indonesia have multiple regulatory bodies with different roles and responsibilities. Thailand's SEC has been proactive in introducing legislative reforms, such as its green bond tokenization rules in 2024, which enable projects like Energy Absolute's $150 million solar farm token offering. At the same time, the Philippines relies on a combination of regulatory bodies and self-regulatory organizations to maintain market integrity.

Key Issues, Challenges, and Opportunities

In recent years, the Southeast Asian markets of Singapore, Malaysia, Thailand, Indonesia, and the Philippines have faced myriad challenges and opportunities, particularly in the context of sustainability and economic growth. While diverse in their characteristics, these markets share common themes that influence their business environments and investment landscapes.

Physical climate risks are a significant concern across the region. Singapore, with its low-lying geography, is particularly vulnerable to rising sea levels and extreme weather events. The government has been proactive in addressing these risks through substantial investments in coastal protection and climate resilience projects. For instance, the Marina Bay Sands has implemented comprehensive sustainability initiatives, including energy-efficient systems and waste reduction programs, setting a benchmark for green buildings (Marina Bay Sands, 2023). Similarly, Malaysia and Indonesia face severe flooding and landslides, exacerbated by deforestation and urbanization. Typhoons and droughts frequently impact Thailand and the Philippines, posing a significant threat to agriculture and water resources. These climate challenges necessitate robust adaptation and mitigation strategies, presenting opportunities for businesses specializing in green technologies and sustainable infrastructure. A report issued by the ADB highlights that the region could lose 26.5 percent of its GDP by 2048 if no action is taken (ADB, 2023). The escalating frequency and intensity of climate-related hazards pose substantial financial risks to the region.

The energy transition in Southeast Asia presents a complex landscape. These markets are at different stages of their energy transition journey. One of the primary issues is the heavy reliance on fossil fuels, which dominate the energy mix in these countries. For instance, Malaysia and Indonesia have significant coal and natural gas reserves, which have historically driven their energy policies. However, this reliance poses environmental challenges, including high carbon emissions and air pollution. In contrast, despite its advanced infrastructure, Singapore faces the challenge of being a net energy importer with limited renewable energy resources, making it heavily dependent on imported natural gas.

The region's transition to renewable energy faces multiple hurdles, including infrastructure gaps and policy inconsistencies. Thailand has made progress in solar energy adoption, particularly through its Eastern Economic Corridor (EEC) Smart City initiative, which integrates IoT and 5G networks to optimize energy use while mandating that 40 percent of buildings meet Leadership in Energy and Environmental Design (LEED) sustainability standards by 2025 (Thailand Board of Investment, 2023). However, grid integration remains challenging, with renewables accounting for just 30 percent of Thailand's energy mix as of 2024 (Energy Policy and Planning Office, 2024).

The Philippines, despite having the world's third-largest geothermal capacity at 1,918 MW (Department of Energy, 2023), struggles with exploration costs reaching $8 million per well and permitting processes that average five to seven years (World Bank, 2023). Indonesia's nickel industry, which supplies 37 percent of global EV battery feedstock (USGS, 2023), highlights the paradox of the transition: its coal-powered smelters emit approximately 52 million tons of CO_2 annually (Climate Trace, 2023), while contributing to deforestation in Sulawesi (Mongabay, 2022).

Across these markets, inconsistent policies—such as Thailand's tax incentives for renewables versus Indonesia's weak carbon pricing create investor uncertainty. The Philippines' delayed geothermal auctions and Indonesia's export bans further complicate long-term planning, underscoring the need for harmonized regulatory frameworks to accelerate the transition. Regulatory fragmentation also complicates ESG implementation. While the ASEAN Taxonomy for Sustainable Finance (Version 2, 2023) provides a regional framework for classifying green activities, national-level ESG standards remain misaligned, creating additional compliance burdens for multinationals (ASEAN, 2023). Investors must carefully assess how these frameworks align—or conflict—with international standards like the ISSB or EU taxonomy.

ASEAN's collective target to increase renewables to 23 percent of total energy supply by 2025 remains active, though progress varies by country. Singapore is pioneering smart grid innovations, including a 15 MW virtual power plant pilot slated to launch in 2025, which aims to integrate distributed energy resources. The Philippines continues to lead in geothermal energy, with Energy Development Corporation adding 141 MWe of new capacity by 2026, including the 28.9-MW Palayan Bayan plant (operational since 2024) (EDC, 2024). Indonesia's $6 billion EV battery ecosystem, set to produce 15 GWh annually by 2026, capitalizes on its nickel reserves. Thailand's agrivoltaics projects and Malaysia's 1,000

MW rooftop solar expansion further demonstrate regional diversity in renewable strategies.

On the other hand, fraud and corruption are pervasive issues that affect the business climate in these markets. While Singapore benefits from strong legal frameworks (ranked 3rd globally in anticorruption by Transparency International 2024), enforcement remains selective— the 2022 Keppel Offshore bribery case resolution (resulting in deferred prosecution) demonstrated prioritization of economic stability over maximal penalties. Digital payment fraud in Singapore nonetheless surged 65 percent YoY in 2023 (Singapore Police Force, 2024), revealing gaps even in advanced markets.

Elsewhere in ASEAN, systemic issues persist:

- Malaysia's 2024 MACC investigations into RM1.2 billion procurement fraud at an SOE (Malaysian Anti-Corruption Commission, 2024).
- Indonesia's 2023 arrest of a Supreme Court justice for case-fixing (Komisi Pemberantasan Korupsi, 2023) and banking fraud cases has underscored vulnerabilities in compliance and regulatory enforcement (World Bank, 2023).
- The Philippines' 2022 Pandora Papers revelations of offshore holdings among officials (International Consortium of Investigative Journalists, 2022).

These cases correlate with declining anticorruption disclosures, as only 41 percent of ASEAN100 firms published detailed fraud prevention reports in 2023 (Association of Certified Fraud Examiners, 2023), down from 58 percent in 2020. AI-driven fraud now compounds these risks, with Indonesia's financial sector reporting a 300 percent increase in deepfake scams in 2024 (Otoritas Jasa Keuangan, 2024). For Malaysia, the lingering effects of the 1MDB scandal (USD 4.5 billion recovered as of 2024) better illustrate the governance challenges facing investors.

Talent mobility is another pressing issue. Singapore and Malaysia, in particular, face fierce competition for high-skilled labor, driven by their ambitions to become regional hubs for finance, green technology, and digital innovation. At the same time, countries like Indonesia and Thailand struggle to retain top talent amid rapid industrialization, with many professionals seeking higher wages and better career prospects abroad, often in Singapore, Australia, or the Gulf states. This "brain drain" is especially acute in sectors such as renewable energy, technology, and finance, where demand far outpaces domestic supply. For investors, these dynamics create both costs and opportunities: companies must invest heavily in workforce development, redesign compensation structures to attract global talent, and increasingly rely on cross-border recruitment or partnerships with regional universities to build pipelines of ESG, tech, and finance professionals (World Bank, 2024).

The U.S.–China rivalry is reshaping Southeast Asia's economic landscape through competing initiatives. China's Belt and Road Initiative (BRI) has funded $1.3 trillion in regional infrastructure projects since 2013 (Belt and Road Portal, 2023), including Indonesia's Jakarta-Bandung High-Speed Rail and Malaysia's East Coast Rail Link (Kereta Cepat Indonesia China, 2023; Malaysia Rail Link, 2023), but concerns over debt sustainability and environmental standards persist. Conversely, the U.S.-led Indo-Pacific Economic Framework (IPEF), launched in 2022, focuses on digital trade standards and supply chain resilience—Vietnam and Singapore were among the first ASEAN members to join its "Clean Economy" pillar for collaboration on green technology (U.S. Department of Commerce, 2023). This duality forces regional players to balance benefits: Thailand leverages BRI financing for its EEC industrial corridor while aligning with IPEF's semiconductor supply chain goals.

The RCEP agreement, implemented in 2022, has become a catalyst for the integration of digital trade. TikTok's expansion illustrates this shift (ByteDance, 2024):

- Tariff Advantages: Under RCEP's simplified rules of origin, Chinese merchants on TikTok Shop avoid Thailand's 30 percent electronics tariff by shipping via bonded warehouses in Guangxi, China, cutting delivery times to five days.
- Market Access: TikTok leveraged RCEP's e-commerce provisions to establish local entities in Indonesia (75 percent stake in Tokopedia) and Malaysia, circumventing social commerce bans and achieving $16.3 billion Gross

Merchandise Value (GMV)in ASEAN by 2023—a four times growth since 2022.

- Talent Mobility: RCEP's service trade commitments enabled TikTok to deploy Chinese livestream trainers to Jakarta, upskilling 15,000 local sellers in 2024 alone.

However, geopolitical tensions persist. The South China Sea disputes have delayed joint oil exploration between China and the Philippines. At the same time, Myanmar's civil conflict has disrupted cross-border logistics, posing key challenges to the full potential of the RCEP. Rising sea levels are now driving unconventional collaborations, such as Vietnam's 2024 partnership with Dutch firms (via IPEF) to fortify the Mekong Delta's supply chains against flooding (Government of Vietnam, 2024). The region's path forward hinges on navigating these dualities: embracing the trade efficiencies of RCEP while mitigating geopolitical risks through diversified alliances.

U.S. trade policies have also played a crucial role in shaping the business dynamics in Southeast Asia. The imposition of tariffs on Chinese goods under the "America First Trade Policy" has led to a reconfiguration of supply chains. This shift has strengthened economic ties between ASEAN and China, creating new business opportunities in the region. For example, the seafood processing industry in Thailand has seen increased investments as companies seek to diversify their supply chains. Similarly, the digital economy in the Philippines has benefited from increased demand for outsourcing services as U.S. companies look for cost-effective alternatives. The recent U.S. tariffs have prompted ASEAN countries to enhance regional cooperation and explore new markets to mitigate the impact of these tariffs. The latest trade reality requires businesses to build regionalized value-creation ecosystems with localized research, production, and distribution capabilities.

In addition, ASEAN remains a hub for growth and innovation. Grab Holdings, for instance, has transformed from a regional ride-hailing service into a Southeast Asian super-app, culminating in its 2021 Nasdaq Special Purpose Acquisition Company (SPAC) listing—the largest ever for a Southeast Asian company (Grab, 2021). Its success underscores the opportunities for companies that can navigate ASEAN's regulatory complexities while scaling digital services across fragmented markets. In parallel, Marina Bay Sands in Singapore exemplifies how foreign investment in hospitality and tourism can leverage strong governance and infrastructure to deliver consistent returns (Las Vegas Sands, 2023).

ASEAN's opportunities are vast, particularly in renewable energy, digital infrastructure, and green finance. Countries like the Philippines are making significant investments in solar and wind projects, while Singapore is positioning itself as a green finance hub through initiatives like the Green Finance Action Plan (Monetary Authority of Singapore, 2023). These developments create openings for foreign investors in sustainable infrastructure, fintech, and advanced manufacturing.

In conclusion, while the Southeast Asian markets of Singapore, Malaysia, Thailand, Indonesia, and the Philippines face significant challenges, they also offer compelling prospects for businesses and investors. These markets can achieve sustainable growth by addressing physical climate risks, enhancing public governance to reduce fraud and corruption, navigating geopolitical complexities, and leveraging regional agreements such as the RCEP. The changing U.S. trade policies further improve the attractiveness of the ASEAN region to the rest of Asia-Pacific, offering new avenues for investment and business expansion. As these markets evolve, businesses prioritizing sustainability and adaptability will be well-positioned to thrive in this dynamic landscape.

Interview With Local Experts

Interview With Julia Tay, Asia-Pacific Public Policy Leader at Ernst & Young

1. What policy measures do you think have been most effective in driving Singapore's sustainability initiatives, and how can they be further enhanced?

   The Singapore Green Plan 2030, launched by the government in February 2021, has been a strong strategic driver of sustainability initiatives. The Green Plan has five pillars—City in Nature, Energy Reset, Sustainable Living, Green Economy, and Resilient Future. This policy measure has been effective firstly because the five pillars are all encompassing and secondly because it is being spearheaded by five ministries and driving a whole-of-nation approach to achieving Singapore's sustainability goals.

2. How can ASEAN countries enhance their sustainability reporting frameworks?

   First movers in ASEAN, including Indonesia, Malaysia, the Philippines, Singapore, and Thailand, have committed to adopting the ISSB standards, with minimal local customization. This facilitates the provision of comparable and decision-useful information to investors. Looking ahead, there remain three priority focus areas: (1) Adoption of ISSB standards by the rest of ASEAN; (2) mandating some form of assurance for sustainability reporting to provide trust and confidence to the capital markets; and (3) capacity building.

3. How can policymakers support the development of auditing practices in sustainability reporting in APAC in the next five years?

   Policymakers need to establish the regulatory framework, which includes (1) adopting the newly launched ISSA 5000 Sustainability Assurance standard; (2) mandating some form of sustainability assurance; and (3) designating the regulatory oversight authority that will license qualified assurance providers and enforce the application of sustainability assurance standards. Given the connectivity between financial reporting and sustainability reporting, policymakers should consider expanding the authority of current audit oversight regulators to also oversee sustainability assurance, in addition to financial statement audits.

Interview With Shireen Muhiudeen, Founder of Corston-Smith Asset Management and Former Nonexecutive Chairman of Bursa Malaysia

1. As the first female chair of the Malaysian Stock Exchange, how can Malaysia's corporate sector improve diversity and inclusion?

   Despite early efforts to increase gender diversity, I have been disappointed with the lack of progress since our research on gender diversity on boards was first released in 2011. The previous 30 percent target for female board representation has now been replaced with a mandate of one woman for certain-sized firms. If one female board member can be required, why not a 30 percent minimum across all boards? This would strengthen diversity and curb groupthink.

2. In *We Are All Stakeholders*, you advocate for radical accountability. How can Malaysian boards address sustainability challenges while maintaining profitability?

   Boards must immediately address any modern slavery issues in their labor practices. Many industries rely on migrant labor, but with today's supply chain scrutiny, failing to meet global labor standards will damage profitability. Environmental responsibility is equally critical. While fossil fuels remain a concern, unmanaged waste is the bigger issue. I would like to see heightened awareness of their supply chains.

3. How do you see sustainable investment practices evolving in Malaysia and across ASEAN in the next decade? What role should policymakers play in this revolution?

   Sustainability has become a box-ticking exercise, focusing on templates rather than impact. There is too much form over substance, and this doesn't address the core issues. Companies need realistic targets. Governance remains the most crucial pillar for progress, and policymakers should prioritize strengthening it.

Interview With Putra Adhiguna, Managing Director at Energy Shift Institute

1. Focusing on Indonesia, what are the biggest opportunities and challenges in advancing the country's energy transition?

   With largely untapped clean energy resources and declining coal financing, Indonesia is approaching an inflexion point for its energy transition—one it may not yet fully grasp. However, addressing the legacy overbuild of coal power, fossil fuel price controls, and under-investment in the grid is crucial. Policymakers must prioritize clear, near-term project pipelines over distant targets. There has been an overemphasis on setting grand targets, but the real imperative is to demonstrate a successful case where green energy drives investment and job creation. Transition requires moving beyond narratives focused solely on emissions.

2. What role do international investors play in accelerating the energy transition in the region? How can they navigate the regulatory complexities?

   International partnerships are crucial, but expectations must be managed, as the transition is a highly complex and politically sensitive process. Private investment is expected to cover at least two-thirds of the region's energy financing. Investors must go beyond capital deployment by actively shaping more green corporate champions and supporting the transformation of legacy businesses. Grounded market knowledge and a nuanced understanding of technology pathways are essential. Investors should assess both large-scale projects and targeted transition opportunities in the commercial and industrial sectors.

3. What key sectors or technologies stand out as the most impactful for driving sustainable change in the region?

   Solar, battery storage, grid upgrades, and interconnections are key enablers. Higher cost technologies, which have struggled to scale in regions with higher carbon prices, are unlikely to gain traction in the broader ASEAN. Transport electrification remains essential, particularly as countries aim to reduce oil imports and subsidies.

Interview With Christopher Leahy, Executive Director at
Barbican Advisory

1. What are the primary drivers of fraud and corruption risks in ASEAN markets, and how do these factors vary across member countries?

   Fraud and corruption are deeply entrenched in ASEAN markets, particularly within governments, civil services, and business groups. Singapore is an outlier, where fraud is minimal, but risks arise from ensuring funds aren't sourced from corruption elsewhere. Many ASEAN economies are dominated by a handful of business groups, often benefiting from rentier monopolies granted by political elites. These groups stifle competition while ensuring continued wealth for incumbents. Business elites hold vast financial power, while political allies use these ties to influence elections and governance through corrupt practices.

2. From an international investor's perspective, what are the key fraud and corruption risks in ASEAN markets that could impact cross-border investments?

   Cross-border investments in ASEAN often require multiple approvals, permits, and licenses—each a potential opportunity for bribery or corrupt dealings. Investors may be unaware of these activities, as local counterparties handle the "paperwork." Ignorance does not shield foreign companies from liability under extraterritorial laws, such as the U.S. FCPA, the UK Bribery Act, or the forthcoming EU anticorruption directives.

3. What steps should investors take to mitigate exposure to fraud when entering or expanding in ASEAN markets, and what warning signs should they watch for?

   Thorough due diligence is crucial, extending beyond country risk assessments and financial checks. Investors must investigate the local partners' sources of wealth, business reputation, financial health, management style, and approach to foreign investment. Warning signs include hidden ultimate beneficial owners, unexpected intermediaries or offshore agencies, unexplained fees, and unusual or illogical business procedures or government approvals.

Key Takeaways

- ASEAN is culturally diverse but unified by relationship-based business practices and strong respect for hierarchy.
- Regulatory systems vary widely, ranging from centralized oversight in Singapore to fragmented and reform-driven models elsewhere.
- Climate and energy transition risks are acute, with policy inconsistencies creating uncertainty for long-term investors.
- Corruption, fraud, and talent mobility remain systemic challenges, requiring enhanced governance and institutional vigilance.
- Regional integration through RCEP and evolving supply chains is reshaping trade, investment, and sustainability strategies.
- Despite risks, ASEAN offers major opportunities in renewables, digital platforms, green finance, and sustainable infrastructure.

Boardroom Briefing

Executives and investors should:

1. Adapt business strategies to local cultural norms, prioritizing trust, hierarchy, and consensus-building across markets.
2. Map and continuously monitor regulatory frameworks in each jurisdiction, recognizing that there is no "single ASEAN model."
3. Anticipate sustainability risks, including climate exposure, fraud, and labor issues, through rigorous and ongoing due diligence.
4. Position portfolios to capture opportunities in digital innovation, energy transition, and regional infrastructure development.
5. Integrate geopolitical analysis, including BRI, IPEF, RCEP, and U.S.–China dynamics, into long-term strategic planning.
6. Invest in talent development, governance systems, and regional partnerships to strengthen execution capacity and market insight.

CHAPTER 10

Sustainability in Australia and New Zealand

[INVESTORS] [CORPORATES] [REGULATORS]
[INTERNATIONAL EXECUTIVES]
This chapter is intended for investors, corporates, regulators, and international executives who need to navigate the sustainability challenges and opportunities in Australia and New Zealand—from climate resilience and governance reform to indigenous partnerships and energy transition opportunities.

Understanding Business Culture

Australia and New Zealand share Anglo-colonial business roots but have evolved distinct cultural approaches that influence their sustainability transitions. Australian business culture prioritizes pragmatic, direct communication—a 2023 study of ASX 200 firms found 78 percent of executives structured sustainability reports around measurable KPIs rather than aspirational goals, reflecting this results-oriented mindset (KPMG Australia, 2023). While less hierarchical than their Asian counterparts, clear corporate structures persist. Cross-class interactions often demonstrate egalitarian norms in practice.

New Zealand's business culture blends this pragmatism with stronger collaborative elements shaped by *Māori whanaungatanga* (relationship-building). The country's 2023 Climate Adaptation Act mandated *iwi* (tribes) consultation for infrastructure projects, institutionalizing consensus-based decision making (New Zealand Government, 2023). However, variations exist—while humility is culturally valued, a strategic balance between modesty and commercial necessity is required.

The two nations also integrate international influences differently. Australia's 2023 adoption of EU-aligned sustainability reporting standards (climate-related financial disclosures) (Australian Treasury, 2023) contrasts with New Zealand's more localized approach, where 72 percent of agribusinesses now align with *Te Ao* Māori (the Māori worldview) environmental principles alongside conventional ESG frameworks (Ministry of Business, Innovation and Employment, 2024). These cultural foundations shape how each country implements sustainability—Australia through compliance-driven targets, New Zealand via community-embedded models—while facing shared challenges in bridging urban–rural divides and decarbonizing legacy industries.

3M Australia's innovation strategy offers valuable insights into adapting global corporate culture to local conditions. Between 2018 and 2022, the company implemented its "15 percent Culture" program locally, allowing Australian employees to dedicate 15 percent of their work time to self-directed projects (3M Australia, 2023). This resulted in 37 patented innovations specifically addressing regional sustainability challenges, including a solar-reflective building film adapted for extreme ultraviolet (UV) conditions (3M Australia Impact Report, 2023). The initiative succeeded because it accommodated Australia's preference for autonomous, results-driven work styles while addressing local environmental needs. However, the program's requirement for detailed quarterly reporting (unlike its more open-ended U.S. counterpart) reflected necessary adaptation to Australia's stronger corporate governance norms.

On the other hand, Fonterra's farmer-owned cooperative model demonstrates both the strengths and challenges of New Zealand's collective approach (Fonterra, 2023). The 2023 capital structure review revealed that while the model provided stability during the 2020–2022 Covid disruptions (paying 95 percent of farmers within 30 days throughout the crisis), it struggled with innovation adoption, taking 18 months longer than competitors to implement methane-reduction technologies (New Zealand Dairy Industry Association, 2023; New Zealand Dairy Industry Report, 2023). This tension between collective decision-making and rapid response highlights a key lesson: cooperative structures excel in risk mitigation but may require complementary governance mechanisms for technological transformation.

These cases illustrate core regional differences. 3M's Australian operations thrived by balancing global frameworks with local flexibility, while

Fonterra's experience shows how deeply embedded collective models require deliberate innovation pathways. For businesses entering these markets, the key takeaway is that successful adaptation requires more than policy translation—it demands structural alignment with each country's cultural and commercial realities. While cultural approaches define how companies operate, long-term participation also requires navigating complex and evolving regulatory frameworks in both countries.

Regulatory Framework

Australia's capital market regulation features a multilayered approach with clearly defined supervisory roles and responsibilities. The primary regulatory bodies include the Australian Securities and Investments Commission (ASIC), the Reserve Bank of Australia (RBA), the Australian Prudential Regulation Authority (APRA), and the Australian Treasury. These entities form the Council of Financial Regulators (CFR), which coordinates the regulation and supervision of the financial system.

ASIC is the primary regulator for corporate governance, financial markets, and financial services. It oversees real-time trading on domestic markets, enforces laws against misconduct, and supervises Australian Financial Service Licence (AFSL) holders. The RBA is responsible for financial system stability, including the oversight of clearing and settlement facilities. APRA regulates banks, insurance companies, and superannuation funds, ensuring their prudential soundness. The Treasury develops economic policy and works closely with the other regulators within the CFR.

The Australian Securities Exchange (ASX) operates under the supervision of ASIC and the RBA, ensuring market integrity and transparency. The ASX Listing Rules govern the conduct of listed companies, and ASIC supervises ASX's compliance with these rules. Also, shareholder bodies such as the Australian Shareholders' Association (ASA) and the Australian Council of Superannuation Investors (ACSI) play significant roles. ACSI, established in 2001, provides a collective voice on ESG issues on behalf of its members, including major asset owners and institutional investors. ACSI's influence is substantial, as its members collectively own a significant portion of ASX 200 companies.

In New Zealand, the regulatory framework is similarly comprehensive, with the Financial Markets Authority (FMA), the Reserve Bank of New Zealand (RBNZ), and the Ministry of Business, Innovation, and Employment (MBIE) as the primary regulators. The FMA oversees the conduct of financial markets, ensuring fair dealing, regulating financial product markets and enforcing the Financial Markets Conduct Act 2013. The RBNZ is responsible for the prudential regulation of banks, non-bank deposit takers and insurers, focusing on maintaining a sound and efficient financial system. MBIE provides policy advice and supports the regulatory framework through legislation and stewardship.

The New Zealand Stock Exchange (NZX) operates under the oversight of the FMA, ensuring market transparency and integrity. The NZX Listing Rules govern the behaviour of listed companies, and the FMA monitors compliance with these rules. Quasi-regulators such as the New Zealand Shareholders' Association (NZSA) advocate for investor rights and promote high standards of corporate governance.

While both Australia and New Zealand have similar regulatory structures, there are notable differences between them. Australia's regulatory framework is more complex, with a greater number of regulatory bodies and a more extensive set of regulations. On the other hand, New Zealand has fewer regulatory agencies and a more streamlined approach to regulation. Both countries, however, emphasise market integrity, investor protection and financial stability.

Australia and New Zealand's regulatory frameworks reflect a careful synthesis of international influences adapted to local conditions. While maintaining strong Commonwealth legal foundations, Australia has selectively incorporated elements from other jurisdictions, adopting U.S.-style continuous disclosure rules in 1994 and modifying EU sustainability standards for local implementation in 2023 (ASIC, 2023). New Zealand's approach similarly blends UK-derived structures with unique Māori governance principles, as exemplified by its 2021 climate risk disclosure rules, which preceded many peers (FMA, 2021). Both countries demonstrate regulatory independence through adaptations, such as Australia's version of the GDPR (Privacy Act amendments, 2023) (Australian Government, 2023) and New Zealand's distinctive Stewardship Code for institutional investors (New Zealand Financial Markets Authority, 2022).

This balanced approach enables compliance with global standards while addressing domestic priorities, from Australia's resource sector needs to New Zealand's indigenous environmental stewardship values. The result is regulatory systems that maintain international credibility without sacrificing local relevance, as seen in Australia's phased climate disclosure roll-out and New Zealand's iwi consultation requirements for infrastructure projects (New Zealand Parliament, 2023).

Key Issues, Challenges, and Opportunities

Australia and New Zealand offer a distinctive mix of opportunities and challenges for corporates and investors, shaped by their advanced economies, strong institutional frameworks and deep integration with global markets. Yet beneath these commonalities lie important differences in their sectoral profiles, regulatory priorities, and exposure to external shocks. For businesses, success in these markets requires not only navigating their shared issues—such as climate risks and labor shortages—but also understanding how each country's unique context influences the way those issues are managed.

In Australia, the growing impact of climate change is a central concern for business leaders. The country's vulnerability to extreme weather, including bushfires, floods, and cyclones, has made climate risk assessments a standard component of strategic planning. The 2019–2020 "Black Summer" bushfires highlighted how climate events can disrupt operations, damage infrastructure, and destabilize supply chains. Rising temperatures and prolonged droughts continue to threaten agriculture and water security, while coastal communities face increasing risks from sea-level rise. Companies in sectors such as energy and insurance have been among the most proactive, using climate scenario analysis to integrate resilience into long-term strategies.

New Zealand contends with a different but equally serious climate profile. Earthquakes, flooding, and storms pose ongoing threats to infrastructure, while changes in rainfall patterns and droughts are reshaping agricultural output—an area central to its economy. Severe flooding in Napier in 2020 demonstrated the vulnerability of urban areas (New Zealand Civil Defence, 2021), while reduced snowfall in alpine regions has begun to affect winter tourism and hydroelectric power generation. These examples show how both countries are confronting climate risks of a similar scale but with distinct characteristics: Australia's challenges are sharpened by heat and bushfire exposure, whereas New Zealand faces a broader spectrum of natural hazards.

Labor market pressures compound these challenges. In Australia, the mining sector continues to grapple with a severe skills shortage, needing an estimated 24,400 new workers by 2026 but likely able to draw on only about 16,000. Competition from other industries offering higher wages and more flexible working conditions has driven companies to expand training and upskilling efforts, though retaining talent remains a persistent struggle. New Zealand faces similar workforce constraints in sectors such as agriculture and construction. Adding to this complexity are social concerns, with mental health issues increasingly affecting productivity and modern slavery risks in global supply chains introducing new ethical and legal dimensions for businesses operating in both countries.

Australia's Modern Slavery Act 2018 already requires large entities to report on modern slavery risks in their supply chains. The law is now under review, with proposals that would strengthen obligations and enforcement. Even before the consultation concludes, the direction of travel is clear: companies will be expected to show not only policies but also outcomes, credible grievance channels, and evidence of remediation where harm is found.

New Zealand is also seeing growing momentum on this front. Cross-party bills are under discussion, backed by investors and corporates calling for stronger safeguards against modern slavery. While the details remain uncertain, the debate reflects how supply chain due diligence is becoming part of the policy conversation across Australasia.

This matters beyond Oceania. The Act has become an early benchmark in APAC, and reform momentum is pushing companies toward higher accountability. Other jurisdictions, including South Korea and Thailand, are moving toward mandatory due diligence, which will slowly reset the regional baseline for supply chain transparency and risk management.

For corporates, due diligence needs to reach deeper tiers, with clear escalation, remediation, and board oversight. For investors, expectations rise for consistent and comparable disclosure to assess how companies manage human rights risks. Even if final details change, the signal is unmistakable: supply chain due diligence is becoming business-critical across the region.

Recent crises have also shaped corporate governance. In Australia, the 2017–2019 Banking Royal Commission exposed widespread misconduct, leading to A\$2.2 billion in customer refunds and catalyzing 76 reform recommendations (Royal Commission into Misconduct in the Banking, Superannuation, and Financial Services Industry, 2019). These reforms—ranging from stronger enforcement powers for ASIC under the Financial Sector Reform Act 2020 to stricter executive accountability measures—have begun to yield results, evidenced by a 43 percent decline in financial complaints to AFCA between 2019 and 2023 (Australian Financial Complaints Authority, 2023; Australian Securities and Investments Commission, 2023). New Zealand's regulatory overhaul followed the collapse of 63 finance companies between 2008 and 2012, costing investors NZ\$3.4 billion. The Financial Markets Conduct Act 2013 introduced adviser licensing and more rigorous disclosure standards, reducing investor losses by 78 percent in comparable stress periods between 2016 and 2020 (New Zealand Financial Markets Authority, 2023). These episodes underscore how tailored regulatory responses can restore confidence: Australia's reforms centered on its banking sector, while New Zealand addressed vulnerabilities in nonbank lending.

Board composition in both countries reflects higher levels of independence and gender diversity than many Asian peers, but gaps remain. Australia's two-strikes rule on executive remuneration has empowered shareholders to hold boards accountable (Australian Securities and Investments Commission, 2023), while New Zealand has made notable progress on gender diversity, though further cultural and ethnic representation is needed. Both countries continue to align corporate governance practices with international standards, ensuring strong oversight of listed companies.

Economic ties with China remain a defining feature of both markets. For Australia, China's demand for minerals, agricultural goods, and education services has been a major growth driver, though investment flows have softened due to geopolitical tensions and stricter regulatory screening. Opportunities remain particularly strong in green energy and technology, where Chinese demand for sustainable solutions aligns with Australia's capabilities. In New Zealand, the trade relationship is more diversified, encompassing dairy, forestry, tourism, and construction, and has benefited from the rising Chinese middle class's appetite for premium food products. The relative stability of this partnership has shielded New Zealand from some of the geopolitical headwinds affecting Australia, though both countries remain sensitive to shifts in global trade dynamics.

Beyond managing risks, there is significant room for growth across multiple sectors. In Australia, the global transition to net zero is opening new investment opportunities in renewable energy, critical minerals, and green hydrogen. The country's abundance of lithium, cobalt, and rare earths positions it as a potential leader in supplying essential inputs for clean technologies. Federal and state governments are also expanding incentives for large-scale renewable projects, presenting opportunities for international investors seeking exposure to energy transition assets.

In New Zealand, agriculture and food production stand out as high-value growth areas, especially in premium and sustainable food exports. The country's reputation for clean, high-quality products, combined with growing global demand for low-carbon food systems, is spurring innovation in regenerative farming and sustainable supply chains. Tourism—especially eco-tourism—is another promising area as borders fully reopen and travelers increasingly prioritize environmentally conscious destinations.

Technology and digital transformation present cross-market opportunities. Both countries are investing in digital infrastructure and innovation ecosystems, with strong potential for collaboration in fintech, agri-tech, and climate-tech. Paired with relatively transparent regulatory environments and deep trade linkages with the United States, European Union, and Asia, these sectors are likely to attract capital inflows in the coming years.

In sum, Australia and New Zealand share many of the same structural challenges—climate risks, labor shortages and the need for ongoing governance reform—but their responses reflect their distinct economic structures and policy priorities. For corporates and investors, this means that success in these markets depends on balancing the management of systemic risks with seizing opportunities in sustainability, innovation, and high-value trade.

Interview With Local Experts

Interview With Louise Davidson, CEO of ACSI

1. What challenges and opportunities do you foresee for Australian companies in aligning their practices with international sustainability standards?

   While challenges exist, a gap will form between Australian and global practices if companies don't align with international climate disclosure standards. ACSI's members, as international investors, value consistent and comparable disclosures, which are crucial in intense competition for global capital. These challenges also present opportunities. Mandatory climate reporting, aligned with international standards, is now in place in Australia. This should elevate the market, improve disclosures from lagging companies, and enhance transparency on climate strategies among Australia's largest firms.

2. How can investors engage with Australian corporations to address climate change and biodiversity loss, ensuring accountability and measurable outcomes?

   We know that concerted engagement and advocacy can have a real impact. ACSI and other investors have engaged with ASX 200 companies on climate risks for several years; by 2023, 70 percent had reported against the TCFD (TCFD, 2021). When climate disclosures became mandatory in 2024, most companies were prepared. Biodiversity risk should be tackled with the same level of urgency. Investors should engage, develop a biodiversity plan, set targets, conduct portfolio assessments, and contribute to policy development.

3. In light of the recent backlash against sustainability practices in the United States, how do you perceive its ripple effects on the Australian market and policy landscape?

   Australia's corporate governance landscape differs significantly from that of the United States. While some U.S. developments impact us, our market and policy settings are unlikely to change dramatically. Research conducted by ACSI last year shows that superannuation fund members strongly support the use of active ownership to ensure the long-term sustainability of companies and their profits.

Interview With Anne-Maree O'Connor, Head of Sustainable
Investment at the New Zealand Superannuation Fund

1. What unique opportunities do you believe New Zealand offers for foreign investors looking to contribute to sustainable development? New Zealand's 85 percent renewable electricity grid, strong wind and solar potential, and geothermal resources create prime opportunities. Nature-based industries, such as food production, forestry, and tourism, have a strong business case for aligning with sustainability goals, while investment in carbon credits forms the basis for the Emissions Trading Scheme. The Māori economy offers valuable indigenous partnerships in land-based industries, seafood, infrastructure, and renewable energy, emphasizing social and environmental impact.

2. How do you see corporate partnerships playing a role in advancing sustainability education in Australia and New Zealand? Corporate partnerships drive sustainability education by integrating financial expertise into policy, as seen in the Sustainable Finance Forum's 2030 Roadmap and Toitū Tahua, the center carrying this forward. Industry groups, such as the Institute of Directors NZ, the Institute of Finance Professionals NZ Inc., and the Responsible Investment Association Australasia, educate leaders across governance, finance, and investment, fostering collaboration across the APAC region to share best practices and accelerate progress.

3. What collaborative strategies do you think could further enhance sustainability efforts in the APAC region? Stronger communication of financial risks and opportunities is key, with investors, banks, and insurers aligning on sustainability themes. APAC leaders should showcase corporate exemplars, promote impact investment, and engage CEOs to drive change. Addressing systemic risks, such as climate change and modern slavery, through policy collaboration is essential. Cross-border cooperation among investors, producers, and consumers can also accelerate the adoption of sustainability.

Key Takeaways

- Australia's pragmatic, compliance-driven business culture contrasts with New Zealand's collaborative, Māori-influenced approach to sustainability leadership.
- Regulatory frameworks are sophisticated but diverge: Australia's multilayered system versus New Zealand's more streamlined FMA-led supervisory model.
- Both countries face significant climate and labor market pressures, though their risk profiles differ markedly across sectors.
- Australia's Modern Slavery Act review and NZ's legislative debates are likely to expand corporate due diligence obligations.
- Reforms following crises illustrate how regulatory change enhances market discipline, transparency, and accountability.
- Opportunities include renewables, green hydrogen, critical minerals, sustainable food, and indigenous partnerships.

Boardroom Briefing

Executives and investors should:

1. Adapt strategies to local context, balancing performance discipline in Australia with stakeholder engagement in New Zealand.
2. Monitor evolving regulatory requirements, including climate disclosure, stewardship standards, and assurance.
3. Prepare for tighter supply chain due diligence as modern slavery and human rights expectations rise.
4. Integrate climate, labor, and transition risks into scenario analysis and capital allocation decisions.
5. Leverage strengths in energy transition, agriculture, and eco-tourism to build resilient growth platforms.
6. Treat both markets as strategic testbeds for sustainability innovation and policy alignment.

CHAPTER 11

The Future of Sustainable Investment in Asia

[ASIAN CORPORATES] [U.S. EXECUTIVES] [INTERNATIONAL
EXECUTIVES] [INVESTORS] [REGULATORS]

This chapter is for Asian corporates, U.S. and international executives, global investors, and regulators who want to understand where Asia's sustainability journey is headed—and what it means for business strategy and governance worldwide.

In this book, I explore the challenges that corporations and investors face as they work to achieve sustainable returns in the Asia-Pacific region. The journey toward sustainability here is complex, shaped by distinct regulatory regimes, cultural contexts, and market conditions. Across the chapters, I share observations from key markets, reflecting on their unique landscapes and the evolving frameworks that influence corporate behavior. In my engagements with boards and regulators across Asia, I have seen firsthand how companies must balance global ESG expectations with deeply local realities—a task that often demands pragmatism and cultural sensitivity.

Achieving sustainable returns in Asia is not only about mitigating risks but also about positioning for growth. The transition to a low-carbon economy, the expansion of green finance and the rising consumer demand for sustainable products are opening new avenues for innovation. From the financial hubs of Hong Kong and Singapore to the rapidly industrializing economies of Southeast Asia, companies that successfully integrate ESG into their core strategies are more likely to navigate these contrasts effectively and emerge as leaders in the new economy.

It is essential to acknowledge that the sustainability landscape is constantly evolving. New regulations, technological advancements and shifting stakeholder expectations are reshaping the way businesses operate. As such, this book cannot provide a comprehensive or definitive guide to sustainability in the Asia-Pacific region. Instead, it aims to offer a foundational understanding of the status quo, equipping readers with the knowledge and tools they need to navigate this rapidly changing field.

In the realm of sustainability practice within the Asia-Pacific region, stakeholders must navigate both quick fixes and long-term challenges. While some areas show promising signs of rapid improvement, others require a more patient and strategic approach.

On the bright side, energy efficiency and the transition to renewable energy sources are areas where significant strides are already being made (International Energy Agency, 2023). Governments and companies across Asia are investing heavily in these initiatives, driven by both regulatory mandates and economic incentives. The adoption of advanced technologies and tighter regulations is also making the tracking of carbon emissions more feasible and accurate, facilitating better compliance and reporting.

Product safety has also improved significantly in recent years, driven by heightened public scrutiny and the amplifying effect of social media (McKinsey, 2023). Companies now recognize that safety failures can quickly escalate into reputational crises, prompting them to adopt more rigorous quality controls and proactive risk management measures. At the same time, the disclosure of sustainability-related information is set to advance markedly over the next five years, with the adoption of ISSB standards expected to enhance transparency and accountability. This shift will provide investors and stakeholders with more consistent, reliable data, reinforcing trust in corporate reporting (ISSB, 2023).

Shareholder engagement is undergoing a gradual transformation across Asian markets, driven by the adoption of stewardship codes and growing emphasis on collaborative investor action. This shift reflects increasing recognition that engaged responsible ownership, contributes to better risk management and decision making over time. However, the effectiveness varies significantly by market maturity and enforcement, with some emerging markets continuing to struggle with token compliance. The long-term potential for improved governance exists, but the challenge remains in ensuring that these engagements translate into tangible improvements in market standards and business resilience.

Not all sustainability challenges can be addressed swiftly. Biodiversity restoration, for instance, is a complex and time-consuming process. Rebuilding ecosystems that have been destroyed requires sustained effort and long-term commitment. Similarly, addressing physical climate risks necessitates a significant increase in awareness and understanding of their impact on businesses operating in the Asia-Pacific region. This is a critical first step before meaningful action can be taken.

The Just Transition (a process of shifting to a green economy in a way that is fair and inclusive for workers and communities affected) across the APAC region will unfold gradually, requiring a careful balance between climate imperatives and social stability. This is particularly relevant for developing Asian economies, where energy affordability, employment protection, and equitable access to solutions remain fundamental priorities. Labor rights improvements are also likely to be slow, given the varying levels of Labor Law implementation and union protection across different markets. Enhancing corporate governance standards is constrained by the prevalent consolidated ownership structures, which will take time to evolve. Cultural issues such as corruption and the diversity of leadership are deeply ingrained and require a fundamental shift in mindset and practices, which cannot be achieved overnight.

Stakeholders must manage their expectations and remain committed to continuous progress, understanding that the journey toward sustainability is a marathon, not a sprint. By recognizing both the quick wins and the enduring challenges, we can collectively work toward a more sustainable and resilient future for the Asia-Pacific region.

Corporations and investors have often underestimated Asia. However, this region's dynamic landscape deserves a more nuanced and forward-thinking approach. The Asia-Pacific region is not only a hub of economic growth but also a leader in innovation and sustainability practices. Companies that fail to recognize the strategic importance of Asia risk missing out on significant opportunities for growth and development.

The current backlash against ESG and sustainability practices in the United States is unlikely to significantly impact Asia for several reasons.

First, the region's commitment to sustainability is driven by a combination of regulatory mandates, market demands, and societal expectations that are largely independent of U.S. political dynamics. Asian markets are increasingly adopting international sustainability standards, which are enhancing transparency and accountability. This regulatory momentum is expected to continue, regardless of shifts in U.S. policy.

Moreover, the economic landscape in Asia is evolving in ways that reduce the region's reliance on the U.S. market. Intraregional trade within Asia has been growing steadily, driven by the deepening economic interdependence among Asian countries. This trend is supported by the rapid growth of manufacturing supply chains that span multiple Asian countries, fostering a strong network of trade in intermediate goods and final products. As a result, Asian economies are becoming more self-reliant and less susceptible to external shocks, including policy moves in the United States.

Furthermore, China's rise as a global economic powerhouse plays a significant role in this game. China's substantial investments in renewable energy, electric vehicles, and green technologies are setting new benchmarks for sustainability practice. The country's commitment to achieving carbon neutrality by 2060 is driving transformation in various sectors, making it a leader in the global energy transition (National Development and Reform Commission, 2021). This leadership position enhances China's influence within Asia and attracts international investors keen to align with sustainable growth trajectories.

Underestimating Asia's potential is a strategic oversight that corporates and investors can ill afford. The region's proactive stance on sustainability and economic dynamism presents unparalleled opportunities for growth and innovation. Only by recognizing and leveraging these trends can businesses achieve sustainable success in the region.

In this book, I have also highlighted several critical considerations for corporate executives and foreign investors operating in the Asia-Pacific region. Understanding these factors is essential for navigating Asia's complex and dynamic business environment.

Corporate executives should be particularly vigilant about a few key areas. First, the regulatory landscape in Asia is continually evolving. Keeping up with these changes to ensure that compliance is needed for maintaining a positive corporate reputation and avoiding legal pitfalls. Additionally, executives must be aware of the rapid technological advancements in the region. Adopting digital transformation and harnessing technologies such as AI, blockchain, and the IoT can offer a competitive advantage and enhance operational efficiencies.

Another important aspect is the cultural diversity across Asian markets. Executives are suggested to develop a deep understanding of local customs, business practices, and consumer preferences to tailor their strategies effectively. Building strong relationships with local stakeholders and adopting a culturally sensitive approach can significantly enhance business success. Furthermore, supply chain resilience is critical, given the region's susceptibility to natural disasters and geopolitical tensions. Diversifying supply chains and implementing thorough risk management practices can help mitigate potential disruptions to supply chains.

For foreign investors, there are several red flags to watch out for. Political instability and regulatory unpredictability in certain markets can pose significant risks. Conducting systematic due diligence and staying informed about the political climate is essential for making informed investment decisions. Moreover, issues related to IP protection and enforcement can be challenging in some Asian countries. Investors should ensure that they have powerful legal safeguards in place to protect their IP rights.

Another red flag is the potential for corruption and unethical business practices. Transparency International's Corruption Perceptions Index highlights varying levels of corruption across the region, and investors must exercise caution and conduct comprehensive background checks on potential partners to mitigate the risk of fraud (Transparency International, 2024). Moreover, understanding the local labor market and ensuring compliance with labor laws and standards is crucial to avoid reputational damage and legal issues.

In light of these risks, what should business leaders actually do? Three imperatives stand out:

1. **Respect differences.** Success requires humility and preparation. Understand local cultures and norms before acting; assumptions from home markets rarely apply directly in Asia.

2. **Think long term.** Behaviors tolerated in the past under opaque systems may no longer be acceptable. Companies must make decisions that will hold up under future scrutiny.

3. **Invest in relationships.** Networks remain one of the most valuable assets in Asia. Trust built with regulators, partners, and communities often determines long-term success as much as financial strength.

Taken together, these imperatives form the foundation for resilient and sustainable operations in Asia. Despite these challenges, the future remains positive for those who manage their business in Asia with caution and strategic foresight. The region's economic growth, technological innovation, and increasing consumer demand present supreme opportunities for businesses and investors. Companies can thrive in the Asia-Pacific region by staying informed, adapting to local conditions, and prioritizing sustainability and ethical practices. The key is to approach the market with a balanced perspective, recognizing both the opportunities and the risks, and to navigate them with diligence and prudence. The potential for success in Asia is immense, provided the right strategies and a commitment to responsible business practices are in place.

Supply chain expectations are also shifting. Australia's review of its Modern Slavery Act highlights how human rights and labor standards are moving from voluntary reporting to regulated due diligence. While the final reforms are still under consultation, the direction is clear: APAC markets are beginning to embed supply chain accountability into the baseline for corporate responsibility. This will ripple across the region, influencing investor expectations and shaping how companies manage global and regional supply networks.

Future Snapshot

Looking ahead, several trends are already reshaping Asia's sustainability journey. Based on recent developments, here are eight predictions that executives and investors should consider:

1. **China's global role will expand.** China is set to become the world's leader in sustainability, already demonstrating global influence through ambitious climate commitments, renewable energy investment, and rapid growth in green finance.

2. **Intra-Asian business will accelerate.** With technological breakthroughs and stronger regional integration, Asia will increasingly generate growth from within, becoming less dependent on U.S. and European markets.

3. **Climate risks will hit Asia hardest.** While climate change will disrupt businesses globally, Asia's exposure to extreme weather events and complex supply chains means that the region will face disproportionate challenges.

4. **Human rights pressures will intensify.** With labor rights, supply chain practices and community impacts coming under sharper scrutiny, companies that fail to anticipate these expectations risk major disruption.

5. **Governance will determine resilience.** As family-owned businesses undergo succession and ownership structures become more dispersed, strong governance will move from an aspiration to a necessity.

6. **Sustainability disclosure will become standardized.** The adoption of ISSB-aligned reporting and assurance frameworks will gradually reduce data fragmentation and improve cross-border comparability.

7. **Green finance will deepen regional capital markets.** Transition finance, sustainability-linked instruments, and blended finance structures will play a growing role in funding Asia's decarbonization and adaptation needs.

8. **Technology will reshape sustainability management.** AI, digital platforms, and advanced data systems will increasingly support emissions tracking, supply chain monitoring, and regulatory compliance.

Key Takeaways

- Asia's sustainability journey is defined by contrasts: quick wins in energy efficiency and disclosure, but long-term challenges in governance, biodiversity, and just transition.
- Climate risks will affect all markets, but Asia's exposure makes resilience planning critical.
- Supply chain due diligence is becoming a baseline expectation in Asia-Pacific, with reforms like Australia's Modern Slavery Act signaling a regional shift toward deeper accountability.
- Intraregional growth and China's global leadership position Asia as the engine of sustainability innovation.
- Executives must adapt to diverse cultural contexts, manage regulatory complexity and prioritize long-term thinking.
- Relationship-building and governance reforms remain the decisive factors for resilience and investment success.

Boardroom Briefing

Executives and investors should:

1. **Respect differences**: understanding local norms, cultures, and practices is not optional but a strategic necessity for building trust and avoiding missteps.
2. **Think long term**: decisions that once slipped under the radar will face future scrutiny.
3. **Build relationships**: networks with regulators, partners, and communities are vital for sustained success.
4. **Prepare for supply chain due diligence**: reforms like Australia's Modern Slavery Act are early signals that executives cannot ignore.
5. **Plan for climate risk**: stress-test supply chains and operations against Asia's unique vulnerabilities.
6. **Position for opportunity**: from renewables to digital innovation, Asia offers unmatched growth if approached with patience and prudence.

Final Reflections

I hope that this book serves as a valuable resource for Asian corporates implementing sustainability strategies, United States and other executives doing business in Asia, and investors who are looking to invest in this region. By understanding the challenges and opportunities that lie ahead, we can work toward a more sustainable and thriving future for the Asia Pacific region and beyond.

Looking back, what strikes me most is the extraordinary diversity of Asia's sustainability journey. There is no single model that fits all markets. Some countries move with speed, while others advance more gradually, driven by their own social, cultural, political, and institutional dynamics. Levels of regulatory capacity, market maturity, and social expectations differ, shaping how sustainability is interpreted and implemented in practice. And yet, there is a common thread: the recognition that sustainability is no longer optional, but central to long term resilience, competitiveness, and social legitimacy.

Finally, a word of perspective: Asia's role in global corporate governance will remain distinctive, but its influence is only growing. Asia will always remain diverse and divided, and that diversity is its strength. The best approach is to identify what works in each market through practice rather than assumption, through engagement rather than prescription, and through learning rather than short term imitation.

It is better to conserve resources at the outset and allow efforts to grow steadily, carefully monitored over time. Sustainability in Asia is a learning by doing process. Persistence to stay and wisdom to know what to keep and when to adapt are equally important. Corporate governance will continue to strengthen, perhaps not always at the pace international stakeholders expect, but progress is steady. Setbacks and periods of uncertainty will remain part of this journey. Blink, and the region may already have moved to the next level of development before you know it.

My hope is that this book sparks not only reflection but also action. If even a few of the ideas here help executives, investors, and regulators approach Asia with greater curiosity, respect, humility, and long-term commitment, then the purpose of this work will have been fulfilled.

Thank you for reading. Ciao.

References

3M Australia. 2023. *3M Australia Impact Report.* Sydney: 3M Australia.

ACFE Singapore. 2023. *Fraud Prevention Reports in ASEAN.* Singapore: ACFE.

Adani Group. 2016. *Annual Report 2015–16.* Ahmedabad: Adani Group.

Adani Group. Various years. *Corporate Filings and Project Reports.* Ahmedabad: Adani Group.

Advertising Standards Authority of Singapore. 2024. *Guidelines on ESG Marketing and Green Claims.* Singapore: ASAS.

Ahmed, S.R., A.P. Shah, Q.H. Tran, V. Khetan, S. Kang, A. Mehta, Y. Bao, and W. Wei. 2025. "Enhancing Retrieval for ESGLLM via ESG CID: A Dataset for Mapping GRI and ESRS." *arXiv.* https://arxiv.org/abs/2503.10674.

Alibaba. 2024. *2024 Environmental, Social, and Governance Report.* Hangzhou: Alibaba Group Holding Limited.

Apple Inc. 2023. *Press Release: Apple Achieves $10 Billion in Revenue in India.* Cupertino, CA: Apple.

Apple Inc. 2024. *Environmental Progress Report 2024.* Cupertino, CA: Apple.

Aricell. 2024. *Post-Accident Safety Investigation.* Hwaseong: Aricell.

ASEAN Secretariat. 2022. *Regional Comprehensive Economic Partnership (RCEP) Agreement Implementation Report.* Jakarta: ASEAN Secretariat.

ASEAN. 2023. *ASEAN Taxonomy for Sustainable Finance, Version 2.* Jakarta: Association of Southeast Asian Nations.

Asia Investor Group on Climate Change (AIGCC). Various years. *Climate Finance & Net Zero Advocacy Publications.*

Asian Corporate Governance Association (ACGA). 2018. *Awakening Governance* and *CG Watch Reports.* Hong Kong: ACGA.

Asian Corporate Governance Association (ACGA). 2023. *CG Watch 2023: Corporate Governance in Asia.* Hong Kong: ACGA.

Asian Development Bank (ADB). 2013. *Same Energy, More Power.* Manila: ADB.

Asian Development Bank (ADB). 2020. *Asian Development Outlook.* Manila: ADB.

Asian Development Bank (ADB). 2022. *Economic Impact of Coral Reef Degradation in Southeast Asia.* Manila: ADB.

Asian Development Bank (ADB). 2023. *Asian Development Outlook 2023.* Manila: ADB.

Asian Development Bank (ADB). 2023. *Asia-Pacific Climate Report 2024.* Manila: ADB.

Asian Development Bank (ADB). 2023. *The Economics of Climate Change in ASEAN: Regional Outlook 2023*. Manila: ADB.

Asian Development Bank. 2024. *Asia–Pacific Climate Report 2024: Catalyzing Finance and Policy Solutions*. Manila: Asian Development Bank.

Association of Certified Fraud Examiners Singapore Chapter. 2023. *Corporate Fraud Risk in ASEAN 2023*. Singapore: ACFE.

Atlassian. 2024. *2024 Impact Report*. Sydney: Atlassian.

Australian Council of Superannuation Investors. Various years. *ESG Reports and Policy Submissions*. Melbourne: ACSI.

Australian Financial Complaints Authority (AFCA). 2023. *Annual Review 2022-23*. Melbourne: AFCA.

Australian Government. 2023. *Privacy Act 1988: Amendments on Data Protection and Consumer Privacy*. Canberra: Attorney-General's Department.

Australian Securities and Investments Commission. 2023. *Corporations Act: Two-Strikes Rule on Executive Remuneration*. Canberra: ASIC.

Australian Securities and Investments Commission. 2023. *Sustainability Standards Adaptation Report*. Canberra: ASIC.

Australian Securities Exchange. Various years. *ASX Listing Rules and Governance Reports*. Sydney: ASX.

Australian Shareholders' Association (ASA). Various years. *Investor Advocacy Publications*. Sydney: ASA.

Australian Treasury. 2023. *Climate-Related Financial Disclosure Framework: Consultation Paper*. Canberra: Australian Treasury.

Australian Treasury. Various years. *Economic and Financial Policy Reports*. Canberra: Australian Treasury.

Bangko Sentral ng Pilipinas. 2025. *Fraud Prevention Framework Report*. Manila: BSP.

Bank Indonesia. Various years. *Monetary and Financial Stability Reports*. Jakarta: Bank Indonesia.

Bank Negara Malaysia (BNM). Various years. *Monetary Policy and Financial Sector Reports*. Kuala Lumpur: BNM.

Bank of Japan (BOJ). Various years. *Monetary Policy and Financial Stability Reports*. Tokyo: BOJ.

Bank of Korea (BOK). Various years. *Monetary Policy and Financial Stability Reports*. Seoul: BOK.

Barbican Advisory. 2025. *Insights on Fraud and Corruption in ASEAN*. London: Barbican Advisory.

Belt and Road Portal. 2023. *Belt and Road Initiative Project Overview 2013–2023*. Beijing: National Development and Reform Commission of China.

Bloomberg. 2021. *Coverage of Adani Group's Infrastructure Projects*.

Bloomberg. 2022. *Global Investor Reactions to BRSR Implementation*.

Bloomberg. 2023. "Chinese Factories Stockpile NVIDIA Chips Amid U.S. Export Ban." December.

Bloomberg. 2023. *India Market Valuations and Apple Revenue Reports.*

Bloomberg. 2023. *Market Reaction to Sime Darby Withhold Release Order.*

Bloomberg. 2023. *Sustainable Investing Trends and Market Outlook 2023.* Bloomberg LP.

Bloomberg. 2024. *Asia-Pacific Sustainable Finance Rankings.* Bloomberg Intelligence.

Bloomberg. 2024. *Equity Valuations in Indian Markets.*

BloombergNEF. 2023. *Solar Power Cost Competitiveness in Asia.* London: BloombergNEF.

Boston Consulting Group (BCG). 2022. *Climate Tech Revenue Opportunities by 2030.* Boston: BCG.

Business Environment Council (BEC). Various years. *Sustainability Insights and Programs.* Hong Kong: BEC.

Business Standard. 2025. *Court Upholds DRI Decision on Adani Over-Invoicing Allegations, Dismissing 2014 Case.* 2025. New Delhi: Business Standard.

BYD. 2024. *BYD 2024 Annual Report: Green Innovation and Global Expansion.* Shenzhen: BYD Company Limited.

ByteDance. 2024. *TikTok Shop ASEAN E-Commerce Report 2023.* Singapore: ByteDance.

Cabinet Office of Japan. 2022. *Report on the July 2021 Heavy Rainfall and Flooding in Kyushu.* Tokyo: Government of Japan.

CDP. 2024. *Mandatory Physical Climate Risk Disclosure in Asia.* London: CDP.

Central Bank of the Republic of China (Taiwan). Various years. *Monetary Policy and Banking Operations Reports.* Taipei: Central Bank.

Centre for Science and Environment. 2021. *Regulatory Challenges in India's Power Sector.* New Delhi: Down to Earth/CSE.

Ceres. 2023. *Investor Guide to Corporate Climate Transition Plans.* https://www.ceres.org/resources/reports/investor-guide-corporate-climate-transition-plans.

CFA Institute. 2024. "What Is ESG Investing?" CFA Institute. Published March 4, 2024.

CFA Institute. Various years. *ESG Guidance and Research Publications.*

Charoen Pokphand Group. 2024. *Sustainability Report 2024.* Bangkok: CP Group.

China Banking and Insurance Regulatory Commission (CBIRC). Various years. *Annual Reports.* Beijing: CBIRC.

China Securities Regulatory Commission (CSRC). 2024. *Mandatory ESG Disclosure Requirements for Listed Companies.* Beijing: CSRC.

China Securities Regulatory Commission (CSRC). Various years. *Annual Reports and Securities Market Updates.* Beijing: CSRC.

China Securities Regulatory Commission. 2016. "Notice on the Suspension of the Circuit Breaker Mechanism." January 7, 2016. Beijing: China Securities Regulatory Commission. http://www.csrc.gov.cn/pub/newsite/zjhxwfb/xwdd/201601/t20160107_290269.html.

China Securities Regulatory Commission. 2024. *Notice on Enhancing ESG Disclosure Requirements for Listed Companies.* Beijing: CSRC.

China SIF. Various years. *Sustainable Investment Forum Publications.* Beijing: China SIF.

Cisco Systems. 2024. *Net Zero Strategy and Community Program Report.* San Jose: Cisco Systems.

Climate Trace. 2023. *Emissions Data on Indonesian Nickel Smelters.*

Confederation of Indian Industry (CII). Various years. *Policy Advocacy Reports.* New Delhi: CII.

Conference Board. 2023. *CEO Survey on Geopolitical Risks.* New York: Conference Board.

Conservation International. 2023. *Biodiversity Hotspots Data.* Arlington, VA: Conservation International.

Corporate Action Japan. Various years. *Corporate Sustainability Reports and Advocacy Publications.* Tokyo: Corporate Action Japan.

Council of Financial Regulators (CFR). Various years. *Financial System Stability Coordination Reports.* Canberra: CFR.

Creary, Stephanie J., Mary-Hunter ("Mae") McDonnell, Sakshi Ghai, and Jared Scruggs. 2019. *When and Why Diversity Improves Your Board's Performance.* Harvard Business Review, March 27, 2019.

DBS Bank. 2024. *DBS Partners with GreenFi to Advance AI-Enabled Environmental Risk Management.* Singapore: DBS Press Release.

Deloitte. 2023. *IP Protection in Asia Study.* Singapore: Deloitte.

Department for Promotion of Industry and Internal Trade. 2022. *FDI Policy in Digital Media.* New Delhi: DPIIT.

Department of Energy (DOE), Philippines. 2023. *Geothermal Capacity Reports.* Manila: DOE.

Department of Public Enterprises (DPE). Various years. *Annual Reports.* New Delhi: DPE.

Down to Earth. 2025. *Environmental Reporting on Adani Projects.*

Economic Times. 2011. *Coverage of Kingfisher Airlines Expansion and Collapse.*

Economic Times. 2021. *Coverage of BRSR Launch and Early Adoption.*

Economic Times. 2022. *Adani Group's Corporate Growth and Investments.*

Ecosperity. 2023. *Climate Risk and Economic Impact Report for ASEAN.* Singapore: Ecosperity.

Elliott Management. 2023. *Investor Statement on Hyundai Elevator Acquisition.* New York: Elliott Management.

eMarketer. 2024. *Asia-Pacific E-commerce Trends Report.* New York: eMarketer.

Energy & Mines. 2023. *Indonesia's Nickel Sector: Illegal Operations and Environmental Costs.* London: Energy & Mines.

Energy & Mines. 2023. *Nickel Sector Sustainability Review.*

Energy Development Corporation. 2024. *Palayan Bayan Geothermal Project Updates.* Manila: EDC.

Energy Policy and Planning Office (EPPO), Thailand. 2024. *Thailand Renewable Energy Reports.* Bangkok: EPPO.

Energy Shift Institute. 2025. *Clean Energy Transition in Indonesia.* Jakarta: Energy Shift Institute.

Environmental Protection Administration (Taiwan). 2023. *Net-Zero Roadmap for Taiwan (2050 Goal).* Taipei: Climate Change Administration. https://www.cca.gov.tw/en/.

Ernst & Young. 2023. *Multinational Supplier Survey on Schedule Inflation.*

European Commission. 2022. *Competition and Markets Authority (CMA) Ruling on H&M's Conscious Collection.* Brussels: European Commission.

EY-Parthenon. 2024. *CEO Survey on Climate Adaptation.* London: EY-Parthenon.

EY-Parthenon. 2024. *CEO Survey on Coastal Asset Risks in Asia.* London: EY-Parthenon.

FAO. 2023. *Global Forest Resources Assessment 2023.* Rome: FAO.

Federation of Indian Chambers of Commerce and Industry. Various years. *Industry Advocacy and Policy Reports.* New Delhi: FICCI.

FICO. 2024. *Synthetic Identity Fraud in Asia: 2024 Outlook.* San Jose, CA: FICO.

Financial Markets Authority. 2021. *Climate-Related Disclosure Framework.* Wellington: FMA.

Financial Services Agency (FSA). 2021. *Japan's Corporate Governance Code.* Tokyo: FSA.

Financial Services Agency (FSA). 2024. *Action Program for Governance Reform and Cross-Shareholding Reduction.* Tokyo: FSA.

Financial Services Agency (FSA). Various years. *Corporate Governance and Stewardship Code Updates.* Tokyo: FSA.

Financial Services Commission (FSC). Various years. *Regulatory Updates and Capital Market Reports.* Seoul: FSC.

Financial Services Commission. 2022. *Regulatory Updates and Capital Market Reports.* Seoul: FSC.

Financial Services Commission. 2024. *Guidelines for Enhancing ESG Disclosures and Foreign Investment Incentives.* Seoul: Financial Services Commission.

Financial Supervisory Commission (FSC, Taiwan). Various years. *Regulatory Updates and Capital Market Reports.* Taipei: FSC.

Financial Supervisory Service (FSS). Various years. *Supervision and Inspection Reports.* Seoul: FSS.

Financial Times. 2021. *Hindustan Unilever Regional Strategy Report.*

Financial Times. 2023. *Adani Market Value Drops $150 Billion After Hindenburg Report.* March 2023.

Financial Times. 2023. *Coverage of Hindenburg Research Allegations Against Adani Group.*

Financial Times. 2023. *Global MBA Sustainability Index 2023.* London: Financial Times.

Financial Times. 2025. *EU Deforestation Regulation Market Impact.*

Fonterra. 2023. *New Zealand Dairy Industry Report.* Auckland: Fonterra.

Food and Agriculture Organisation (FAO). 2023. *Global Forest Resources Assessment: Asia Regional Report.* Rome: FAO.

FSC Taiwan. 2024. *Corporate Governance Roadmap 2023–2026.* Taipei: Financial Supervisory Commission.

G7 Impact Taskforce. 2021. *Time to Deliver: Mobilising Private Capital at Scale for People and Planet.* https://www.gsgii.org/reports/time-to-deliver-report-2021/.

Gartner. 2023. *Geopolitical Risk Management Report 2023.* Stamford, CT: Gartner.

General Motors (GM). 2005. *GM-SAIC Joint Venture Case Study.* Detroit: GM Corporate Archives.

Global Capacity Building Coalition. 2023. *Launch Report: Strengthening Climate Finance Capacity in Emerging Markets.* Dubai: GCCB.

Global Energy Monitor. 2024. *Global Renewable Energy Installations.* San Francisco: GEM.

Global Energy Monitor. 2024. *Global Solar Power Tracker and Global Wind Power Tracker.* San Francisco: Global Energy Monitor. https://globalenergymonitor.org.

Global Reporting Initiative (GRI). Various years. *Sustainability Reporting Standards.* https://www.globalreporting.org.

Google People Analytics. 2020. *APAC Leadership Academy Survey Results.* Mountain View, CA: Google.

Government of Australia. 2021. *Australia's Long-Term Emissions Reduction Plan.* Canberra: Department of Industry, Science, Energy and Resources. https://www.dcceew.gov.au/energy/climate-change/strategy/long-term-emissions-reduction-plan.

Government of China. 2021. *Working Guidance for Carbon Dioxide Peaking and Carbon Neutrality before 2060.* Beijing: State Council. https://www.gov.cn/zhengce/content/2021-10/24/content_5644613.htm.

Government of Hong Kong SAR. 2021. *Climate Action Plan 2050.* Hong Kong: Environment Bureau, Climate Change Secretariat. https://www.climateready.gov.hk/files/pdf/CAP2050_en.pdf.

Government of India. 2022. *India's Long-Term Low Emissions Development Strategy.* New Delhi: Ministry of Environment, Forest and Climate Change. https://www.moef.gov.in/.

Government of Indonesia. 2021. *Long-Term Strategy for Low Carbon and Climate Resilience 2050.* Jakarta: Ministry of Environment and Forestry. https://www.menlhk.go.id/.

Government of Indonesia. 2023. *Nusantara Capital City Development Master Plan.* Jakarta: Ministry of National Development Planning.

Government of Japan. 2020. *Green Growth Strategy towards 2050 Carbon Neutrality.* Tokyo: Ministry of Economy, Trade and Industry. https://www.meti.go.jp/english/press/2020/1225_001.html.

Government of Japan. 2023. *Japan's Green Growth Strategy towards 2050 Carbon Neutrality.* Tokyo: METI.

Government of Korea. 2020. *2050 Carbon Neutrality Roadmap.* Seoul: Ministry of Environment. https://www.me.go.kr/eng/.

Government of Korea. 2023. *Korea's 2050 Carbon Neutrality Roadmap.* Seoul: Ministry of Environment.

Government of Malaysia. 2021. *12th Malaysia Plan: Advancing Sustainability for 2050.* Putrajaya: Economic Planning Unit. https://www.epu.gov.my/en.

Government of New Zealand. 2019. *Climate Change Response (Zero Carbon) Amendment Act.* Wellington: Ministry for the Environment. https://www.legislation.govt.nz/.

Government of Singapore. 2022. *Singapore Green Plan 2030: Net-Zero Commitment Update.* Singapore: Ministry of Sustainability and the Environment. https://www.greenplan.gov.sg/.

Government of Thailand. 2021. *Nationally Determined Contribution and Long-Term Low Emissions Development Strategy.* Bangkok: Ministry of Natural Resources and Environment. https://www.mnre.go.th/.

Government of the Philippines. 2022. *Nationally Determined Contribution Implementation Plan.* Manila: Climate Change Commission. https://climate.gov.ph/.

Government of Vietnam. 2024. *Press Release: IPEF Partnership on Mekong Delta Supply Chain Resilience.* Hanoi: Ministry of Planning and Investment.

Grab Holdings. 2021. *Form F-1 Registration Statement: Grab Holdings Limited.* Washington, DC: U.S. Securities and Exchange Commission.

Green Plan 2030. 2021. *Singapore Green Plan Framework.* Singapore: Government of Singapore.

GreenFi. 2024. *Digitising ESG Risk Management for Financial Institutions: A Case Study with DBS.* Singapore: GreenFi Whitepaper.

Greenpeace Italy. 2023. *Shell Litigation Summary.* Rome: Greenpeace.

Harvard Business Review. 2021. "Cross-Cultural Management at Microsoft Singapore." *Harvard Business Review.*

Harvard Business Review. 2022. *Cultural Drivers of Overcommitment in Indian Business.*

Hindenburg Research. 2023. *Adani Group: How the World's Third Richest Man Is Pulling the Largest Con in Corporate History.* New York: Hindenburg Research.

HK Government. 2024. *Hong Kong Talent Engage Scheme 2024 Progress Report.* Hong Kong SAR Government.

HKEX. 2024. *Enhancements to ESG Reporting Framework: Consultation Conclusions.* Hong Kong Exchanges and Clearing Limited.

Hong Kong Exchanges and Clearing Limited. 2019. *Consultation Conclusions on Listing Regime for Companies from Emerging and Innovative Sectors.* Hong Kong: HKEX.

Hong Kong Exchanges and Clearing Limited. 2024. *Corporate Governance Code and Listing Rules Update.* Hong Kong: HKEX.

Hong Kong Insurance Authority. Various years. *Annual Reports.* Hong Kong: IA.

Hong Kong Mandatory Provident Fund Schemes Authority (MPFA). Various years. *Annual Reports.* Hong Kong: MPFA.

Hong Kong Monetary Authority (HKMA). Various years. *Monetary Policy and Banking Stability Reports.* Hong Kong: HKMA.

Hong Kong Privacy Commissioner for Personal Data. 2019. *Investigation Report on Cathay Pacific Airways Data Breach.* Hong Kong: PCPD.

Hong Kong Tourism Board. 2024. *Tourism Recovery and Outlook Report 2024.* Hong Kong: HKTB.

HSBC Holdings plc. 2024. *Leveraging AI for Enhanced Customer Lifecycle Management.* London: HSBC.

HSBC. 2023. *Mandatory ESG Training Program for Relationship Managers.* London: HSBC.

Hunt, Vivian, Sundiatu Dixon-Fyle, Celia Huber, María del Mar Martínez Márquez, Sara Prince, and Ashley Thomas. 2023. *Diversity Matters Even More: The Case for Holistic Impact.* McKinsey & Company, December 5, 2023, 52 pages.

Hurun Report. 2024. *Global Unicorn Index 2024.* Shanghai: Hurun Research Institute.

Hyundai Motor Group. 2021–2023. *Corporate Governance and Acquisition Reports.* Seoul: Hyundai.

IAASB. 2024. *ISSA 5000: Sustainability Assurance Standard.* New York: IAASB.

IFC. 2023. *Women in Leadership: Asia Snapshot.* Washington, DC: IFC.

IFRS Foundation. 2023. *IFRS Sustainability Disclosure Standards.* London: IFRS Foundation.

IKEA. 2024. *IKEA Sustainability Report 2024*. Delft: Inter IKEA Systems B.V.

Indian Ministry of Commerce. 2021. *Trade and Tariff Data*. New Delhi: Ministry of Commerce.

Indonesia Corruption Eradication Commission (KPK). 2023. *Annual Report on Corruption Cases*. Jakarta: KPK.

Indonesia Financial Services Authority (OJK). Various years. *Banking and Financial Sector Reports*. Jakarta: OJK.

Indonesia Stock Exchange (IDX). Various years. *Annual Reports and Market Updates*. Jakarta: IDX.

Institute of Directors NZ. Various years. *Governance Guidance and Education Reports*. Wellington: IoD NZ.

Institute of Finance Professionals New Zealand. Various years. *Industry Publications*. Wellington: INFINZ.

Insurance Commission, Philippines. Various years. *Insurance Sector Reports*. Manila: Insurance Commission.

Insurance Regulatory and Development Authority of India (IRDAI). Various years. *Annual Reports*. Hyderabad: IRDAI.

Intel Penang. 2021. *Payroll Transparency Program Progress Report 2019–2021*. Penang: Intel Corporation.

Intel. 2022. *Supplier Diversity Report*. Santa Clara: Intel.

Intergovernmental Panel on Climate Change. 2022. *Climate Change 2022: Impacts, Adaptation, and Vulnerability. Sixth Assessment Report*. Geneva: IPCC.

International Consortium of Investigative Journalists (ICIJ). 2022. *Pandora Papers: The Philippines Edition*. Washington, DC: ICIJ.

International Energy Agency (IEA). 2023. *World Energy Outlook 2023*. Paris: IEA.

International Energy Agency (IEA). 2024. *Clean Energy Transitions Programme Annual Report 2024*. Paris: IEA. https://iea.blob.core.windows.net/assets/d41d8925-4a85-4b1f-9d59-80d9c871d675/CETPAnnualReport2024.pdf.

International Energy Agency (IEA). 2024. *Southeast Asia Energy Outlook 2024*. Paris: IEA. https://www.iea.org/reports/southeast-asia-energy-outlook-2024.

International Energy Agency (IEA). 2024. *World Energy Outlook 2024*. Paris: IEA. https://www.iea.org/reports/world-energy-outlook-2024.

International Energy Agency Bioenergy. 2025. *Country Reports 2024 Update: Trends of Bioenergy in Member Countries*. IEA Bioenergy. https://www.ieabioenergy.com.

International Labour Organisation. 2023. *Asia Labour Market Trends 2023*. Geneva: ILO.

International Labour Organisation. 2023. *Productivity Trends in Asia's Financial Services Sector*. Geneva: ILO.

International Labour Organisation. 2024. *Labour Practices in Palm Oil Supply Chains*. Geneva: ILO.

International Monetary Fund (IMF). 2023. *World Economic Outlook, October 2023*. Washington, DC: IMF.

International Sustainability Standards Board (ISSB), IFRS. 2023. *IFRS S1 and S2: International Sustainability Disclosure Standards*. London: IFRS Foundation. https://www.ifrs.org/sustainability.

International Union for Conservation of Nature (IUCN). 2023. *Red List of Threatened Species – Asia Regional Summary*. Gland: IUCN.

Interpol. 2023. *Cybercrime Trends in Asia*. Lyon: Interpol.

Interpol. 2023. *Dark Web Economy and Healthcare Data Risks*. Lyon: Interpol.

Interpol. 2024. *ASEAN Cybercrime Threat Assessment*. Lyon: Interpol.

Interpol. 2024. *Emerging Cyberthreats in Asia 2024*. Lyon: Interpol.

Japan Exchange Group (JPX). Various years. *Market Operation and Compliance Reports*. Tokyo: JPX.

Japan Exchange Group, Tokyo Stock Exchange (TSE). Various years. *Listing and Governance Rules*. Tokyo: TSE.

Japan Government Pension Investment Fund (GPIF). 2023. *Annual Report 2023*. Tokyo: GPIF.

Japan Government Pension Investment Fund (GPIF). 2023. *Investment Stewardship Guidelines*. Tokyo: GPIF.

JD.com. 2025. *Audit Report on Dairy Supply Chains*. Beijing: JD.com.

Johnson & Johnson. 2023. *Corporate Governance and Ethics Framework*. New Brunswick: Johnson & Johnson.

Johnson & Johnson. Various years. *Corporate Governance Reports and Healthcare Market Partnerships*. New Brunswick: Johnson & Johnson.

Kaspersky. 2024. *ASEAN Cybercrime Loss Report*. Moscow: Kaspersky.

Kaspersky. 2024. *Cybercrime and Digital Security in Southeast Asia*. Moscow: Kaspersky Lab.

Keidanren (Japan Business Federation). Various years. *Policy Advocacy and Economic Reports*. Tokyo: Keidanren.

Keppel Offshore & Marine. 2022. *Bribery Case Resolution Statement*. Singapore: Keppel.

Kereta Cepat Indonesia China (KCIC). 2023. *Jakarta-Bandung High-Speed Rail Project Update*. Jakarta: KCIC.

KFC China. Various years. *Market Expansion and Localisation Reports*. Shanghai: Yum China.

Komisi Pemberantasan Korupsi (KPK). 2023. *Annual Report 2023: Major Case Updates*. Jakarta: KPK.

Korea Capital Market Institute (KCMI). Various years. *Policy and Market Research Reports*. Seoul: KCMI.

Korea Creative Content Agency. 2024. *2024 Korean Content Industry Export Report*. Seoul: KOCCA.

Korea Deposit Insurance Corporation (KDIC). Various years. *Annual Reports.* Seoul: KDIC.

Korea Exchange (KRX). 2023. *Market Statistics and Value Enhancement Disclosure Initiative.* Seoul: KRX.

Korea Exchange (KRX). 2024. *Value Enhancement Disclosure Initiative: Consultation Paper.* Seoul: Korea Exchange.

Korea Fair Trade Commission (KFTC). Various years. *Antitrust and Competition Policy Reports.* Seoul: KFTC.

Korea Institute of Corporate Governance and Sustainability (KCGS). Various years. *Corporate Governance and ESG Ratings Reports.* Seoul: KCGS.

Korea Listed Companies Association (KLCA). Various years. *Corporate Governance Advocacy Publications.* Seoul: KLCA.

Korea Securities Depository (KSD). Various years. *Custody and Settlement Reports.* Seoul: KSD.

Korean Government. 2024. *Press Briefing: Martial Law Declaration and Economic Response Measures.* Seoul: Government of the Republic of Korea.

Korean Statistical Information Service (KOSTAT). 2022. *Population Statistics.* Seoul: KOSTAT.

KPMG Australia. 2023. *Sustainability Reporting in the ASX200: From Aspirations to KPIs.* Sydney: KPMG Australia.

KPMG. 2022. *Industry Readiness for Scope 3 Emissions Reporting.*

Lancet. 2021. *Research on Medical Poverty in India.*

Lazard. 2023. *Shareholder Activism Data Report 2023.* New York: Lazard.

Leanwares JSC. 2025. *Sustainability Impact Report.* Hanoi: Leanwares JSC.

Levi Strauss. 2016. *Supply Chain Audit Program Results.* San Francisco: Levi Strauss & Co.

Lloyd's of London. 2024. *Lloyd's Risk Report 2024.* London: Lloyd's.

Mainwaring, Simon. 2025. *Why Sustainability Is Critical for Business Success in 2025 (And the Data to Prove It).* Forbes, January 30, 2025.

Malaysia Rail Link Sdn Bhd (MRLSB). 2023. *East Coast Rail Link Project Overview.* Kuala Lumpur: MRLSB.

Malaysian Anti-Corruption Commission (MACC). 2024. *Press Release: Investigation into Procurement Fraud at State-Owned Enterprise.* Putrajaya: MACC.

Marina Bay Sands. 2023. *Sustainability and Green Building Initiatives Report.* Singapore: Marina Bay Sands.

MAS (Monetary Authority of Singapore). 2023. *Green Finance Action Plan 2023 Progress Report.* Singapore: MAS.

McKinsey & Company. 2020. *Climate Risk and Response in Asia.* New York: McKinsey.

McKinsey & Company. 2021. *Study on Indian Executive Workload and Deadlines.*

McKinsey & Company. 2022. *Labour Practices Report.* New York: McKinsey.

McKinsey & Company. 2022. *Post-Pandemic Productivity Insights.* New York: McKinsey.

McKinsey & Company. 2022. *The Net-Zero Transition: What It Would Cost, What It Could Bring.* https://www.mckinsey.com/business-functions/sustainability/our-insights/the-net-zero-transition.

McKinsey & Company. 2023. *Asia's ESG Imperative: Leading the Transition.* McKinsey Sustainability Insights.

McKinsey & Company. 2023. *Corporate Governance and Social Impact Study.* New York: McKinsey.

McKinsey & Company. 2023. *Product Quality and Consumer Safety in Asia: The Social Media Effect.* New York: McKinsey & Company.

McKinsey & Company. 2024. *Digital Payments Fraud Monitoring Report.* New York: McKinsey.

McKinsey & Company. 2024. *Negotiation and Partner Retention Study in ASEAN.* New York: McKinsey.

McKinsey & Company. 2024. *Reimagining Climate Risk Disclosure in Asia.* McKinsey Global Institute.

McKinsey & Company. 2024. *Study on Indian CEO Stakeholder Engagement.*

McKinsey & Company. 2024. *Supply Chain Resilience and Geopolitical Risk Report.* New York: McKinsey.

McKinsey Global Institute. 2020. *Climate Risk and Response in Asia: Physical Hazards and Socioeconomic Impacts.* Singapore: McKinsey Global Institute. Published November 2020.

Medigen Vaccine Biologics Corporation. 2024. *Corporate Update: Global Vaccine Deployment and WHO Technology Partnership.* Taipei: Medigen.

Medigen Vaccine Biologics. Various years. *Biotech Innovation and COVID-19 Vaccine Reports.* Taipei: Medigen.

MIIT (Ministry of Industry and Information Technology). 2024. *China's Digital Economy Development Report 2024.* Beijing: MIIT.

Ministry for the Environment (New Zealand). 2024. *Second Emissions Reduction Plan (2026–2030).* Wellington: Ministry for the Environment. https://environment.govt.nz/.

Ministry of Business, Innovation and Employment (MBIE). 2023. *Integrating Te Ao Māori in Agribusiness Sustainability Practices.* Wellington: MBIE.

Ministry of Business, Innovation, and Employment. 2024. *Agribusiness Alignment with Te Ao Māori Principles.* Wellington: MBIE.

Ministry of Economy and Finance (MOEF). 2020. *Korean New Deal Comprehensive Plan.* Seoul: MOEF.

Ministry of Economy, Trade and Industry (METI). 2020. *Japan's Stewardship Code.* Tokyo: METI.

Ministry of Economy, Trade and Industry (METI). 2023. *GX Basic Policy: Japan's Green Transformation Roadmap.* Tokyo: METI.

Ministry of Economy, Trade and Industry (METI). Various years. *Green Transformation (GX) and Industrial Policy Reports.* Tokyo: METI.

Ministry of Employment and Labour, Republic of Korea. 2024. *Aricell Factory Fire Investigation Report.* Seoul: MOEL.

Ministry of Finance (MoF). Various years. *Economic and Financial Policy Reports.* New Delhi: MoF.

Ministry of Finance (MOF). Various years. *Financial Market and Regulatory Reports.* Tokyo: MOF.

Ministry of Justice (MOJ). Various years. *Legal and Corporate Regulatory Framework Reports.* Tokyo: MOJ.

Ministry of Justice (Republic of Korea). 2024. *Amendments to the Commercial Code on Intra-Group Transactions.* Seoul: Ministry of Justice.

Ministry of Manpower (Singapore). 2023. *Gender Pay Gap Data.* Singapore: MOM.

Ministry of Manpower (Singapore). 2024. *Workforce Participation Statistics.* Singapore: MOM.

Ministry of Trade, Industry and Energy. 2024. *South Korea's Green Hydrogen Investment Roadmap.* Seoul: MOTIE.

Minority Shareholders Watch Group (MSWG). Various years. *Shareholder Activism Reports.* Kuala Lumpur: MSWG.

Mint. 2013. *Coverage of Kingfisher Airlines Bankruptcy.*

MOEA (Ministry of Economic Affairs, Taiwan). 2024. *Taiwan Renewable Energy Investment Outlook 2024.* Taipei: MOEA.

Monetary Authority of Singapore (MAS). Various years. *Financial Stability and Market Supervision Reports.* Singapore: MAS.

Mongabay. 2022. *Deforestation Impacts of Nickel Mining in Indonesia.*

Morgan Stanley. 2023. *India E-Commerce Market Forecast to 2030.* Mumbai: Morgan Stanley Institutional Securities.

Morgan Stanley. 2023. *India's E-Commerce Market Forecast 2030.* New York: Morgan Stanley.

Morgan Stanley. 2023. *Indian Online Retail Market Projections.*

MSCI Inc. 2025. *Financial Relevance of Sustainability Risks and Opportunities.* New York: MSCI Inc.

MSCI. 2023. *Climate Risk and Corporate Adaptation Budgets in Asia.* New York: MSCI.

MSCI. 2023. *ESG Fund Performance Study.* New York: MSCI.

MSCI. 2023. *MSCI ESG Leaders Performance Report 2023.* New York: MSCI.

Mumbai High Court. 2022. *Commercial Case Resolution Data.* Mumbai: Mumbai High Court.

National Company Law Tribunal (NCLT). 2024. *Insolvency and Bankruptcy Resolution Timelines.* New Delhi: NCLT.

National Development and Reform Commission (NDRC). 2021. *China's 2060 Carbon Neutrality Roadmap.* Beijing: NDRC.

National Development and Reform Commission. 2024. *Implementation Plan for Advancing the Dual-Circulation Development Strategy.* Beijing: NDRC.

National Pension Service (NPS). Various years. *Corporate Governance and ESG Reports.* Jeonju: NPS.

Netflix. 2018. *Press Release: Netflix to Build Special Effects Studio in Seoul to Support Korean Original Content.* Los Gatos, CA: Netflix.

New Belgium Brewing Company. 2023. *Sustainability and Environmental Impact Report.* Fort Collins, CO: New Belgium Brewing Company.

New Zealand Civil Defence. 2021. *Napier Flood Response and Recovery Report.* Wellington: Ministry of Civil Defence & Emergency Management.

New Zealand Dairy Industry Association. 2023. *Dairy Sector Capital Structure and Innovation Review 2023.* Wellington: NZDIA.

New Zealand Financial Markets Authority (FMA). 2022. *Stewardship Code for Institutional Investors.* Wellington: FMA.

New Zealand Financial Markets Authority (FMA). 2023. *Review of the Financial Markets Conduct Act 2013: Investor Outcomes.* Wellington: FMA.

New Zealand Government. 2023. *Climate Adaptation Act 2023.* Wellington: Ministry for the Environment.

New Zealand Parliament. 2023. *Climate Disclosure and Iwi Consultation Requirements Report.* Wellington: New Zealand Parliament.

New Zealand Shareholders' Association (NZSA). Various years. *Investor Advocacy and Corporate Governance Publications.* Auckland: NZSA.

New Zealand Stock Exchange. Various years. *NZX Listing Rules and Governance Reports.* Wellington: NZX.

Nike Inc. 2024. *Nike Impact Report 2024: Move to Zero and Community Engagement.* Beaverton, OR: Nike.

Nikkei. 2023. "Japanese Trading Houses Handle 41% of ASEAN Commodity Flows." *Nikkei Asia.*

Nikkei. 2024. *Oasis Wins Canon Concessions on Cross-Shareholdings.* Tokyo: Nikkei Asia.

Nomura Research Institute. Various years. *Corporate Governance and ESG Research Publications.* Tokyo: Nomura Research Institute.

NVIDIA Corporation. 2023. *Sustainability Report.* Santa Clara: NVIDIA.

OECD. 2023. *Regional ESG Governance Trends.* Paris: OECD.

OECD. 2024. *OECD Employment Outlook 2024.* Paris: Organisation for Economic Co-operation and Development.

Office of Insurance Commission (OIC), Thailand. Various years. *Insurance Market Reports.* Bangkok: OIC.

Office of the United States Trade Representative. 2024. *2024 Report to Congress on U.S.–China Economic and Trade Relations.* Washington, DC: USTR.

Office of the United States Trade Representative. 2024. *2024 Report on the U.S.–Korea Economic and Technology Partnership.* Washington, DC: USTR.

Ola Electric. 2023. *Corporate Announcement: Electrification of 10,000 Rickshaws.* Bangalore: Ola Electric.

Otoritas Jasa Keuangan (OJK). 2024. *Financial Sector Cybersecurity and Fraud Trends Report.* Jakarta: OJK.

Oxfam. 2023. *India Inequality Report.*

Panasonic Corporation. 2024. *Panasonic Group Sustainability Data Book 2024.* Osaka: Panasonic.

Patagonia. 2023. *Chemical Management and Supply Chain Policy.* Ventura: Patagonia.

Pension Fund Regulatory and Development Authority (PFRDA). Various years. *Annual Reports.* New Delhi: PFRDA.

People's Bank of China (PBOC). Various years. *Monetary Policy and Green Finance Reports.* Beijing: PBOC.

People's Bank of China. 2024. *Green Finance Development Report 2023–2025.* Beijing: PBOC.

People's Republic of China, National Development and Reform Commission. 2019. *Outline Development Plan for the Guangdong-Hong Kong-Macao Greater Bay Area.* Beijing: NDRC.

Pfizer. Various years. *Joint Ventures and Market Development Reports.* New York: Pfizer.

Philippine Stock Exchange (PSE). Various years. *Market Reports and Updates.* Manila: PSE.

Press Information Bureau, Government of India. 2024. *Digital Payments and Connectivity Report: March 2024 Update.* New Delhi: Government of India.

Principles for Responsible Investment (PRI). Various years. *Responsible Investment Resources.*

Privacy Act Amendments. 2023. *Australia's GDPR-Style Privacy Reforms.* Canberra: Australian Government.

Procter & Gamble (P&G). Various years. *Market Strategy and HR Development Reports.* Tokyo: P&G Japan.

Procter & Gamble Japan. 2005. *Marketing Transformation in Japan: The Camay Case Study.* Tokyo: P&G Japan.

PUB (Singapore). 2021. *Water Tariff Reform Impact Study.* Singapore: PUB.

Qualcomm. 2023. *Shanghai R&D Hub Report.* San Diego: Qualcomm.

Ramsar Convention Secretariat. 2022. *Global Wetlands Status Report*. Gland: Ramsar Secretariat.

Reliance Industries Limited. 2023. *Annual Report 2022–23*. Mumbai: Reliance Industries Limited.

Reserve Bank of Australia (RBA). Various years. *Financial Stability and Prudential Oversight Reports*. Sydney: RBA.

Reserve Bank of India (RBI). 2022. *Wealth Distribution Report*. Mumbai: RBI.

Reserve Bank of India (RBI). 2023. *Report on Digital Payments 2022–23*. Mumbai: RBI.

Reserve Bank of India (RBI). 2023. *UPI Transaction Data Report*. Mumbai: RBI.

Reserve Bank of India / National Payments Corporation of India. 2025. *Annual Digital Payments Report 2024–25*. Mumbai: RBI.

Reserve Bank of New Zealand (RBNZ). Various years. *Prudential and Financial System Reports*. Wellington: RBNZ.

Responsible Investment Association Australasia. Various years. *Sustainable Finance Publications*. Sydney: RIAA.

Reuters. 2020. *Volkswagen Dieselgate Financial Penalties*.

Reuters. 2023. "China-Philippines Tensions Escalate in the South China Sea." August.

Reuters. 2023. "DWS, Goldman Sachs, and BNY Mellon Fined for Misleading ESG Claims." June 2023.

Reuters. 2023. *India Markets Regulator to Tell Court Adani Inquiry Began in 2014 But Hit Dead End*. October 5, 2023. Bengaluru: Reuters.

Reuters. 2024. "Lloyd's of London Risk Report Highlights South China Sea Shipping Premiums." August 2024.

Reuters. 2024. "Southeast Asia Needs to Boost Investments Five-Fold by 2035 to Meet Climate Goals, IEA Says." *Reuters*, October 21, 2024. https://www.reuters.com/sustainability/southeast-asia-needs-boost-investments-five-fold-by-2035-meet-climate-goals-iea-2024-10-21.

Reuters. 2024. *Dieselgate Criminal Case Updates*.

Reuters. 2024. *Palm Oil Labour Investigations*.

Royal Commission into Misconduct in the Banking, Superannuation and Financial Services Industry. 2019. *Final Report*. Canberra: Australian Government.

Royal Dutch Shell. 2023. *Greenpeace Italy v. Shell Court Filings*. The Hague: Shell.

S&P Global Inc. 2025. *Corporate Sustainability Assessment and Sustainability Benchmarking Services*. New York: S&P Global Inc.

Salesforce. 2023. *Philanthropic Impact Report*. San Francisco: Salesforce.

Samsung Electronics. Various years. *Corporate Reports and Market Disclosures*. Seoul: Samsung.

Schneider Electric. 2024. *Zero Carbon Project Reporting*. Paris: Schneider Electric.

Securities and Exchange Board of India (SEBI). 2019. *Order in the Matter of Satyam Computer Services Limited.* Mumbai: SEBI.

Securities and Exchange Board of India (SEBI). 2023. *Enforcement Action in the Jane Street Insider Trading Case.* Mumbai: SEBI.

Securities and Exchange Board of India (SEBI). 2023. *FPI Rules and Market Updates.* Mumbai: SEBI.

Securities and Exchange Board of India (SEBI). 2024. *Report on Adani Group Promoter Holdings.* Mumbai: SEBI.

Securities and Exchange Board of India (SEBI). Various years. *Sustainability Disclosure Regulations (BRSR).* Mumbai: SEBI.

Securities and Exchange Commission (SEC), Philippines. Various years. *Annual Reports and Regulatory Updates.* Manila: SEC.

Securities and Exchange Commission (SEC), Thailand. Various years. *Securities Market and Derivatives Reports.* Bangkok: SEC.

Securities and Exchange Surveillance Commission (SESC). Various years. *Market Surveillance and Enforcement Reports.* Tokyo: SESC.

Securities and Futures Commission (SFC). Various years. *Annual Reports and Market Supervision Updates.* Hong Kong: SFC.

Securities Commission Malaysia (SC). Various years. *Capital Market Reports.* Kuala Lumpur: SC.

Seventh Generation. 2023. *Sustainability Report.* Burlington, VT: Seventh Generation.

Shanghai Automotive Industry Corporation (SAIC). 2005. *GM-SAIC Partnership Retrospective.* Shanghai: SAIC.

Sime Darby. 2024. *Sustainability Report.* Kuala Lumpur: Sime Darby.

Singapore Exchange (SGX) Regulation. 2023. *Mandatory Climate Reporting Framework.* Singapore: SGX.

Singapore Exchange (SGX). 2023. *ESG Training Programs for Listed Companies.* Singapore: SGX.

Singapore Police Force. 2023. *Digital Payment Fraud Report.* Singapore: SPF.

Singapore Police Force. 2024. *Annual Crime Brief 2023.* Singapore: Singapore Police Force.

SK Hynix. Various years. *Annual Reports and Industry Disclosures.* Icheon: SK Hynix.

South China Morning Post. 2024. "Hong Kong Sees Surge in Finance and ESG Professionals Relocating to Singapore." *South China Morning Post*, March 10, 2024.

Starbucks Coffee Japan, Ltd. 2024. *Starbucks Japan Sustainability and Localisation Report 2024.* Tokyo: Starbucks Japan.

State-owned Assets Supervision and Administration Commission (SASAC). Various years. *Annual Reports.* Beijing: SASAC.

State-owned Assets Supervision and Administration Commission. 2024. *Guidelines for Decarbonisation in State-Owned Enterprises.* Beijing: SASAC.

Statista. 2023. *Demographic and Industry Data 2023.* Hamburg: Statista.

Statista. 2024. *Industry Data on Global Smartphone Production 2022–2023.* Hamburg: Statista.

Statista. 2024. *Industry Data on Global Vehicle Markets 2024.* Hamburg: Statista.

Statistics Bureau of Japan. 2023. *Population Projections for Japan: 2023–2040.* Tokyo: Ministry of Internal Affairs and Communications.

Statistics India. 2024. *Internet Subscriber and Connectivity Data, March 2024.* New Delhi: Ministry of Communications.

Statistics Korea. 2024. *Population and Demographic Statistics.* Seoul: Statistics Korea.

Statistics Korea. 2024. *Population Projections for Korea 2023–2050.* Daejeon: Statistics Korea.

Stock Exchange of Thailand (SET). Various years. *Market and Governance Reports.* Bangkok: SET.

Straits Times. 2024. "Singapore Traders Use RCEP Tariff Differentials to Bypass Sanctions." January.

Suntory Holdings Limited. 2024. *Suntory Group Integrated Report 2024.* Tokyo: Suntory.

Supreme People's Procuratorate (China). 2025. *Annual Report on Commercial Bribery Cases.* Beijing: Supreme People's Procuratorate.

SustainAbility Institute by ERM. 2023. *The State of ESG Disclosure in Asia.* ERM Group.

Sustainable Finance Forum. 2020. *2030 Roadmap for Sustainable Finance in New Zealand.* Wellington: Sustainable Finance Forum.

Swiggy. 2023. *Corporate Announcement: Launch of 19-Minute Delivery Service.* Bangalore: Swiggy.

SynTao. Various years. *Corporate Sustainability Research and Reports.* Beijing: SynTao.

Taipei Times. 2024. "Taiwan Faces Brain Drain in ESG and Tech Sectors." *Taipei Times*, February 25, 2024.

Taishin Financial Holdings. Various years. *Investor Relations and Sustainability Reports.* Taipei: Taishin.

Taiwan Semiconductor Manufacturing Company (TSMC). 2023. *Q4 2023 Earnings Call Transcript.* Hsinchu: TSMC.

Taiwan Semiconductor Manufacturing Company (TSMC). 2024. *TSMC Sustainability Report 2024.* Hsinchu: TSMC.

Taiwan Semiconductor Manufacturing Company (TSMC). 2025. *Shareholder Meeting Transcript.* Hsinchu: TSMC.

Taiwan Semiconductor Manufacturing Company (TSMC). Various years. *Corporate Sustainability Reports.* Hsinchu: TSMC.

Taiwan Stock Exchange (TWSE). Various years. *Market Operations and Listing Rules*. Taipei: TWSE.

Task Force on Climate-Related Financial Disclosures (TCFD). 2021. *Guidance on Climate-Related Financial Disclosures*. Basel: TCFD.

Task Force on Climate-related Financial Disclosures (TCFD). 2021. *Guidance on Metrics, Targets, and Transition Plans*. https://www.fsb-tcfd.org.

Tencent. 2024. *Social Responsibility Initiatives*. Shenzhen: Tencent.

Tesla. 2023. *Renewable Energy and Solar Products Report*. Austin: Tesla.

Texas A&M University. 2023. *South Korea Has the Lowest Fertility Rate in the World—and That Doesn't Bode Well for Its Economy*. College of Arts & Sciences, June 2023.

Thailand Board of Investment (BOI). 2023. *Eastern Economic Corridor Smart City Initiative Report*. Bangkok: BOI.

The Conference Board. 2025. *C-Suite Outlook 2025: Seizing the Future*. Report published January 12, 2025. New York: The Conference Board.

The Hindu BusinessLine. 2023. "Xiaomi's $1 Billion Investment in Tamil Nadu Assembly Lines." March.

The Lancet. 2022. *Catastrophic Health Expenditure and Poverty in India: An Analysis of National Health Accounts*. London: The Lancet.

Toitū Tahua: Centre for Sustainable Finance. Various years. *Sustainable Finance Reports and Guidance*. Wellington: Toitū Tahua.

Tokyo Metropolitan Government. 2022. *Ordinance on Mandatory Installation of Rooftop Solar Panels for New Buildings by 2025*. Tokyo: Tokyo Metropolitan Government.

Tokyo Stock Exchange. 2021. *Japan's Corporate Governance Code: Seeking Sustainable Corporate Growth and Increased Corporate Value over the Mid- to Long-Term*. Revised June 2021. Tokyo: Tokyo Stock Exchange. https://www.jpx.co.jp/equities/listing/cg/index.html

Tokyo Stock Exchange. 2023. *Prime Market Listing Requirements and Governance Reform Update*. Tokyo: TSE.

Tokyoesque. 2024. *The Impact of Japan's Ageing Population on the Business Landscape*. Tokyoesque, March 15, 2024. https://tokyoesque.com/the-impact-of-japans-ageing-population-on-the-business-landscape/.

Toyota Motor Corporation. 2021. *Press Release: Temporary Suspension of Kyushu Production Facilities Following July 2021 Flooding*. Toyota City: Toyota.

Toyota Motor Corporation. 2024. *Toyota Sustainability Data Book 2024*. Toyota City: Toyota.

Toyota Motor Corporation. Various years. *Corporate Governance and Sustainability Reports*. Toyota City: Toyota.

Transparency International. 2023. *Corruption Perceptions Index*. Berlin: Transparency International.

Transparency International. 2024. *Corruption Perceptions Index 2024*. Berlin: Transparency International.

Transparency International. 2024. *Corruption Perceptions Index*. Berlin: Transparency International.

TrendForce. 2023. *Global Smartphone and Semiconductor Market Share Report 2023*. Taipei: TrendForce.

TSMC. 2024. *TSMC Sustainability Report 2024*. Hsinchu: Taiwan Semiconductor Manufacturing Company.

U.S. Chamber of Commerce. 2024. *Intellectual Property Index 2024*. Washington, DC: U.S. Chamber of Commerce.

U.S. Department of Commerce. 2023. *Export Control Updates on Advanced AI Chips*. Washington, DC: Department of Commerce.

U.S. Department of Commerce. 2023. *Indo-Pacific Economic Framework for Prosperity (IPEF): Clean Economy Pillar*. Washington, DC: U.S. Department of Commerce.

U.S. Environmental Protection Agency. 2015. *Volkswagen Dieselgate Settlement Documents*. Washington, DC: EPA.

U.S. Environmental Protection Agency. 2017. *Volkswagen Dieselgate Consent Decree*. Washington, DC: EPA.

U.S. Geological Survey. 2023. *Global EV Battery Nickel Supply Report*. Reston, VA: USGS.

U.S. Securities and Exchange Commission. 2023. *Enforcement Actions on ESG Disclosures and Fund Marketing*. Washington, DC: SEC.

U.S. Securities and Exchange Commission. 2024. *Financial Institutions ESG Marketing Violations*. Washington, DC: SEC.

U.S. Securities and Exchange Commission. 2024. *Keurig Recycling Settlement Report*. Washington, DC: SEC.

UBS. 2025. *Global Wealth Report 2025*. Zurich: UBS Group AG.

UK Competition and Markets Authority (CMA). 2022. *H&M Conscious Collection Ruling*. London: CMA.

UN Women. 2023. *Gender Equality in Corporate Leadership: Asia-Pacific Snapshot*. UN Women Regional Office for Asia and the Pacific.

UNCTAD. 2024. *World Investment Report 2024: Investing in Sustainable Industries*. Geneva: United Nations Conference on Trade and Development.

UNEP FI. 2022. *A Legal Framework for Impact: Sustainability in Investment Decision-Making*. United Nations Environment Programme Finance Initiative.

UNESCO. 2023. *Science Report 2023*. Paris: UNESCO.

Unilever Southeast Asia. 2023. *Sustainability Report 2023*. Jakarta: Unilever.

Unilever. 2024. *Sustainability Plan Progress Report*. London: Unilever.

United Nations Environment Programme (UNEP). 2021. "Scientists Warn of Dangerous Decline in Asia-Pacific's Biodiversity." *UNEP News and Stories,* May 18, 2021. https://www.unep.org/news-and-stories/story/scientists-warn-dangerous-decline-asia-pacifics-biodiversity.

United Nations. 2022. *World Population Prospects 2022.* New York: UN.

ValueAct Capital. 2024. *Engagement Report: Seven & i Holdings Corporate Strategy Review.* San Francisco: ValueAct.

Verizon. 2024. *Renewable Energy Goals and ESG Plan.* New York: Verizon.

Vietnam Customs. 2024. *Trade Statistics Report April 2024.* Hanoi: Vietnam Customs.

Vietnam Food Administration. 2024. *Blockchain Milk Traceability Study.* Hanoi: VFA.

Vietnam Plus. 2025. *Sustainable Manufacturing in Vietnam: Case Studies in the Textile Sector.* Hanoi: Vietnam News Agency.

Visionify. 2025. *AI-Powered Workplace Safety Solutions.* Singapore: Visionify.

Walmart Inc. 2023. *Investor Presentation: Flipkart Acquisition and E-Commerce Strategy in India.* Bentonville, AR: Walmart.

WeLab. Various years. *Digital Banking and Fintech Reports.* Hong Kong: WeLab.

World Bank. 2016. *Peatland Fires Impact.* Washington, DC: World Bank.

World Bank. 2020. *Ease of Doing Business Report.* Washington, DC: World Bank.

World Bank. 2022. *Container Shipping Cost Report.* Washington, DC: World Bank.

World Bank. 2022. *Geothermal Development Cost and Permitting Challenges in the Philippines.* Washington, DC: World Bank.

World Bank. 2022. *Global Container Shipping Cost Report.* Washington, DC: World Bank.

World Bank. 2022. *Resource Management and Climate Reports.* Washington, DC: World Bank.

World Bank. 2022. *Wealth and Informal Economy Data.* Washington, DC: World Bank.

World Bank. 2022. *World Development Report 2022: Finance for an Equitable Recovery.* Washington, DC: World Bank. https://www.worldbank.org.

World Bank. 2023. *ASEAN Energy Transition and Business Environment Report.* Washington, DC: World Bank.

World Bank. 2023. *Global Wealth Databook 2023.* Washington, DC: World Bank.

World Bank. 2023. *India Income and Business Environment Report.* Washington, DC: World Bank.

World Bank. 2023. *Vietnam Solar Development Progress Report.* Washington, DC: World Bank.

World Bank. 2024. *ASEAN Labour Market Outlook 2024: Workforce Trends and Policy Challenges*. Washington, DC: World Bank.

World Bank. 2024. *Infrastructure and Regulatory Approval Report*. Washington, DC: World Bank.

World Economic Forum. 2023. *ASEAN Supply Chain Council: Early-Warning Systems Report*. Geneva: WEF.

World Economic Forum. 2023. *Global Gender Gap Report 2023*. Geneva: World EconomicForum.https://www.weforum.org/reports/global-gender-gap-report-2023.

World Federation of Exchanges (WFE). 2023. *ESG Reporting Guidelines*. London: WFE.

World Health Organisation (WHO). 2024. *WHO Technology Transfer Hub for Vaccine Development*. Geneva: WHO.

World Meteorological Organisation (WMO). 2024. *State of the Climate in Asia 2024*. Geneva: WMO.

World Meteorological Organisation (WMO). 2023. *State of the Climate in Asia 2023*. Geneva: WMO.

World Wide Fund for Nature (WWF). 2022. *Mekong Sediment Crisis Report*. Gland: WWF.

Yahoo Finance. 2024. "China's Regulators Face Talent Loss amid Structural Reforms." *Yahoo Finance*, April 12, 2024.

YTL Power International. 2024. *Sustainability and Energy Transition Reports*. Kuala Lumpur: YTL.

About the Author

Nana Li is Head of Sustainability & Stewardship, Asia-Pacific at Impax Asset Management, where she leads sustainability and ESG research, stewardship strategy and engagement, and policy advocacy across the region.

Before joining Impax in 2022, Nana served as Research and Project Director at the Asian Corporate Governance Association (ACGA). She authored and co-authored influential research on corporate governance in Asia and led dialogue with regulators, stock exchanges, listed companies and institutional investors. Since 2018, she has chaired ACGA's China Working Group, which brings together more than 80 large global institutional investors, and she continues to serve as a Specialist Consultant to ACGA.

Nana is actively involved in global standard-setting and policy discussions. She serves on the Stakeholder Advisory Council of the International Auditing and Assurance Standards Board and the International Ethics Standards Board for Accountants, and is a member of the IFRS Sustainability Reference Group, the International Corporate Governance Network's Global Policy Committee, and the Principles for Responsible Investment's Global Policy Reference Group. She is a frequent speaker at leading international and regional forums and regularly contributes to policy consultations and industry research across Asia-Pacific.

Nana co-authored *Awakening Governance (2018)*, one of the first reports to explain China's corporate governance system to foreign investors, and *Unlocking Corporate Success by the Power of Diversity (2024)*, the first investor-led book on gender diversity in Japan. In 2025, she received the International Corporate Governance Network's Excellence in Stewardship Award (Individual), becoming the first Asian recipient in the award's history.

She holds an MBA from the University of Chicago (Honours), a Master of Finance from the University of Hong Kong (Dean's List), and a Bachelor of Commerce from the University of New South Wales (Distinction).

Nana is a CFA charterholder, and she has completed the HKICPA Qualification Programme. She is fluent in English, Mandarin and Cantonese.

Index

www.ingramcontent.com/pod-product-compliance
Lightning Source LLC
Chambersburg PA
CBHW061504180526
45171CB00001B/34